Nimitz at Ease

Captain Michael A. Lilly, USN
(Ret.)

Nimitz the warrior. Nimitz the strategist. Both aspects of this World War Two American hero are well documented. Now, Michael Lilly has provided insight into Nimitz, the man, in this engaging, well documented, and heretofore unpublished account of the private and social life of the Fleet Admiral in Hawai`i during his pressure-filled years as Pacific Commander in Chief. Lilly has done a masterful job of humanizing this American icon, while telling a story of Hawaiian lifestyle and friends, and conveying a "sense of place" about Hawai`i, Nimitz, and his close association with the prominent Walker family throughout the war. A great, significant, and informative read.
—Adm. R.J. "Zap" Zlatoper, USN (Ret.), Former Commander in Chief, U.S. Pacific Fleet

Michael Lilly's "At Ease" is an important contribution to the history of the U.S. Navy in World War II and Hawaii during the 1940's. Drawing on his Honolulu family's extensive collection of letters and documents from the war period, the recollections of family members about their close friendship with Admiral Nimitz, public records, and books about naval actions in the Pacific, Lilly has drawn a singular portrait of the Five Star Admiral from the perspective of one of Hawaii's most prominent families. This book will fascinate everyone interested in the war in the Pacific and Old Hawaii with its new and unique insights into Admiral Nimitz when he was "At Ease."
—William J. Cassidy Jr., Former Deputy Assistant Secretary of the Navy

Nimitz at Ease

Also by Michael A. Lilly
If You Die Tomorrow

Nimitz at Ease ©2019 Michael A. Lilly, All Rights Reserved

Print (color) ISBN 978-1-949267-26-6
Print (grayscale) ISBN 978-1-949267-36-5
ebook ISBN 978-1-949267-27-3

This book is sold subject to the condition that it shall not, by way of trade or otherwise, be lent, resold, hired out or otherwise circulated without the publisher's prior consent in any form of binding or cover other than that in which it is published and without a similar condition including this condition being imposed on the subsequent purchaser.

Cover design by Guy D. Corp
www.grafixCORP.com

STAIRWAY≡PRESS

STAIRWAY PRESS—APACHE JUNCTION

www.stairwaypress.com
1000 West Apache Trail, Suite 126
Apache Junction, AZ 85120 USA

Dedication

Una & Sandy Walker and Fleet Admiral Chester W. Nimitz

1944 Map of Oʻahu

Foreword

By Chester Nimitz Lay and Richard Freeman Lay

ON 27 OCTOBER 1945, Navy Day, our grandfather, Fleet Admiral Chester W. Nimitz, sent a photo of himself to Una and H. A. "Sandy" Walker. Beneath the photo it is written, "To Una and Sandy Walker with best wishes and great appreciation of all you have done for me and our Officers and men throughout the war with the Japanese. Affectionately, C. W. Nimitz, Fleet Admiral."

Theirs was an old and deep friendship that began when our grandfather, then a 35-year-old Lieutenant Commander, had been ordered to Oʻahu to build a de novo submarine base at Pearl Harbor in the early 1920s. Nimitz reconnected with the Walker's, an old and prominent island family, in December of 1941, as he assumed command of the Pacific Fleet. For the next three years, until he transferred his CinCPac [Commander in Chief, Pacific Fleet] team to Guam, the Walkers' Laʻie beach house, "Muliwai," would become our grandfather's weekend (and occasional weekday) refuge from the stresses of high command. It was there that he could walk, swim, dine and play poker with the Walker family, often accompanied by members of his command. Our grandfather enjoyed his own private "USO with the Walkers," the author (their grandson) tells us. And it was true.

Outside the Walker and Nimitz families, this story of enduring love and friendship is little known; indeed, E. B. Potter, in his biography, *Nimitz*, devotes a scant three paragraphs to it. *Nimitz at Ease* lays out this story in wonderful detail, much of it through correspondence to the Walkers from our grandfather—carefully preserved by Una—and from her own diary for the year 1944, which the author calls "Truly a treasure trove of history."

We already knew a great deal about our grandfather, growing up with him and our mother Kate; and there has been little written about Fleet Admiral Nimitz that we did not consume. We have learned so much more about his personal side during the war, after reading *Nimitz at Ease*. Sandy, who is brought to life in the book, had a lot in common with his close friend, Chester Nimitz—both refined and yet easy-going and relaxed. Our grandfather also admired and talked about "men of good will." Sandy and his wife Una were certainly among them. We read a draft manuscript of *Nimitz at Ease* to our late mother Kate after she turned 100 on February 22, 2014. She loved it and was delighted that the book included the story about "Umlaut," her fictitious prisoner of war, for the first time in print.

Nimitz at Ease is beautifully written and filled with history, some of it unknown until now. Michael Lilly is in a unique position, with his family history, growing up in Muliwai, papers and his own background as a naval officer and historian. His use of the Nimitz Graybook, "Interviews with Hal Lamar," his own recollections, and numerous other sources, brings this period to life in amazing detail. Surely, no one else alive could have related this story with such richness and preserved it so well for posterity.

Preface

FLEET ADMIRAL CHESTER W. Nimitz commanded all the armed forces in the Pacific during World War II—the largest military power that ever existed in history. Victorious over the Japanese Empire, he was elevated to the highest rank in the United States Navy—a five-star Fleet Admiral. From my earliest memory, Nimitz was a part of my life.

While I first met him when I was too young to remember, he was the distinguished white-haired gentleman in the photo reproduced on the cover of this book, taken by my mother at my grandparents' La'ie, Hawai'i, beach house, Muliwai.

The photo symbolizes this book.

Pictures of Nimitz are usually in uniform or civilian suit. At Muliwai, he is wearing swim shorts with my young sisters, Maile and Sheila crawling all over him. He is relaxed, though the war rages in the western Pacific.

Behind him is another man, also in swim shorts, who has never been to Muliwai before. Retired Adm. Thomas Hart was briefly in Hawai'i on an important mission, conducting the Hart Inquiry into the attack on Pearl Harbor. He was taking testimony that morning, but joined Nimitz for a relaxing weekend at ease.

From a young age, I heard stories of Nimitz's close

relationship with my grandparents Una and H. Alexander "Sandy" Walker, Sr. My Uncle Henry ("Hanko") Walker, Jr., in his autobiography, relates that soon after Nimitz took over the Pacific Fleet in Pearl Harbor, he saw his parents Una and Sandy Walker whom Nimitz had met earlier on a previous posting, and they became close personal friends.*

Our family reports that Nimitz spent every weekend during the war with the Walkers at Muliwai and that Nimitz and the Walkers alternated dinners between Nimitz's quarters in Pearl Harbor and the Walkers' home in Honolulu, some eight miles apart. Hanko, too, recorded that Nimitz "literally spent most weekends with them at Muliwai.[1]

While stories about Nimitz's relationship with the Walkers became family legend, I wondered if the time they spent together was exaggerated. The pictures certainly prove that they saw one another—but every weekend?

As a retired Navy Captain, I personally observed the heavy demands of a fleet admiral during the Vietnam War and later those of Nimitz's successors in command of the Pacific Fleet.

Nimitz's demands were exponentially greater. He wore two challenging hats at the time, positions that are currently held by two different four-star admirals in Hawai`i—Commander in Chief, Pacific Fleet (CinCPac), and Commander in Chief, Pacific Ocean Areas (CinCPOA). Under the latter hat, he had operational command of all Allied forces—air, land and sea—in the Pacific. He was the supreme commander, overseeing the enormous effort fighting World War II in the Pacific; so, could Nimitz really have found the time to socialize with the Walkers every weekend?

Then I made an astounding discovery.

Among the papers found after Una's death was her blue-cover diary for the year 1944, which resided unopened in my garage for

---

* Walker, Henry A., Jr, *Memoirs*, self-published, 1990, p.31.

[1] *Ibid.*, pps.31-2.

three decades. I was close to throwing it out, when I decided to thumb through it. "Still at War!" wrote Una in her elegant calligraphy on January 1, 1944. A few days later, she served Nimitz fish salad for dinner at their home.

What emerged from the diary were contemporaneous notes of every encounter my grandparents had with Nimitz and other military leaders and dignitaries that year.

The diary was a treasure trove of history.

Instead of merely periodic encounters, I discovered that Nimitz and my grandparents were nearly constant companions. Of the days that Nimitz was physically on Oahu in 1944, he and the Walkers were together at least every other day—indeed, sometimes every day for days on end! Not only did Una detail how often they were together, but she noted what they did—walking Kailua Beach, hiking in the mountains, listening to symphonies in the evenings at Muliwai, while the stars rose over the horizon, pitching horseshoes, playing tennis and poker, dancing, singing, and dining at Makalapa and Nuʻuanu.

I also found a box filled with Nimitz photos and memorabilia maintained by my grandparents, over a hundred letters from Nimitz, his aide, and subordinate admirals, sent to the Walkers.

Final new source material arrived in the mail from Nimitz's grandson Chester Nimitz "Chet" Lay in the form of a CD. In February 2014, the U.S. Naval War College completed digitizing and publishing online the previously top-secret Graybook a 4,023-page log maintained by Nimitz's headquarters, providing a daily snapshot of Nimitz's war in the Pacific.

With Una's diary, letters, the Graybook and the other source materials spread out on my desk, I was in the unique position to track Nimitz's daily activities in war and peace, much of which has never been published.

What follows is the true and untold story of the grand relationship that developed between Nimitz and the Walkers during the war and how it fit into the extraordinary circumstances of their lives.

It is an account of a fascinating friendship in unusual times and a look at how the Walkers helped relieve Nimitz of the tremendous pressures of leading in wartime. The Walkers gave Nimitz a place, space and time free of command or demand which, in a small but meaningful way, helped him cope with and win the war in the Pacific.

I hope you find this history as fascinating as I did, when I turned the first page in my grandmother's diary. Attributions to my grandmother or family members are from personal recollections, letters, or her diaries.

Any errors of history are solely my fault. All photographs, unless otherwise noted, are from my family collection.

Nonfootnoted references to my grandmother are from her diary, letters or my personal recollections.

Table of Contents

Chapter 1 3
   Admiral Chester W. Nimitz 3

Chapter 2 9
   Refuge in Hawai'i 9

Chapter 3 16
   Have You Ever Heard of Pearl Harbor? 16

Chapter 4 22
   Yes, Ginger, We Did Hear of Pearl Harbor! 22

Chapter 5 36
   Nimitz: "This is Mr. Walker's Beach!" 36

Chapter 6 49
   1944: "Still at War!" 49

Chapter 7 75
   Nimitz's Refuge from War: Muliwai 75

Chapter 8 88
   Kwajalein, Truk & "Umlaut!" 88

Chapter 9 103
   A Stressful Brisbane Trip 103

Chapter 10 111
   The Hart Inquiry and Admirals at Muliwai 111

Chapter 11 129
   An L.S.T. Tragedy in Paradise 129

Chapter 12 140
   Nimitz's Fall at Muliwai 140

CHAPTER 13 148
   Nimitz, MacArthur and Roosevelt: Philippines or Formosa? 148

Chapter 14 162
   Hanko Joins the Navy 162

Chapter 15 173

Michael A. Lilly

Nimitz finds Relief from War Demands 173
Chapter 16 187
Leyte and a Record Cache of Japanese Glass Balls 187
Chapter 17 203
Ambassador Grew on Japanese Tenacity 203
Chapter 18 213
A Pentagon of Stars 213
Chapter 19 225
1945: Path to Victory 225
Chapter 20 238
"Guam Bombed!" 238
Chapter 21 251
Una: "The Number 1 Exponent of Hawaiian Hospitality" 251
Chapter 22 261
Columbus: "An Early MacArthur?" 261
Chapter 23 272
The Woo Pen 272
Chapter 24 278
War's End: The Atomic Bomb 278
Chapter 25 291
Victory: September 2, 1945 291
Chapter 26 306
Post War 306
Afterword 328
Acknowledgments 348
About the Author 351
Endnotes 352

Chapter 1

Admiral Chester W. Nimitz

A MIDDLE-AGED gentleman in a plain dark suit and overcoat entered through arched porticos patterned after Rome's Fourth Century Arch of Constantine. From the crowded main hall of Union Station, Washington D.C., he found the track for the Baltimore & Ohio Railroad's overnight sleeper to Chicago. It was December 19th, and Washington was icy cold without a leaf on any tree. He was movie star handsome with a rosy complexion, white hair, crisp blue eyes and an athletic build, his countenance giving no evidence of the tremendous weight he bore. His companion, a good-looking younger man with receding hair, clutched a canvas case of papers marked *Top Secret*. He was traveling under an assumed name. The older man was Mr. Freeman, named after his wife's family.

He traveled by train, his preferred method of travel when he had much to ponder. Though the soporific rhythm of wheels clattering on rails and the sway of his coach, along with a nightcap or two of Old Grand-Dad bourbon, administered by his younger companion, might have helped him overcome chronic insomnia, his swirling mind thwarted their effects.

Michael A. Lilly

After a short layover in Chicago, the pair connected to the Santa Fe Railroad's plush Super Chief Pullman to the west coast. The younger man soon handed *Mr. Freeman* the case. Inside were photographs and summaries revealing the worst nightmare of any Navy admiral. They detailed "the magnitude of the Pearl Harbor disaster." [1]

One photo stood out from the devastation—the infamous, mangled remains of the World War I-era Battleship, USS *Arizona* (BB 36) with its superstructure tilting at an acute angle. The photo hit *Mr. Freeman* particularly hard, since he had commanded a group of battleships just two and a half years before. *Arizona* had been his own flagship.

The Japanese sneak attack on Pearl Harbor outraged the public, but few knew the lurid details contained in the files. For the first time, the incoming Commander in Chief of the Pacific Fleet (CinCPac) realized how devastating the defeat really was and the enormity of the task facing him: the entire fleet was under water, the Hawaiian Islands were open to invasion, and the public was angry and demoralized.

At the time, Chester W. Nimitz was a two-star Rear Admiral in charge of the Navy's Bureau of Navigation. The younger man was his trusty aide, Lt. H. Arthur "Hal" Lamar. Ironically, the previous January, Adm. Ernest King, the head of the United States Navy, had offered Nimitz command of the Pacific Fleet. CinCPac was a desirable post. Even today, it is one of the most prestigious and envied positions in the United States Navy. The admiral in charge wears four stars on his collar and commands all of the naval forces throughout the Pacific Ocean. Nimitz would have leapt over dozens of more senior admirals. But he did not think he was ready. With a prescience that was to serve the nation well throughout the Pacific War, Nimitz wisely turned down the honor. Instead, a more senior Admiral, Husband E. Kimmel (Nimitz's friend), was given the command, which he assumed in January of 1941. After the debacle of Pearl Harbor eleven months later, President Roosevelt told Secretary of the Navy (SecNav) William Franklin "Frank" Knox to "tell Nimitz to get the hell out to Pearl and stay there till the war is won." [2]

Here was the mission for which he had trained throughout a 36-year career since graduating from the U.S. Naval Academy in 1905. Unlike the previous offer, this was an order from the President of the United States—a weighty responsibility that he could not turn down. Three weeks after the attack, Nimitz arrived in San Diego.

On Christmas Eve 1941, after two frustrating days of aborted departures, Nimitz again boarded a four-engine PB2Y-2 Coronado Flying Boat bound for Pearl Harbor. The noisy, unpressurized seaplane took 17 hours to arrive on Christmas morning. Even the photographs in his Top Secret files had not fully prepared Nimitz for the massacre displayed below him. His mind had imagined how bad the damage was, only to find its reality so much worse. One of the pilots recorded that Nimitz "kept shaking his head and clucking his tongue."

> We were looking at the West Virginia, the California, the Utah, and the Arizona—all crumpled hulks. We were looking at skeletons of what were once hangars and flight lines filled with the junk of what were once military planes. The carnage was sickening.[3]

Nimitz's flying boat landed in Pearl Harbor's East Loch, where the Adm. Bernard A. "Chick" Clarey Causeway has linked Oahu with Ford Island since 1998. Emerging wearing civilian clothes, cold and partially deaf from the Coronado's engines, Nimitz surveyed the scene from sea level before being conveyed ashore by whaleboat through oily waters and rain showers. The Navy's mighty Pacific Fleet lay in ruins.

Japan might have struck a tactical blow, but Nimitz already knew the enemy had made a colossal strategic blunder. The Navy's massive oil reserves, repair yards, and submarine base were untouched. The fleet's three aircraft carriers had been safe at sea, an ominous portent for Japan. Those carriers could thwart any Japanese offensive in the western Pacific. Because the Japanese failed to destroy the Pearl Harbor dry docks, all but three of the twenty-one ships sunk or damaged in the attack were refloated, soon to wreak vengeance against the enemy over the next three and a half years. Most of the fleet's destroyers and cruisers were still intact.

Unbeknownst to many in the tradition-laden United States Navy, battleships were becoming archaic, having fought their last major battle during World War I. By December 6, 1941, battleships as a class were almost obsolete. By December 7, they were obsolete.[4]

As Rear Adm. Claude Bloch later said, "The Japanese only destroyed a lot of old hardware. In a sense, they did us a favor."[5]

The tragedy helped the Navy adopt a more effective naval strategy already deployed by the Japanese—the carrier task force. Although he may never have said it, the quote often attributed to Japanese Admiral Isoroku Yamamoto, that the attack may have "awakened a sleeping giant," correctly described its aftermath.

While most Americans had never heard of Pearl Harbor, suddenly the entire country learned the Japanese had attacked the Pacific Fleet, killing more than two thousand people. The Day of Infamy aroused the anger of the country, as if the president had been assassinated; silenced the isolationist America First Committee; and galvanized Congress to declare war the next day.

On the other hand, the ease with which the Japanese destroyed the Pacific Fleet also created a false sense of invincibility among some in the Japanese military, a euphoria that soon turned into desperation. Within days of the attack, Yamamoto realized, too late, that they should have invaded and captured Hawai'i—a strategy that could have materially altered the whole course of the war in their favor.

Less than two weeks after the attack, the two leaders of the Navy and Army in the Pacific, Admiral Kimmel and Gen. Walter Short, were relieved of their commands in disgrace and replaced by

Nimitz and Lt. Gen. Delos Emmons, respectively. Emmons was fifty-two, fair-haired and called himself Military Governor of Hawai'i. Nimitz graciously told a dispirited Kimmel (who immediately reverted to his permanent two-star rank of Rear Admiral), "The same thing could have happened to anybody." [6] (Nimitz certainly must have had in mind his own fortuitous decision to decline the Pacific Command the previous January.)

Catherine Nimitz could not accompany her husband of twenty-eight years to Hawai'i, because it was in a war zone. As a Navy wife, she was accustomed to long separations, although not such extraordinary circumstances that lasted nearly four years. The new CinCPac moved into his bachelor quarters on the rim of an old volcanic crater, with commanding views of the otherwise peaceful waters of Pearl Harbor, where the canted mast of *Arizona* still haunted the scene of desolation. His fleet surgeon, Capt. Elphege Alfred M. Gendreau, and Chief of Staff, Rear Adm. Raymond Spruance, lived with him in the spacious two-story home at 37 Makalapa Drive, which every CinCPac has occupied since.

Nimitz last had duty in Hawai'i from 1920 to 1922 when, as a 35-year-old lieutenant commander, he built the first submarine base in Pearl Harbor and lived in Manoa Valley, which is when he and the Walkers first met and became friends. Sandy Walker had such a generous and warm-hearted spirit that upon meeting him, one felt a lifetime kinship. My grandmother Puna,[*] to her family, Una, to her friends, was an intelligent and witty woman of the world, with whom most felt instantly at ease. Even before he assumed command of the Pacific Fleet on the last day of December 1941, Nimitz's

---

[*] Puna is short for *Kupuna Wahine*, loosely meaning Grandmother. Una adopted the name, Puna, in 1937 when my sister Maile was born. Una told Pauline King, wife of the Hawai'i Territorial Senator Samuel W. King, that she did not want to be called, Tutu or Grandma. "Be sure they call you Puna," replied Pauline, "which is the correct name for a grandparent." Una enthusiastically agreed and was known thereafter in the family as Puna.

friendship with the Walkers had been rekindled.

When I was troubled or stressed while growing up, my parents and grandparents soothed me with a Hawaiian word for patience that gracefully rolls off the tongue with the undulating rhythm of long ocean swells—*ho`omanawanui*. "All things work out in the fullness of time," my grandmother wisely advised. The Walkers passed that word on to Nimitz, because he needed a lot of patience with his Pacific Fleet under water and the Japanese juggernaut grinding through the western Pacific.

The day after Nimitz took command of the Pacific Fleet, he called on the Walkers' Hawaiian word while being interviewed by the press.

"You asked several questions about the future, many of them no doubt pressing," said Nimitz. "I'm a *Kamaaina** myself, and I'd like to reply in a Hawaiian word. This word is *Hoomanawanui*, meaning, 'Let time take care of the situation.'" [7]

Indeed, it did. By not following up on their success at Pearl Harbor, Nimitz later remarked that the Japanese "left their principal enemy with the time to catch his breath, restore his morale, and rebuild his forces." [8]

Soon, Nimitz would be introduced to the physical manifestation of *ho'omanawanui*, magical Muliwai.

---

* *Kama'aina* means "child of the earth"—literally, born in Hawai`i. Colloquially, it is also used to describe someone who has been in Hawai`i for a long time.

Chapter 2

Refuge in Hawai'i

MY FAMILY HAS lived in Nu'uanu Valley since the mid-nineteenth century. This lush, tree-filled crevice that stretches five miles from downtown Honolulu to the cliffs of the Ko'olau Mountains, known as the Pali, is the main valley of the *ahupua'a** of Honolulu. In the late 18th Century, King Kamehameha annihilated the army of O'ahu's King Kalaikupule by forcing them upslope to the precipitous Pali cliffs over which they plunged to their deaths some 1,000 feet below.

Nimitz's friends, Sandy and Una Walker, resided in an historic Victorian manor house in the Classical Revival style about two miles up Nu'uanu Valley from Honolulu. Since the 19th Century, most of the prominent families of O'ahu lived in Nu'uanu for its temperate climate and handsome shade trees.

"I love our valley," Una often said. "Nu'uanu translates to chilly heights and air. Many Hawaiian songs and even *hula* depict the cool breezes of Nu'uanu."

---

* *Ahupua'a* is Hawaiian for a pie-shaped wedge of land that reaches from the top of the mountains to the sea.

Their house was staffed with maids, cook and a combination butler/chauffeur. Its long, circular, Royal Palm-lined driveway led to a large, hip-roofed porte-cochère. The granite driveway curbs and flagstone paths came to Hawai'i in the early 19th Century as ballast on sailing ships that carried aromatic Sandalwood to China and returned empty. Streams of fragrant dendrobium superbum and anosmum orchids cascaded from the trunks of dozens of tall tree ferns flanking the driveway and surrounding a lighted pagoda on an island-like honor guard. The property comprised seven acres of lush and luxuriant orchid gardens and Hawaiian flora. One of their Lychee and Macadamia nut trees were the oldest in the islands.

Sandy's mother, Jane, was one of the first to grow orchids in Hawai'i. The Walkers followed her example, raising orchids in what became world-famous gardens in their Nu'uanu property, still recalled today as Walker Gardens.

Author with his mother, Ginger Lilly, Walker Japanese Garden—1948

In 1905, a magnificent Japanese Garden was constructed on the property by a world-class Japanese architect. Its stones, lanterns, bridges, pagodas and authentic teahouse were imported from Japan. The Japanese Garden was and remains the oldest and finest in Hawai'i.

Sandy was a third generation *keiki o ka 'aina*[*] on his mother's side. His father J. S. Walker, Sr. was a successful Scottish-born businessman and Minister of Finance and Attorney General *ad interim* to King David Kalakaua. "Sandy," to his friends, and "Gramps," to his grandchildren, grew up speaking Hawaiian as easily as English.

"While I was growing up," he often said with smiling eyes, "my neighbors were the Kings and Queens of Hawai'i." After a moment, he would enlighten that his childhood home—*Mauna`ala* for sweet mountain—was "next door to the Royal Mausoleum, where those Kings and Queens are entombed."

Sandy & Una Walker—1944

---

[*] Literally, "Child born of the earth."

Michael A. Lilly

Sandy was a giant of a man. Wide of girth, with massive hands, he made a striking figure. He was a lively storyteller, who speckled his tales with vivid anecdotes that brought them to life. With a marvelous twinkle in his eye, you never knew whether he was telling you something very important or merely pulling your leg. He was also a most generous-hearted host. While playing poker, he sometimes intentionally lost, just to make his guests feel at home. Finishing eating before others, he continued pushing his knife and fork around until they were done. Sandy was so humble and self-effacing, one would not at first realize how successful he was in life. So endearing and likeable was he that in his twenties, he served as the best man in the weddings of thirteen of his Harvard classmates! It is hard to imagine someone so loved by so many. Throughout his life, Sandy won the confidence and affection of most of those around him.

Sandy's Scottish father was leading wagon trains of Mormons to Utah, when he contracted Rocky Mountain spotted fever and was told to convalesce in the tropics, winding up in Hawai'i in 1854. Mirroring his father, after attending Harvard (class of 1907), Sandy contracted tuberculosis and similarly sought the mild Hawaiian climate to recuperate. Being from a wealthy family and not having to work, he was content to loiter on Waikiki beach (in a customary suit and tie no less) and enjoy life. There he met Una, a vivacious and athletic young lady from California, who was tanned a deep brown from surfing, and sometimes surfing with Olympic champion, Duke Kahanamoku. She was fit, cultured, and alluring. Sandy fell instantly in love with Una and asked her to marry him, but Una resisted, because he was not employed.

"An endless significance lies in work," she often instructed, quoting Thomas Carlyle. "In idleness alone is there perpetual despair. You get a job, Sandy, and then I'll marry you."

Sandy acceded to her suggestion, and he soon became secretary of the Hawaiian Sugar Planters' Association (HSPA)—an alliance of sugar plantations to promote and develop the sugar industry. His marriage to Una came soon after, on a date whose anniversary would later live in infamy, December 7, 1920.

In 1933, when A. W. T. Bottomly tragically drowned in a boating accident, Sandy replaced him as President of American Factors, Ltd. (later, Amfac), a corporation comprising forty-five sugar plantations on five islands and the largest of Hawai'i's Big Five businesses, which together controlled the economy of the islands.

Sandy had the intelligence, background, and wit to succeed in anything he chose to do. As a businessman, he followed several principles. "Always learn the job of the person ahead of you," he told me. "Soon he will be unnecessary, and you will have his job.

"Always learn the jobs of those around you. When [the business] is cutting personnel, you will be retained. Never tell anyone all you know. Otherwise, he will know as much as you, and you will no longer be needed." And, importantly, "Always volunteer."

In addition to his innate abilities, he had at his side his extraordinary partner, who was intensely ambitious herself, a woman who motivated him to soar to great heights. Una Craig Walker was born in Calaveras County, California, the location of Mark Twain's celebrated jumping frog. Her father Nute Craig served briefly in the Civil War at age fifteen ("A Yankee," Una loathed to admit) before venturing west. In Wyoming he became a member of the Territorial Legislature and, three years after the infamous Long Branch Saloon Gunfight at Dodge City, KS, he was elected Sheriff of Cheyenne. With his Swedish immigrant wife, they later moved to a large ranch in California called *Casa Bianca,* where he raised thoroughbred horses and eventually wrote and self-published his gripping wild-west autobiographies, *Stepping Stones to Eighty* and *Thrills.*

Una, Nute's youngest daughter, was a remarkable woman, whose personality had many contrasts. Sophisticated, witty and elegant, she was altogether enchanting. Though not a stunning beauty, she had a feminine charisma that charmed men and women, kings and paupers alike. In fact, she was as much at ease with the King of Thailand as with her Filipino yardmen. Most who encountered Una instantly liked her.

However, genteel ladies of Honolulu were shocked with Una's surfing and tanned skin (considered disreputable by some in that time). Once, she lost her large redwood surfboard, and the famous Duke Kahanamoku surfed by on a wave, scooping her from the water without stopping!

Una could herd cattle astride a horse at Maui's Haleakala Ranch in the morning and dance until midnight at a formal ball that evening. She played tennis, swam, and strummed the ukulele. An article in the March 20, 1940, issue of the *Washington Times-Herald* accurately captured her eclectic nature at the age of 52:

> *Her days are always full...she knows the dangerous thrill of surf-board and surf-boat riding...She is an admirable horsewoman, and when she and her husband, on vacation, go to the vast sugar plantations and cattle ranches of friends on nearby islands, she often takes part in the cattle drives ... She's a first-rate swimmer and tennis player and a beautiful rumba dancer...*
>
> *She devotes a great part of her time to her two daughters and son...She grows orchids and raises Kerry blues and Scottish terriers...As the wife of one of the most prominent businessmen in Honolulu, she has many responsibilities... active in welfare and social life of her community...She thoroughly enjoys people...dislikes formality...plays the ukulele, and to its plaintive melodies sings native songs...On her biennial trips to the mainland, she...keeps fit by taking up dancing, ice and roller skating...*
>
> *She is a tall, handsome woman...Her beautifully coiffed hair is touched with silver, and her large eyes mirror intelligence and a warm and understanding personality...Her name: Mrs. H. Alexander Walker.*

In the 1930s, Sandy spent months at a time in Washington D.C., lobbying Congress for legislation to support the sugar industry against foreign competition. He was successful in the passage of the Sugar Act, effectively defeating sugar-beet states' and Eastern refiners' efforts to denigrate Hawaiian sugar as foreign and not American. "Walker was prominent in gaining Congressional recognition of Hawai'i as an 'integral' part of the United States." [9]

While Sandy befriended those in the halls of government, Una became close friends with the wives of industry and government leaders. Among them was one of the wealthiest women in the world—Marjorie Merriweather May Post, founder of General Foods, Inc. Post invited Una to join a group of ladies who were purchasing and preserving Stratford Hall Plantation, the Virginia birthplace of Confederate Gen. Robert E. Lee.

While the family reports that Una asked Sandy whether she should join the Stratford Hall ladies, more likely, she presented the idea to Sandy in such a way that he could only concur with a *fait accompli*. Sandy agreed because the reason they were on the East Coast was to advance Hawai'i and its sugar industry, and by befriending influential people such as the ladies preserving Stratford Hall, Una would advance that effort as well. Hence, she became its director from the Territory of Hawai'i in 1934, a post she held for 50 years, until she turned it over to her daughter Ginger.

The Walker family enjoyed a charmed and peaceful life in their remote refuge of Hawai'i—until war clouds darkened the horizon.

Michael A. Lilly

Chapter 3

Have You Ever Heard of Pearl Harbor?

THE WALKERS RAISED three children—Virginia ("Ginger," my mother), Henry, Jr. ("Hanko"), and Ann.

Ginger Lilly Dancing the Hula at a Garden Party at her Parents' Home, circa 1941

Because Sandy grew up speaking Hawaiian, he ensured that each of the children were instructed once a week by a Hawaiian teacher, including the great *kumu hula*[*] 'Iolani Lauhine, in Hawaiian songs, language and dance. Ginger became an outstanding hula dancer and ukulele player. At the time of Pearl Harbor, Hanko and Ann were in East Coast boarding schools. Ginger was a young divorcee with two babies—Maile and Sheila.

December 7th was a surprise to most people in America, but Hawai'i had been preparing for it for years. Even before World War I, the Army fortified the Hawaiian Islands with a chain of batteries in defense of a future Pacific war with Japan, after she defeated Russia in 1905.

On May 18, 1939, May 23, 1940, and as late as May 20, 1941, the Territory conducted island-wide blackouts in preparation for war. The May 20th blackout simulated an attack by enemy planes for thirty minutes, starting at 9:00 p.m. "When warning bells are rung or sirens sounded," the announcement instructed, "IMMEDIATELY put out all lights…inside and outside…BLACKOUT COMPLETELY."

The Hawai'i Red Cross had been mobilizing for war for months and by mid-1941 was already training in response to an expected air attack by Japan and possible invasion and its effect on the civilian population.[10]

As Chair of the Red Cross Surgical Dressings Corps, Una had been building her corps of volunteers for two years until there were five thousand women working daily.[11] This was in character for her lifelong service to the community. During the First World War, Una was the first woman in the islands to don the new Red Cross cap and veil.

Ginger relates that she "joined the Red Cross in early 1941 because, as everyone in Hawai'i knew, there was going to be a war with Japan. I wanted to be prepared."

She attended three Red Cross first aid courses at Queen's

---

[*] *Kumu hula* literally means teacher of the *hula*.

Hospital.

Meanwhile, she and forty-one other women with their own station wagons trained to become members of the American Red Cross Women's Volunteer Motor Corps. Their studies were difficult. They learned to drive and maintain heavy army trucks, trailer rigs, and ambulances; change massive tires and fix engines; and first aid, emergency delivery of babies, blackout driving, military drills, and defense against gas attacks.[12]

In March 1941, Ginger wrote her sister, Ann: "I can change tires all by myself now and fix mechanical ailments too...Next week we have police tests and have to all drive in a convoy from Honolulu to Waimanalo."

The *Honolulu Advertiser* front page for March 23, 1941 sported a picture of Ginger and two other volunteers repairing a tire in their final test. Having passed that test, she earned her certificate as a Red Cross Motor Corps volunteer. Soon, Ginger's training came to good use when casualties mounted during the attack on Pearl Harbor.

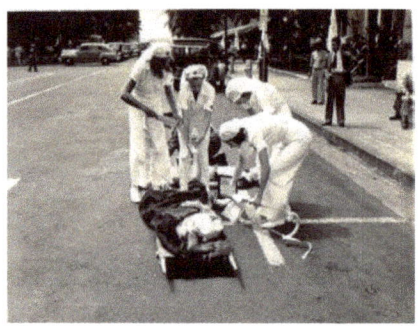

Red Cross Motor Corps Volunteers Practicing First Aid on Bishop Street in Downtown Honolulu.
Appearing (left-to-right) are Alice Judd, Chimey Walker, Cappy Cooke, and Ginger Lilly; the "victim" is Martha Hayworth. Ginger's "Woodie" station wagon is in the background. March 3, 1941.[13]

Nimitz at Ease

On July 20th, Ginger, along with her other Red Cross Motor Corps drivers, began regular duties and were given a complete list of assignments for Attack Day.[14]

In case of invasion, families along the coast were to evacuate to homes in the valleys and hills. Each of the Walkers' three *lanais* (Hawaiian for large porches) were allocated to friends. Sandy anticipated a Japanese assault and began importing massive supplies of drugs, dry goods, and food, which he stuffed into empty warehouse space and even boxcars rented from his friend Walter Dillingham's Oahu Railway and Land Company.[15] His stockpiles proved a Godsend when the attack finally came.[16]

As a result, not only did Sandy anticipate civil defense needs, but his retail stores had sufficient merchandise for the public, while other businesses ultimately had to ration products.

The *Honolulu Advertiser* headline on Sunday, November 30, 1941, one week before the actual attack, carried a prophetic if premature warning.

Headline: Japanese to Strike

If only the military leaders in Hawai'i had been with Ginger the day before the attack when the following transpired:

> *With war only 24 hours away, at 8:00 a.m. on December 6, Ginger Walker, dressed in a heavy khaki Motor Corps uniform with a broad, leather belt and rakish fore-and-aft cap, drove her "Woodie" station wagon to meet a Royal Australian ship at Aloha Tower. The ship carried officers destined for pilot training in Canada and ultimately to England to fight the*

Luftwaffe.

"I was assigned six handsome young boys," she said, "to tour Oahu before a one o'clock lunch at Bellows Field in Waimanalo."

"Have you ever heard of Pearl Harbor?" Ginger asked the six flyers.

"No," they replied in unison.

"Well ... someday you might. I'll take you here."

She drove them up Aiea Heights from which Pearl Harbor appeared below in a wide panorama of 96 warships, including eight battleships, nestled peacefully at their berths.

"My God!" the Royal Australian pilots gasped. "This is fabulous. Look at all those warships in the harbor."

Each officer took a turn photographing Ginger with Pearl Harbor in the background.

"Suppose the Japanese used a submarine to block the harbor?" an obviously anxious officer asked. "The entire Pacific Fleet would be a sitting duck."

"You're right," replied Ginger who said that she worried about the comment the rest of the day.

After dropping the pilots off at Aloha Tower from which they departed at 6:00 p.m., a troubled Ginger attended a dinner party at the home of Kahala Beach friends. She watched a magnificent full moon slowly rise above the Koko Head crater to the east. The cool trade winds—Ginger always called them caressing—ruffled the trees. It was a splendid tropical evening, but she fretted about the fleet nestled unprepared at its moorings.

After dinner, she played bridge with Lt. Charles Bryant, who was flying daily PBY Catalina patrol missions from Pearl Harbor.

"Charlie," Ginger began in a stern voice and serious eyes penetrating through her glasses that her children learned meant business, "*I went to Aiea Heights with six Australian officers today. It seemed to us that every ship in the Pacific Fleet was in the harbor. They are sitting ducks for a Japanese attack.*"

Bryant only laughed.

At that, Ginger repeated her fear that the Pacific Fleet was in peril. "*If the Japanese block the entrance to the harbor, all our ships will be trapped.*"

"Ginger," an exasperated Bryant finally declared, "*Every day, we fly PBY search missions around the Islands. It is impossible for the Japanese to get within one thousand miles of Hawai'i without our spotting them.*" He emphasized this with a conviction untrammeled by the slightest doubt.

It was obvious to Ginger that Bryant's attitude was cast firmly in stone. She returned home that last antebellum evening with the vision of an unprotected fleet gnawing at her mind and interrupting her sleep.[*]

---

[*] Ironically, Adm. Kimmel's predecessor, Adm. James O. Richardson, argued against moving the fleet from San Pedro, California, to Pearl Harbor in 1940, calling Pearl Harbor a "god-damned mousetrap." Miller, Nathan, *War at Sea: A Naval History of World War II*, Oxford University Press, 1995, 197.

Michael A. Lilly

Chapter 4

Yes, Ginger, We Did Hear of Pearl Harbor!

DECEMBER 7, 1941, just before 8:00 a.m., Bryant ate his fateful words, for his search planes were not patrolling to the northwest of Hawai'i from which six Japanese aircraft carriers, two battleships, and supporting warships bore down on the Hawaiian archipelago and launched their surprise attack on Pearl Harbor.

Ginger's breakfast was interrupted by distant explosions. She raced to her front yard and looked up to see a squadron of Zeros, with bright red dots painted under their wings—American pilots called them red meatballs—flying down Nu'uanu valley from the Pali. "[They were] Japanese war planes," Ginger later said, her brown eyes aflame. "How wrong Charlie Bryant was!"

As reported by Stanley Weintraub's *Journey into War*, Sandy Walker thought at first the distant explosions were gunnery practice:

> In an elegant Victorian mansion on six lushly landscaped acres at 2616 Nuuanu Avenue, Una and H. Alexander Walker awoke to the noise of what seemed like distant gunnery practice. Chief executive officer of American

> *Factors, a sprawling mercantile conglomerate...the politically conservative Walker was outraged.**
>
> *Here they go again,"* he spluttered to Una, *"wasting taxpayers' money on a Sunday morning. This fellow Roosevelt even spoils my sleep.*
>
> *Walker's wife reminded him that a display of bad temper was not a way to begin their twenty-first wedding anniversary. It would be a big day.*[17]

Since December 7th was the Walkers' wedding anniversary, they had planned a sit-down dinner for fifty guests, complete with musicians, dancers and caterers. Flowers were ordered from florists. Guests of honor included the two military leaders in the Pacific—Admiral Kimmel, Commander in Chief, Pacific Fleet, and General Short, Commander of the Army's Hawaiian Department.

Una said, "No one dreamed of the devastation and death which were to mark that portentous date."

As Hanko later wrote, faithfully chronicling what Una related to me:

> *No one showed up. In later years my parents marveled, not over the fact that the party did not take place, but that not one of the invited guests, the musical performers or the kitchen help, called to say they would not be coming. Everybody huddled near their radios, because it was widely expected that the Islands themselves would be invaded and eventually occupied.*[18]

---

* Like Nimitz, Sandy was too gentle and politic ever to become outraged.

Ginger Lilly in Red Cross Motor Corps Gabardine Uniforms, May 1942

Ginger Lilly in Red Cross Motor Corps Gabardine Uniforms, May 1942

Ginger reported for duty in her gray gabardine Red Cross uniform, tin helmet and gas mask. From Pearl Harbor, she transported the wounded, "…many of whom were in great pain and shock and terribly worried about their wives and children," to makeshift first aid stations set up in all the local schools, such as Farrington and Ma'ema'e Elementary in Nu'uanu Valley. "They pressed upon me scraps of paper telling their names and which hospital they'd be in and begged me to find their wives and children. I said I would."

Some local residents opened their homes to people who had to be evacuated, when their quarters were destroyed.

Ginger heard "firing going on most of the day, and there were great clouds of smoke billowing forth, especially from the direction of Pearl Harbor." As night descended, her headlights were "blacked out, with only a tiny blue beam looking downward, to help [me] drive all night." With "the sky red with flames still shooting upwards," she "went from warehouses to hospitals, taking supplies for the wounded and for the women and children in the schools," where they were sheltering. Over the following weeks, she remained on duty for days, operating out of the Motor Corps headquarters at Castle Kindergarten in downtown Honolulu. For the rest of the war, she kept her wagon stocked with first aid kit, food, water, blankets, sheets, bandages, and reading materials.

Meanwhile, Sandy filled every container and bathtub in their Nu'uanu home with water, eerily anticipating reports (later turning out to be false) that O'ahu's water supply was poisoned. False reports of Japanese invasion forces terrified everyone on O'ahu. The radio reported Japanese paratroops in the hills above Kalihi Valley and Alewa Heights. Japanese transports were marshalling offshore. Accounts of beach landings swept the Island. "Saboteurs Land Here," warned the *Honolulu Advertiser* headline the next morning. The Japanese had laid mines in Honolulu Harbor. Fortunately, none of these frightening news accounts were true.

If the expected invading Japanese army marched up Nu'uanu Valley and arrived at the Walkers' driveway, their loyal Japanese national gardener, 74-year-old Suetaro Goto, was prepared to tell them in his native tongue that the Walkers were good people. Happily it never happened.

The Walkers cabled to Hanko and Ann in the east coast that they were alive and unharmed. They may have been uninjured, but Una told me they were under such excruciating tension that day that they "each lost eleven pounds of weight!" The Walkers might have lost even more weight had they read the ominous warning, marked "Secret," which the Chief of Naval Operations sent to Adm. Kimmel two days later:

Nimitz at Ease

> *Because of the great success of the Japanese raid on the seventh, it is expected to be promptly followed up by additional attacks in order render Hawaii untenable as naval and air bases, in which eventuality it is believed Japanese have suitable forces for initial occupation of islands other than Oahu including Midway Maui and Hawai`i...Under present circumstances it seems questionable that Midway can be retained...*[19]

Even ten days after the attack, the Secretary of the Navy was not yet satisfied that Hawaiian Islands [were] safe from capture and could not guarantee that landings by Japanese troops [would] not be made against undefended islands of the Hawaiian group.*

Una Walker in Red Cross Uniform, December, 1941

---

* *Graybook.*, 73. A principal architect of Pearl Harbor, Commander Minoru Genda, urged the attack be followed by an invasion. Had they successfully done so, the U.S. forces would have been thrown back to the mainland from which it would have been extremely difficult to prosecute a Pacific war, especially with Japan controlling the strategically vital Hawaiian Islands. Japanese military leaders belatedly began serious plans for an invasion in the months after the attack, of which Midway was the opening gambit. With Nimitz in command at Pearl Harbor and having won that gambit, Japan forever lost any hope for victory.

An immediate concern of Una's on December 7th was getting a supply of surgical dressings to the many wounded in Pearl Harbor and at the various first aid stations. She arrived at the Honolulu Academy of Arts from which her surgical dressing team operated, and was surprised to find not one of her dozens of female Japanese volunteers present. She called "one of her Japanese volunteers, Mrs. Asahina, to ask when she would be coming in, since no Japanese ladies had shown up. Mrs. Asahina replied, 'We'll be there in a minute.' Mrs. Asahina later told Mrs. Walker that hearing her voice was one of the great moments of her life because she hadn't known what was expected of her." [20]

One-by-one, Una called each of the Japanese ladies on the team, all of whom expressed shame and anger by the attack on Pearl Harbor, tearfully telling Una they thought they would not be welcome. On the contrary, Una told them, "You are our best workers. We cannot operate without you. And you had nothing to do with the attack." The Japanese volunteers were relieved, and all immediately began showing up for work.

Una Walker (far right) & Her Red Cross Surgical Dressing Corps, Sacred Hearts Academy, 1943

By December 7th, Una's group had produced almost two hundred thousand dressings, expected to last six months of war.[21] However, the supply was exhausted that first day. In the next six months, the ladies created an additional million and a half dressings![22]

By 1945, they were producing a million dressings a month.[23] They also made plaster of Paris bandages for Army amputation cases and face masks for use by surgical teams.[24] Una later remarked, "We made all the dressings that were used at Aiea Naval Hospital, the penicillin sponges for the forward areas and all the battle dressings for the LSTs going to the Pacific."[25] (A Landing Ship Tank, or LST, was a flat-bottomed amphibious cargo ship with a bow ramp capable of landing supplies and men directly onto a beach.) Una told me that whenever a ship stopped in Pearl Harbor asking for a special supply of bandages, she always knew it was headed for an undisclosed battlefront.

General Delos Emmons, Military Governor of Hawai'i and Una Walker (center) at the Honolulu Academy of Arts with her Red Cross Surgical Dressing Corps Volunteers[26]

The day after the attack was the annual meeting of the Hawaiian Sugar Planters' Association over which Sandy had presided as president for eight years. Under his direction, the board set aside its published agenda and passed the following war resolution:

> Be it resolved that in light of the existing emergency, the Hawaiian Sugar Planters' Association does pledge its fullest cooperation to the government of the United States, and places all its facilities, services and membership at the disposal of our government.[27]

One government project carried the resolution into effect. It was conducted by HSPA's scientists who studied the growth of the miracle drug, *penicillin notatum,* under local conditions to determine which strain would yield high enough concentrations of the antibiotic.[28]

Several days after the attack, Una awoke to an urgent phone call at 4:00 a.m. from Army Air Corps Brig. Gen. Howard C. Davidson, fifty-one at the time and who commanded a wing at Wheeler Field. He asked her to assemble a list of twenty bright, reliable women to be the nucleus of a secretive Army job.[29]

Una immediately awoke Sandy with whom she compiled a list for General Davidson, which formed the initial roster of what became known as the *Women's Air Raid Defense* (WARD) in Hawai'i, based at Fort Shafter.

Davidson and Una met the recruits at the Royal Hawaiian Hotel in Waikiki the day after Nimitz's arrival, Christmas 1941. Davidson explained that the women were needed to relieve men ordered to forward combat areas and the duties and demands that the secret work entailed.[30]

The "Shuffleboard Pilot" WARDs plotted and interpreted radar and other information and used long "shuffleboard" sticks to move contacts around a large map table in a concrete bunker at Fort Shafter.

Meanwhile, President Roosevelt directed Hawai'i's Governor

Joseph B. Poindexter to place the Hawaiian Islands under Martial Law, suspending Habeas Corpus—the "Great Writ" guaranteed by the U.S. Constitution. General Short, whose days were numbered, announced:

> *I have this day assumed the position of military governor of Hawai`i, and have taken charge of the government of the Territory.*[31]

By that fiat, the lives and livelihoods of every person in the islands became subordinate to military control, under the most austere restrictions ever placed on American citizens since the Civil War.

Curfew and blackout requirements were imposed between 6:00 p.m. to 6:00 a.m. At night, not so much as a struck match was permitted.[32] Wages were frozen. Phone calls, mail and newspapers were censored. The Army ran everything—food supply and distribution, communications, traffic, hospitals and health, price control, civilian defense, liquor distribution, gasoline rationing, and fiscal matters—even to a large extent the courts.[33]

Because the Japanese had used poison gas against the Chinese, every citizen received a gas mask. Gas rationing of ten gallons a month severely restricted travel by car. Speed was limited to 20 mpg in town and 25 outside of town. Utility services were reduced. Paper currency was eventually overprinted with the word HAWAII, rendering it worthless in case of a Japanese invasion.

"Every household, every industry, every business place," an editorial proclaimed "became a unit in the war machine."[34] After the war, Martial Law was ruled unconstitutional by the United States Supreme Court.[35]

Michael A. Lilly

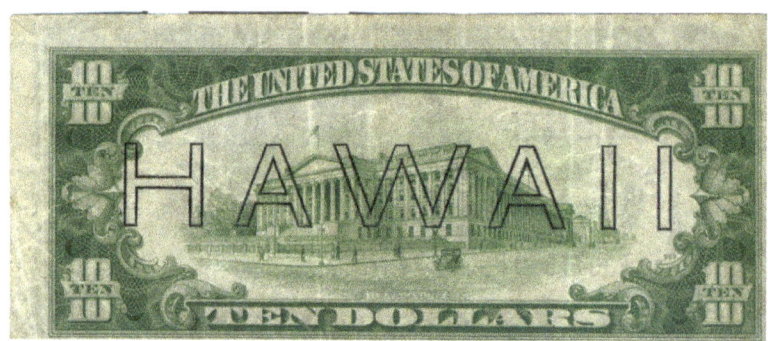

Hawai'i Overprint Note[36]

In addition to her volunteer work for the Red Cross, Ginger also spent nearly every day at the Blood Bank. "The judge here under Martial Law," Una wrote to daughter Ann at Ethel Walker School in Connecticut, "punishes all speeding, etc., by their giving blood, and Ginger holds their heads and gives them coffee."

Because Sandy was a prominent businessman and had long served with the Territorial Government, he had become close friends with Gen. Delos Emmons, when he was stationed in Hawai'i from 1934 to 1936. Emmons later replaced Short as Military Governor, and he asked Sandy to serve as his volunteer Director of Food Control, responsible for importing, storing and distributing food supplies for the Hawaiian Islands and its burgeoning military population.

"My God," cried Sandy, "the people are crying for rice, and the warehouses are filled with rotting potatoes. What shall I do?" Fortunately, there was no one better positioned to take on the thankless chore, for Sandy was already a major importer of commodities and knew the buying patterns and volume of business done by the various suppliers of the civilian community.[37]

Sandy toiled half of every day of the war from an office in 'Iolani Palace where, as the sole volunteer executive, he directed staffs of subordinates, some uniformed, and issued edicts from which there was no appeal.[38] His first act was to immediately close grocery stores, until an inventory of food in the islands could be completed. The inventory demonstrated that, without uninterrupted shipments from the mainland, the islands would soon exhaust their food supplies. Grocers were allowed to reopen after being issued a license, but Sandy began stockpiling enough food to feed the island population for six months.

Augmenting that effort, Sandy's sugar plantations set aside hundreds of acres to expand local cultivation of vegetables. Still, there were chronic shortages of fresh meat and other consumables from Mainland scarcities, delays in overland transportation, lack of Pacific shipping, and inadequate warehouse and refrigeration space in Honolulu.[39]

One news article reported that Sandy's appointment as Food Control Director "met with general satisfaction throughout the business community," because he was "one of Hawai'i's best known business men and [had] taken an active part in civic and community affairs."[40] An editorial extolled him as "one of the topnotch businessmen of the territory, endowed with plenty of common sense and accustomed to forthright dealing."[41]

"The fact that throughout the entire war, Hawaii was not rationed like mainland communities, speaks volumes for the fairness and efficiency" of Sandy's skillful management.[42]

Still, because of a scarcity of fresh meat, Hawai'i's population largely turned to canned meats, and still is today the largest per capita consumer of Spam.[43] Locally, citizens grew vegetables in victory gardens set up in parks, vacant lots, and in an estimated 15,000 home gardens by August 1942.[44]

The other half of the day Sandy ran American Factors at the base of Bishop and Fort Streets. Since sugar was the lifeblood of Hawai'i industry, American Factors continued to thrive during the war years under Sandy's management. Still, with sugar land converted to vegetables and military use, its plantations were reduced by "more than 22,000 acres." [45] While excess profit levies increased American Factors' taxes fourfold, Sandy ably increased its net income slightly during the war years.[46] The war also disrupted the company's development plans. For the remainder of the war, the company's principal function became the procurement and distribution of basic items essential to the life of the Territory.[47]

Between his full-time job as president of American Factors and several sugar plantations, Director of food distribution, and chairman of the Territory's Board of Leper Hospitals and Settlements, Sandy toiled seven days a week. He did not take a day off from December 7, 1941, until Easter weekend, 1943. Sandy, in suit and tie and a panama hat with feather lei on his head, departed for work in the morning "before the black-out is over," Una wrote, and is "so weary by night," that he was in bed under mosquito nets on his lanai by 8:00 p.m. Unable to exercise much, Sandy "gained quite a lot, but feels fine on the whole." Una concluded, "War is the limit!"

Ginger wrote her sister Ann that their father bet "$10 that the war would be won by us and over by August 1942. I'd gladly pay the 10 bucks if he's right." Unfortunately, she won the bet. Ginger also requested that Ann send bobby pins. "Honolulu has long been out of them—and my hair could use a couple."

Later, she pled for five eyelash curlers, saying the government only imports things here that are vitally necessary to our existence; curlers were not deemed necessary. They had also "been canning guavas and making juice, which we are drinking in place of orange juice," which had disappeared from grocery shelves. Ginger had a permanent wave one day, but complained that "most of the hairdressers are leaving for the coast—as there aren't *enuf* females to do the hair here."

Meanwhile, Ginger could hardly wait to confront Charlie Bryant for maintaining the same mistaken opinion that cost Admiral Kimmel and General Short their commands. Once she did, said Ginger, it was perhaps the only time in Bryant's life that he was left speechless.

Months later, Ginger received letters from the six Australian flyers, enclosing photos of her at Aiea Heights and satirically writing, "Yes, Ginger, you were right. We did hear of Pearl Harbor!"

Michael A. Lilly

Chapter 5

Nimitz: "This is Mr. Walker's Beach!"

IN THE 1930s, the Walkers bought a six-acre parcel with a thousand feet of undeveloped beachfront in La'ie, an hour's drive from downtown Honolulu on the winding two-lane Kamehameha Highway, near what is now the popular Polynesian Culture Center.

Wailele (dancing water) stream snaked through the property under canopies of Kamani, Pandanus and Ironwood trees to a large brackish pond contained by a broad sandbank separating it from the sea. In heavy rains, mountain freshets flooded the stream, which broke through the sandbank, forming torrents and rapids that the Walker grandchildren rode like a roller coaster to the sea. *Muliwai* is Hawaiian for "river," especially one breaking through the sand and into the sea. Hence, the derivation of the name Una gave to the property.

With one of her signature pastel parasols over her head, Una had directed monstrous sugar plantation bulldozers to build huge sand berms around the property to protect it from prevailing winds. She sat next to the driver, directing every push of the blade.[48]

Abutting the highway across the stream, they built a caretaker's house and a grass paddle tennis court outlined in lime.

Access to the court was over a picturesque arched bridge spanning Wailele stream.

On flat ground facing south to the ocean and the towering volcanic Ko'olau Mountains beyond, she built a large shake-roofed main house with a vaulted ceiling and open beams from which hung nets of large Japanese glass balls. Glass balls were hand blown on Japanese fishing sampans and used to float their nets at sea, where they would break loose. Thousands were carried on Pacific currents until they were thrown on a beach. Though they have been replaced today with plastic floats, glass balls are still trapped in swirling pockets of currents from which they sometimes escape and wind up on Muliwai's beach, to the delight of early-morning walkers. They are treasured finds.

Two walls of the main house were glass-paned panel doors that disappeared into pockets. With those doors open, the outdoors became an extension of the living room. Three bedrooms, accessed from the outside ranch-style, flanked obliquely to the left. Each room had a full bath and shower with a door opening from the shower directly outside. A large kitchen and pantry were in the back. A long Koa dining table, fashioned from two large slabs of Koa wood, occupied a covered outdoor dining area flanked by Koa chairs. Inside the eaves of the main house was a line of large Koa "Missionary" rocking chairs facing the ocean. The back of the living room sported a huge Hawaiian bed (*hikie*) banked with pillows, against which visitors lounged and, more often than not, fell asleep to the somnolent sounds of the ocean and leaves rustling in the trade winds.

On the walls, Sandy had hung Hawaiian artifacts he had collected while growing up, including a curved *lomilomi* (massage) stick and Hawaiian war clubs. A large glass case was filled with small glass balls collected on the beach. All of the hardware (locks, doorknobs, and hinges) were of the highest quality solid brass to prevent corrosion, and are still in perfect condition over seven decades later. The lawn between the main house and sea was of Zoysia grass, perfect for lawn bowling, croquet, archery and pitching horseshoes.

A separate two-bedroom, one-bath cottage erected on a bluff overlooking the ocean served as the Walkers' quarters, except when Nimitz was in residence.

Access to the property was by a narrow grass driveway winding between Wailele stream and an Ironwood hedge, pruned to a keen edge with a sharp cane knife wielded by the live-in caretaker, Takeo Higuchi. Turning a bend to the right, the driveway suddenly opened to a wide lawn and panoramic garden surrounded by tropical trees and Spider Lilies. Several layers of thick vegetation muted noise from the road. In the 19th Century, a narrow-gauge railroad carried raw sugar from Kahuku Sugar Mill to a pier fronting the property. All that remained of the pier were its vestigial iron pilings that appeared like eerie aliens emerging in rows from the sea and marching ashore.

To drive into Muliwai was to leave the everyday world behind and enter an enchanting and peaceful Garden of Eden. Spend three days there, and you become so relaxed as to have been Muliwai-fied.

Sandy's Favorite View from the Muliwai Main House, circa 1950

Nimitz at Ease

Muliwai Main House, 1944

As Military Governor, General Emmons oversaw implementation of the Martial Law he inherited from General Short, who had been relieved of his command ten days after the attack. Emmons nervously feared a Japanese invasion of the Hawaiian Islands and began daily inspection trips around Oahu. He always stopped at La'ie, half way around the island on its north shore, to eat his box lunch, and asked Sandy if he could do so at Muliwai. Sandy agreed. As a result, Muliwai began its role as a military sanctuary throughout the war and long afterwards. Soon, Nimitz would regularly retreat there.

Wherever a stream entered the sea, such as Muliwai, its fresh water killed coral, creating a navigable channel—perfect for an enemy landing force. To thwart Japanese amphibious forces, the beaches all around the Island were ringed with huge rolls of barbed wire.[49] All told, some four million feet of wire were strung on private land in the islands.[50]

The Walkers were unaware that nine rows of barbed wire, guards, and an underground corrugated-iron-framed command post blocked the Muliwai beachfront. The weekend after the barbed wire was strung, Sandy donned floral bathing shorts, walked to the edge of the yard for his regular swim and found himself confronted by a confusing maze of barbed wire for the first time. With difficulty, he threaded his way through a frustrating zigzag path, until a soldier in Army greens and bearing a rifle suddenly jumped out of the hidden command post.

"Halt!" commanded the soldier.

Sandy was shocked at being accosted by an armed soldier blocking his way. He told the guard that he was going for a swim.

"Sorry, Sir," replied the soldier sternly, "but this beach is off limits."

"But," an exasperated Sandy protested, "This is my beach. I always swim here!"

"I am sorry, Sir, but I have my orders. No one is allowed on the beach."

After composing himself, Sandy said as he retreated, "Well, we'll see about that next weekend."

On Monday, Sandy called Nimitz. "Chester, would you like to spend the weekend at our La'ie beach house?"

"I'd love to," replied Nimitz who already knew about the Walkers' beautiful hideaway known as Muliwai.

After Nimitz arrived the following Saturday morning, Sandy asked, "Chester, would you like to take a swim in the ocean?"

Nimitz, a lifelong lover of exercise and swimming, replied, "I'd love it!"

Sandy and Nimitz donned floral swim shorts and started working their way through the strands of barbed wire.

"Halt!" said the uniformed soldier blocking their way. He began to say the beach was off limits when he recognized the well-known, white-haired commander of all the military forces in the Pacific.

Nimitz informed the soldier, "This is Mr. Walker's beach! He and his guests may swim here any time he wants to!"

From then on, the beach was no longer off limits to Sandy and his guests. Nimitz spent nearly every weekend and many weekdays of the war with the Walkers relaxing at magical Muliwai. However, Una later said Nimitz had the hardest time getting through all that barbed wire to get out to swim.[51]

After their swim, as he did with all guests, Sandy cautioned Nimitz to use the outdoor shower by the end of the main house to remove salt, sand and any remnants of a rare, noxious seaweed he called "poison limu" (*Lyngbya majuscula*). If it was allowed to dry on bare skin, especially tender areas under swim shorts, the seaweed's toxins left painful red blistering welts which, in severe cases, bled. On the beach, Sandy pointed out the seaweed growing in loose clumps of fine black filaments floating with undulating ocean currents. Many an unhappy swimmer who failed to shower never forgot the lesson.

Sandy also warned about stinging Portuguese Man-o-War jellyfish that sometimes arrived in large colonies, their blue sails catching the wind like sailing ships and trailing long tendrils that stung prey. Its strands can wrap around a swimmer's arms and neck, causing sharp pains that can last all day. Rear Adm. Forrest P. Sherman, Nimitz's Deputy Chief of Staff, once was stung badly enough to be hospitalized.[52]

Nimitz wondered, that first weekend, where the Walkers kept their telephone. Mortified, Sandy explained they did not have one at Muliwai. They never intended to install a phone, because it was their country retreat. He soon realized that if Nimitz was going to spend nights there, they needed a phone, so the commander in chief could remain in contact with his headquarters. By the next weekend, the Walkers had installed the first telephone at Muliwai.

In addition to weekends at Muliwai, Nimitz and the Walkers alternated dinners between Nu'uanu and Nimitz's quarters, some eight miles apart. The Walkers also often hosted garden parties for military, government and business VIPs. One included a Who's Who of military leaders, including the plump Secretary of the Navy, Frank Knox.

Michael A. Lilly

Walker Garden party, August 1942 (left-to-right): Nimitz; Sandy; unknown Commander; unknown Captain; Nimitz chief of staff, Rear Adm. Charles H. "Soc" McMorris; Secretary of the Navy, Frank Knox; Vice Adm. Raymond Spruance; Unknown Rear Admiral; and Nimitz's flag lieutenant, Lt. Cdr. Hal Lamar[53]

Nimitz, Sandy and Spruance[54]

Between the end of 1941 and the start of 1944, the U.S. Pacific Fleet had known disaster and triumph. Today, the Arizona

Michael A. Lilly

Memorial building in Pearl Harbor sits athwart the remains of the World War I-era *Arizona*. At its entrance, the memorial's roof is high, representing America pre-war: strong and resilient, even after a decade of the Great Depression. The roof sags toward its center, representing despair after the tragedy and losses at Pearl Harbor. At the far end, the roof begins to rise, returning to the height of its entrance, representing victory at the end of the war. Its twenty-one windows signify a twenty-one gun salute after victory.

However, 1941 ended with a great deal of angst and fear, especially among those residing in Hawai'i, so far into the Pacific and completely vulnerable to invasion by Japan. America was at its nadir. Many fled the islands for the U.S. mainland. Those stationed in Hawai'i were, like Nimitz, unaccompanied. Wives remained on the mainland, although Nimitz's wife Catherine moved to Berkeley, California, in 1942 to be nearby for her husband's regular strategy meetings with Adm. Ernest King, the wartime head of the Navy, in San Francisco.

It wasn't until June 1942, with the victory at Midway and Japan's first defeat since its fleet was routed by the Korean navy in 1598, that a glimmer of hope for a favorable outcome to the Pacific war returned to the American and Hawaiian psyche. Nimitz later agreed that the victory at Midway was a turning point in the Pacific war that enabled us to take future offensive actions.[55]

There were, in fact, several turning points. The Battle of the Coral Sea, the month before Midway, was a turning point that saved Australia from Japanese invasion and occupation. In the fall of 1942, Guadalcanal in the Solomon Islands was a major turning point that halted the Japanese advance into the South Pacific. The year 1943 was not one of turning points, but rather a year of defense, consolidation, and inexorable advance, as our forces slowly island-hopped toward Japan.

"The true consequence of Midway," wrote historian John Keegan, "lay far in the future, when the Americans penetrated the Japanese [defense] perimeter in the southern and central Pacific at the end of 1943…by which time Japan had lost its superiority in naval airpower." [56] At the start of the next year—1944—the Son of Heaven, Emperor Hirohito, blinked through his spectacles as he predicted, with unusual frankness, "the future of the war situation permits absolutely no optimism." [57]

The year 1944 was a Leap Year and indeed, it was one of triumphal, if costly, leaps across the Pacific, all directed by Adm. Chester W. Nimitz from his white concrete headquarters in Makalapa, Pearl Harbor. His fleet ground relentlessly westward, defeating Japanese forces on the Marshalls, Marianas, and Palau Islands. The Philippines were all but subdued. Thirteen major Japanese bases were taken while others were left to wither in isolation.

Since his arrival in 1941, Nimitz and the Walkers had solidified a rich and comfortable relationship with its own familiar rhythm. One might socialize with a close friend or relative today, perhaps once or twice a week or a handful of times a month, at most. By contrast, while Nimitz was commanding the largest armed forces ever assembled in history, two and a half million men, and a war spanning sixty-five million square miles of ocean and islands, he spent nearly every weekend and every other day of the war with the Walkers!

Shakespeare's King Henry IV could have been talking about Nimitz when, after longing for "gentle sleep," he concluded, "Uneasy lies the head that wears the crown."

As Commander in Chief, Nimitz was under the most extreme stress that any military leader could ever expect to experience. Reading *Graybook*, one is struck by the weight and variety of issues and problems, great and small, that Nimitz dealt with every day with cool determination. He presided over a force fighting a war in the northern, western, southern and southwestern Pacific. He was a master at selecting the best men for the jobs, to whom he delegated enormous on-scene authority.

But Nimitz was not totally hand's-off. He followed, prodded and sometimes guided every detail of the war, for he was ultimately responsible for its success or failure. With limited resources,

Nimitz moved units around the Pacific like players on a chessboard to employ optimum use. He moved Battle Divisions or Destroyer Squadrons and even particular ships to proceed best speed of advance to support various fleet commanders or operations. He directed plans for amphibious landings or attacks, coordinated with allied forces, established and disestablished forward staffs, and deployed tankers and air and surface forces. While the war progressed, Nimitz established new commands in forward areas. Once an island was under U.S. control, Nimitz delineated command relationships and control of shore-based forces while giving senior officers total authority to employ all forces in his vicinity to meet a serious emergency.[58]

Handling the imperious MacArthur, who controlled the southwestern Pacific to which Nimitz provided naval support, was a constant challenge. And, while fighting a war in the west, he maneuvered the political mine field in the east, skillfully handling the Joint Chiefs of Staff, Admiral King, and the president. As one author put it, Nimitz "lay like a valley of humility between two mountains of conceit: Ernest King and General Douglas MacArthur." [59]

Nimitz was also the ultimate disciplinary and administrative authority in the Pacific. He promoted, demoted, and rewarded. Discipline ran the gamut from non-judicial punishment to courts-martial. Nimitz courts-martialed five officers running a large gambling ring. As much as four thousand dollars was won or lost in a single night.

"They will hate me," Nimitz lamented to Catherine, "but as is usual in such high stake games—troubles—forgery—blood, etc., results, and [is] bad for our military effort." Nimitz acknowledged that "everyone knows I do not object to gambling for small stakes for amusement or entertainment," but this was too much.[60]

He also stopped men from moonlighting in civilian jobs, some working eight extra hours a day. "I stopped all of that in the theory that if they did that, they could not possibly do their duty to the government. Besides, their liberty hours are for the purpose of relaxation and rest and doing their shopping…So you see—I have minor problems besides the Japs." [61]

Worse, Nimitz acknowledged to his aide, Lt. Cdr. Hal Lamar, that "One of the responsibilities of command" was, "you have to send some people to their deaths." [62] In planning a strategy, Nimitz hated to know that he was issuing an order that would mean the loss of so many lives, lamenting an order was "going to cost me 10,000 people." [63] In the battle for Okinawa alone, Nimitz was ultimately responsible for over twelve thousand servicemen going to their graves.

Those deaths brought awful letters from bereaved parents, whose sons had died on some atoll. "You killed my son on Tarawa," one bitter parent painfully wrote.[64] Lamar tried to hide them, but Nimitz insisted reading each heartbreaking letter and ensured that they received a respectful response. In a letter to Catherine from Guam in March 1945, Nimitz regretted "receiving two or three letters a day signed, 'a Marine Mother,' and calling me all sorts of names. I am just as distressed as can be over the casualties, but don't see how I could have reduced them." [65]

In the spring of 1945 he expressed sadness to the Walkers, after attending purple heart ceremonies at three hospitals in the western Pacific, about seeing "so many sick and wounded men, and I hope and pray that the war's end will come quickly to stop this killing and maiming." After Catherine visited the forty-year-old Mare Island Naval Hospital, Nimitz was "particularly glad to hear of the high morale of the men who have lost arms or legs…I have seen these men on their way back to the coast, [and] it is very heart wrenching." [66] Left unsaid were the many thousands who perished in combat.

Clark Gable portrayed an army general in the 1949 movie *Command Decision,* who similarly sent hundreds of fliers to their deaths over Germany. Nicknamed Iron Butt for his perceived insensitivity, at the end of the film he poignantly admitted to his softhearted successor that he got "their faces all mixed up sometimes. Kids just coming in on the replacement trucks, and the ones you've already killed. But when you start feeling sorry for yourself, you think of what they've got to go through. There's only one thing you can really do for them, Cliff. Make every one of them count. See that they're not used up for nothing. Maybe you can keep their kid brothers from coming over here."

Like Gable's character, Nimitz was utterly alone in sacrificing so many young sons, brothers, and fathers in the defense of freedom. He tried his best to ensure that every single death counted, so that, with victory, their kid brothers stayed home.

It was for these reasons that his friendship with the Walkers was so important to the war effort. It allowed him precious time away from the pressure-cooker strains of command. Theirs was not just a friendship; the time Nimitz spent with the Walkers became essential to his state of mind.

In Pearl Harbor, Nimitz fought a difficult war; but with the Walkers and Muliwai, the war was left behind, and he became the gentle boy next door. For Nimitz, the gulf between his warfighting and friendship with the Walkers was wider than the Pacific. Una said they felt the part they played in Nimitz's personal life while in Hawai'i was essential to victory in the Pacific.

Chapter 6

1944: "Still at War!"

"STILL AT WAR!" began Una's diary of 1944.

After more than two years at war, the Walkers awoke at the palatial Castle estate* in the hills above Kailua. Fifty-four-year-old Harold K.L. "Hal" Castle, a missionary descendant, owned Kaneohe Ranch Company, Ltd, comprising most of the land on the east side of the Ko'olau Mountains. Una admired Hal as a great horseman, polo player and a dog-lover. Another couple present was Martha ("Matty") and Stanley Kennedy, Sr. Kennedy was fifty, President and founder of Hawaiian Airlines and the Coca-Cola Bottling Company of Honolulu. Matty headed Hawai'i's Red Cross Canteen Corps. On the morning of December 7, 1941, she had passed the entrance to Pearl Harbor aboard an inter-island steamer a mere hour and a half before the attack. Once home and the attack underway, she mobilized the Canteen Corps, which began feeding medical unit workers, officials, truck drivers, guards, emergency police, civilians, or anyone who needed food.⁶⁷

Nimitz was in San Francisco attending a regular war strategy

---

* The Castle estate is now St. Stephens Seminary.

meeting with Admirals King and William "Bull" Halsey at the offices of Adm. D. W. Bagley, Commander, Western Sea Frontiers. President Roosevelt had appointed Admiral King, who was sixty-five, to overall command of the U.S. Navy with the title, Commander in Chief, U.S. Fleet. In the aftermath of Pearl Harbor, King wisely changed its acronym from the ill-conceived CinCUS (pronounced "sink us") to CominCh. During this period, Under Secretary of the Navy James Forrestal, a World War I aviator, was lobbying for more aviators in senior Navy positions. Nimitz, a submariner, was vulnerable, but he had a staunch supporter in Admiral King, with whom he became very close while fighting the war in the Pacific.

Fortunately, Nimitz remained in charge, although he was forced to accept a sometimes difficult Vice Adm. John H. "Jack" Towers, an aviator, as his second in command—Deputy Commander in Chief, Pacific Fleet. Towers graduated from the Naval Academy a year after Nimitz in 1906 and flight school in 1911 and was the Navy's third aviator. He designed the gold wings that every naval aviator wears today. Towers rivaled Forrestal in his advocacy of appointing aviators to high Navy positions, deeming non-aviators as black shoe sons of bitches and derisively calling his own boss, submariner Nimitz, as Uncle Sink.[68] He was so outspoken in support of naval aviation that he became a cover story in *Time* magazine in June 1941. At fifty-six, Towers was ruggedly handsome with receding hair, aquiline nose and a tense face with squinty blue eyes that peered at you, as if straining. In a photo of the Walkers' summer garden party, Towers is bending over with a fierce expression. Nimitz thought Towers was a little arrogant, so there wasn't much love lost between them.[69]

The three admirals—Nimitz, Halsey and King—had very little in common outside the Navy and war. King, according to historian, Samuel Eliot Morison, was "A sailor's sailor who neither had nor wanted any life outside the navy...He had no toleration for fools or weaklings...and was more feared than loved...a hard, grim, determined man."[70] His chiseled features mirrored his take-no-prisoner's personality. Humorless, tough, and imperious, he ruled the Navy with an iron fist. Roosevelt facetiously said he "shaves with a blowtorch."

Halsey, then sixty-one, was stocky with a barrel chest, bulldog face and bushy eyebrows. He was coarse, outgoing, [hard-drinking], sprinkled his language with "sailor's tongue" expletives, and harbored a violent temper. He was also outspoken, aggressive and gregarious. His slogan was, "Hit hard, hit fast, hit often." [71]

Nimitz's public relations chief described Halsey as "a colorful figure, audacious in battle and fun-loving in repose." [72] Sailors loved him.

By contrast, Nimitz was the consummate southern gentleman. Hanko recalled that he was "very calm, soft-spoken and had a great sense of humor and a hearty laugh. He was also a man of great courage and kindness…" [73]

Nimitz's youngest daughter Mary, a Dominican nun, described her father as gentle, "very warm and down-to-earth," and "with a great sense of humor." [74] In the many years Lamar served him, "Admiral Nimitz never raised his voice, and I never heard him curse." [75]

He was "gentle but exacting, gracious but hard and fearless, like a mailed fist in a satin glove." [76] An Army Air Force general "recognized the vein of merry humor that flowed beneath a sometimes-stern visage." [77]

He was unflappable under stress. Within five minutes of taking off from Pearl Harbor in his flag flying boat, two engines failed. A dead-stick landing back in the Harbor punctured a hole in the plane, which began to sink. "Everybody was kind of shook up about this," said Lamar. Everyone, "except the Admiral … who never got shook up. He was very calm." [78]

Nimitz fit the character of the military genius in Carl von Clausewitz's 18th Century book on military theory, *On War*. The genius of such a leader was his strength of mind and character, which overcame the extreme mental and physical challenges inherent in war: uncertainty, chance, danger, physical effort, and suffering. Brilliant military leaders like Nimitz and Patton are born, not made. As Winston Churchill wrote, in describing one of England's most victorious generals, his ancestor the Duke of Marlborough, "Genius, though it may be armed, cannot be acquired, either by reading or experience." [79]

Nimitz also had an innate ability to pick the best man for the job. Then he gave him his direction and got out of the way. "When an operation is underway," wrote one account, "and radio silence prevents battle reports, Nimitz is extremely calm. He gives his taskforce commanders a free hand and never advises them during battle. Every naval engagement can be second-guessed, but Admiral Nimitz's officers know they have his full confidence." [80]

Nimitz was generally abstemious, never consuming more than two drinks before dinner. Hanko wrote that he enjoyed a special old-fashioned recipe:

> He placed a cube of sugar in the bottom of the glass, placed one drop of Angostura bitters on the cube, melted the cube with a little hot water, added cracked ice, two ounces of straight bourbon whiskey and then, as a final touch, floated a tablespoon full of dark Jamaica rum on the surface. This was his special drink. He drank very carefully, however, never to excess. [81]

Nimitz also concocted his own CinCPac Special, when liquor was rationed [to] a bottle a week a man. Three quarts of bourbon and 1/4 of a fifth of gold label rum was poured into a gallon jug. Sugar syrup was added cautiously until you can just detect the presence of sugar. The jug was then filled with tap water. It was desirable but not necessary to add two whole vanilla beans, which could remain for years of refills. The powerful mixture was poured over ice and served.

With such a strong drink, "How did we ever win the war?" mused Nimitz's grandson, Chet Lay.

Lamar wrote, "His other favorite was a Scotch and Soda, in a tall glass with lots of ice and lots of soda." Nimitz complained, however, "that the soda in Honolulu was not strong enough and did not have any pep." So, Lamar contacted Sandy Walker, from whom he was able to obtain three cases of soda, which were specially charged for the Admiral's benefit.

"Unfortunately, the charge was so strong that when I opened the first bottle, the entire contents went clear across the living room, much to Admiral Nimitz's amusement" [82] and, perhaps, to Lamar's chagrin.

After the attack on Pearl Harbor, liquor was initially rationed, although Sandy had his own covert supply. One night, the Walkers' oldest child Ginger peered out to see a car creep up the driveway with two ribbons of light stabbing the concrete from blacked out headlights. Sandy emerged from the front door to greet the driver, who opened his trunk. The trunk light illuminated the driver, a sheriff, and cases of whiskey that Sandy spirited into the house.

Sandy and Nimitz had many similar traits that made them kindred spirits. Both were kindly, generous and of gentlemanly demeanor. "Happiness," Sandy often said, "is not built on other's unhappiness." They both had infectious smiles and twinkling eyes.

Rear Adm. Edwin T. Layton, Nimitz's intelligence chief, later said, "He had that brilliant white smile—it just lights up—like somebody let in the sun by raising a window shade; his smile and his blue eyes would go right through you." [83]

So, too, Sandy's eyes were so friendly and affable they warmed your heart. And both were inveterate optimists. When Nimitz asked Sandy how he was, he invariably replied, "Never felt better in my life," or "I'm on the crest of a wave!"

Sandy and Nimitz each made one feel good, just being in their presence.

Each was thrifty.

"Waste not want not," said Sandy; "Teach him he must deny himself," Una quoted Gen. Robert E. Lee, traits borne out of Protestant work ethic upbringing (Nimitz was Lutheran; the Walkers were Episcopalian) and the Depression.

Like the Walkers, Nimitz was punctilious to a fault. They lived by the clock. If [Nimitz] was to visit a new ship coming into Pearl Harbor whose arrival was 11:00, Lamar sent the barge out early in the morning to exactly time the thing. He wanted the barge to hit the bottom of the gangway at 11:00.

When he was invited to the governor of Hawai'i's palace and [was] to be there at 6:45, he wanted his car to drive up at 6:45, not a minute before or a minute later.[84]

So, too, the Walkers. When I was to pick them up at a particular time, I showed up at that precise moment with not a second to spare. Arriving late was rude, Una said. Nimitz was particularly irked by the unpunctuality of politicians.[85] Neither the Walkers nor Nimitz tolerated carelessness about being on time for their appointments.[86]

They were also perfectionists. Una never tolerated bad manners or fractured language, often correcting one of her children's or grandchildren's improper use of the "King's English."

Appropriately, Nimitz enjoyed telling the story about a husband whose wife caught him kissing the housemaid. The wife rebuked her husband, saying, "I'm surprised." In response, he corrected his wife, "No, my dear. I am surprised—and you are astonished."[87]

Meanwhile, during the San Francisco Conference, the Navy leaders discussed the upcoming assault against the Marshall Islands, called, Operation Flintlock. The Japanese were in great strength in the Marshalls, which straddled the route of the Allied advance toward Japan. The center of the Marshalls was the strong base at Kwajalein. Nimitz asked his senior commanders whether to attack the fringe or go in and knock Kwajalein out.

When they all suggested the fringe, Nimitz decided, "Well, that's fine. We'll hit Kwajalein."[88]

Nimitz "returned from [the] coast," Una told her diary, on January 6th. The following evening Una invited a large group including Nimitz for cocktails and dinner.

"Nimitz," Hanko wrote, "was regularly accompanied to

dinners at our house in Nu'uanu" by fleet surgeon, Captain Elphege A. M. Gendreau,* (and in 1943, his successor, Capt. Thomas C. "Doc" Anderson), flag lieutenant Hal Lamar, and chief of staff, Rear Adm. Raymond A. Spruance.

Spruance was fifty-four, wiry and enjoyed exercise perhaps even more than Nimitz. He was ruggedly handsome, with a square jaw and chiseled features, with an uncanny resemblance to Walter Huston's character in Howard Hughes' 1943 movie, *Outlaw*. An officer told Potter that while Nimitz was an easygoing, amiable sort of old shoe type, Spruance was the neat, rigid, down-to-earth type of person who was always all business.[89] Shy, plodding and abstemious, this steely-eyed admiral won the Battle of Midway against superior forces with skillful direction.

When, in August 1943, Spruance took command of the largest armada in history, the Central Pacific force (later named, the Fifth Fleet), which won all the major Pacific battles, Rear Adm. Charles H. "Soc" McMorris, then fifty-three, replaced him as chief of staff. Thereafter, Soc normally accompanied Nimitz to events with the Walkers.

Tall and cadaverous like Disney's Ichabod Crane, with a high, balding forehead, McMorris was nicknamed "Socrates" or "Soc" by his U.S. Naval Academy classmates for his abilities as a thinker and strategist.[90] Described as having a face resembling a fried egg, Soc called himself the ugliest man in the Navy.[91]

As chief of staff, Soc was essential to shielding Nimitz from routine matters, which relieved him of many burdens. Soc was brilliant, caustically blunt, and offended aviators with his candid opinions about their inexperience in ship tactics. While Soc had the friendliest relations with the Walkers, he could be brutally harsh to others. When an army colonel wanted to know why he was denied a jeep, Soc replied, "Because I'm a born sonofabitch and I'm going to stay that way."[92] Unlike Spruance, Soc avoided exercise and

---

* Gendreau sadly died aboard an LST during combat in the South Pacific in July 1943.

wouldn't walk across the street if he could ride.[93]

Lamar, whose job as flag lieutenant or aide was to cater to the needs of Nimitz, was rarely beyond the Admiral's beck and call. They had been together for so long that, even before Nimitz came to Hawai'i in 1941, he implicitly knew what Nimitz needed, sometimes before Nimitz realized it. Lamar said he had a kind of extrasensory perception by which he always anticipated what he was going to want.[94]

That was the hallmark of a successful flag lieutenant. Ginger nicknamed Lamar "Hedy" for the then-famous and gorgeous Austrian film actress, Hedy Lamarr. A handsome man with a slightly receding hairline, Lamar eagerly participated in Nimitz's walking, swimming, hiking and other exercises and became as close to the Walkers and Ginger as Nimitz was.

Walker Mansion

From its porte-cochère Nimitz climbed several granite steps to a covered porch supported by square-fluted columns, and entered the mansion through a large, beveled-glassed door. Inside was a large hall foyer and grand staircase, with a high-ceilinged sitting room to the left. The library to the right, and beyond the library was a large dining room with two massive Italian crystal chandeliers and space for twenty-two people to sit comfortably.

"For a seated dinner," said Una, "I think sixteen to eighteen persons is ideal."

Una Walker's "Secret Garden" Off Side Lanai

Ironically, the dining room served as a fictional Nimitz's office, and the sitting room as his dining room in Otto Preminger's 1965 war epic, *In Harm's Way*.[*]

No matter how warm and humid the evening, Sandy and Una greeted their guests in eveningwear, Sandy in a suit and tie and Una

---

[*] The five-minute scene, which took three days to film, can be watched in its entirety on line at Turner Classic Movies:
http://www.tcm.com/mediaroom/video/348030/In-Harm-s-Way-Movie-Clip-The-Navy-s-Never-Wrong.html

in a gown. Guests assembled on a side lanai of tropical rattan furniture. In the center of the room was a unique coffee table—a gigantic, South Pacific white coral head, sheathed in plastic, rising up from a thick stem to a flat canopy of jagged spikes, a gift from Marjorie Post. The lanai overlooked Una's favorite garden surrounded by canopied Monkey Pod trees, areca palms, orchids, heliconias, anthuriums, and gingers.

"It is only visible from this lanai," explained Una, "I call it my Secret Garden."

Long sprays of aromatic *dendrobium superbum* orchids streamed from the massive limbs of a large Milo tree like a frozen waterfall.

Sandy stocked a cart with an array of delicious cheeses. Their cheerful Japanese maid, Kauai-born Matsuko Goto, dressed in crisp white uniform,[*] circulated with canapés of warm cheese puffs, Roquefort cheese on toast, Spanish sausage and other *hors d'oeuvres*.

Dinners were lavish affairs in the main dining room, with Hara the cook concocting a delectable menu, which included fruit cocktail, soup, fish entrée, and main course served by Matsuko. Sandy never let a guest leave a dinner table without a dessert of partially melted ice cream. At curfew hour, blackout curtains were drawn, or lights turned out. Not a light, nor even a match, glowed in the dark outside. While creeping down the driveway at night to Nu'uanu Avenue, as Una and Sandy sometimes did, Honolulu was invisible to the eye, as it was hoped it would be to Japanese warships and planes.

"After dinner in Nu'uanu," Hanko continued, "Nimitz and his senior military commanders, as well as my father, would play poker in a large upstairs sitting room. Nimitz loved to play poker, and he was a fine player."[95]

Sandy and Una occupied two large upstairs bedrooms, each with a separate covered lanai, the size of a large living room. On hot nights, they slept in four-poster beds encased in mosquito

---

[*] Maids in wealthy Honolulu homes wore kimonos until the war, when they insisted on wearing anything but, from shame.

netting on their adjacent lanais. Poker was dealt in the sitting room next to Sandy's bedroom. Cigar and cigarette smoke fouled the air and hung in a thick blue cloud against the ceiling. Una cheered from the sidelines and, when they were short-handed, she joined in the card game.

By these gatherings, whether swimming at Muliwai, walking Kailua beach or playing tennis at the Walkers' court, Nimitz relieved his mind of the demands of command, which helped him overcome chronic sleeplessness. The talk was of anything but war. Amusing tales were expected. Nimitz had hundreds of these stories, which he could tell all night long.[96] Many of them were humorous or risqué yarns, which might be politically incorrect today. Sometimes he repeated a story, as he once started to do to his son Chester, Jr. and wife Joan. "Aw, Dad," interrupted the son, "you told that one last night."

"Then," instructed his father with a smile, "listen this time for technique." [97]

One of Nimitz's choicest mixed-company jokes was about a fat hypochondriac who needed his appendix removed, but, because of his age and disposition, he had a hard time finding a surgeon willing to do it. Emerging from the operation, the patient asked the surgeon about his condition.

"You're doing fine," said the surgeon.

"But doctor," the patient inquired with his hand to his neck, "there's something I don't understand. I have a terrible sore throat, which I did not have when I entered the hospital. What causes that?"

"Well," replied the doctor, "I'll tell you. In view of the circumstances, your case was a very special one[,] and a big group of my colleagues came to watch the operation. When it was over they gave me such a round of applause that I removed your tonsils as an encore." [98]

Nimitz's wry writ could sometimes be appreciated only by a few. His wife Catherine had complained about a prudish woman who gave her a hard time at a San Francisco club. Nimitz responded satirically that the woman was "a good candidate for the conundrum: 'If a corset cover covers a corset, what does a corset cover?' Answer: 'A naval base, two canteens and a recreational center.' Tell her I sent it to her in one of my more serious moments and that I am joining you ruining the morals of the old ladies." [99]

What was the conundrum and how might the answer ruin the woman's morals? My wife deciphered it. Nimitz's naval base corset covered the woman's naval, the two canteens her breasts, and the recreational center her private parts. A very gentile way of putting the prudish woman in her place!

Sandy was full of stories, as well, which he and Nimitz shared for hours with hardly a word about the carnage in the western Pacific. One of Sandy's favorite D.C. stories from the 1930s was meeting Roosevelt's Secretary of the Interior, Harold L. Ickes, who had a reputation for independent Republicanism, honesty, and pugnacity.[100] Roosevelt's Attorney General, Francis Biddle, who knew Ickes well, said he was combative, shrewd, [and] belligerent, but never a bore.[101] If Sandy had any inkling of Ickes' nature, he would not have been surprised by the fierce tirade to which he was subjected.

Ickes paced back and forth before the seated Sandy, shaking his fist, and shouting angrily, "You are nothing but a tyrant and a filthy capitalist!"

Ickes harangued the silent Sandy for at least a quarter of an hour, sat down and smugly said, "Well, Mr. Walker, what have you got to say for yourself?"

"Nothing," Sandy replied with a smile, "I'd say you just about covered it all."

After a short pause, Ickes burst out laughing, reached out his hand and said, "Put 'er there, Mr. Walker. We're going to be good friends!" And they were.

That is not to say that war was never a topic of discussion with Sandy. Presiding over American Factors, he provided endless supplies and assistance to the military. His plantation trucks moved military and medical equipment. Hundreds of acres of sugar land were turned over to the military for bunkers and housing.

Thousands of blankets were provided when needed. At 2:00 a.m. one morning, Sandy received a call from an Army colonel needing one ton of yellow laundry soap, which he promptly had delivered.[102] But normally, Sandy and Nimitz did not discuss the travails of war.

On Saturday January 8th, Una awoke at her normal time, 5:30 a.m., and paced herself through a series of exercises and ballet stretches before breakfast and greeting her yardmen as they arrived for work. She spent several hours each day in the garden working and supervising her yardmen. A lifelong gardener, she revealed the secrets for her success. It was very important for the owner to supervise her garden and workers. "The eye of the owner," she said with a *kolohe* (mischievous) smile, "is worth a ton of manure."

One secret to gardening, she revealed to me, was to only plant things where they are happy. Plants are not happy in a climate or at an elevation where they don't belong. Another secret was giving plants and gardens intensive care.

Una pointed to a riot of yellow *Oncidium* orchids growing in a Lychee tree. "They look like they belong there, don't they? Because orchids grow naturally in the crotches of trees, they catch the sun and rain and flourish. That's what I mean about growing plants only where they are happy."

Throughout her seven acres of gardens were some thirty varieties of orchids of every imaginable color growing in profusion in flower beds, potting sheds and yards, and streaming from tree limbs or from crotches of trees.

When he was not at work, Sandy donned a wide-brimmed woven planter's hat and blue checked *Palaka* (Hawaiian cowboy) shirt and denim shorts and worked with Sueki Goto, Matsuko's husband, tending to orchid propagation. In a shed, they potted young orchid shoots in small terracotta pots of fern fibers and gravel, which were lined up in the greenhouse or one of several lath houses. As the orchids matured, they were repotted and placed in outdoor storage areas on raised rows of perforated metal Marsden Mats he had obtained from the military.

Michael A. Lilly

Later that morning, Nimitz and Lamar took the Walkers to Kailua to walk the beach. They drove up Nu'uanu Valley on the snaking two-lane Old Pali Road through a tunnel of Monkey Pod, Ear Pod and Mango trees to a narrow pass in the mountain, called the Pali, and down a thousand-foot defile leading to Kailua beach on the eastern side of Oahu for an afternoon of hiking and swimming.

Earlier, Sandy had pointed out to Nimitz that in his youth, the road over the mountains was little more than a footpath. When bubonic plague broke out in Kailua, Sandy was one of several teenagers stationed at the cleft of the Pali with a rifle and orders to prevent anyone from crossing the mountain pass and spreading the disease to the rest of the island.

With a mischievous grin, Sandy called Nimitz's attention to the rounded twin peaks of *Konahuanui,* which formed the tallest mountain of the Ko'olau Range next to where he had stood watch as a teenager. Out of earshot of the ladies, Sandy translated the Hawaiian name as meaning, "his large fruit" or "big balls." The dual-mounded peaks were formed, according to a visually painful and peculiar Hawaiian legend, when a giant tried to catch a *wahine* (woman) he was chasing by throwing his testicles at her, and they landed instead on the ridge.

Nimitz was a physical fitness advocate and loved long walks, pitching horseshoes, tennis and swimming. These allowed Nimitz to relax and stimulate idle conversation and [get] one's mind off the vital and sometimes-depressing business at hand.[103] From Nimitz's Guam headquarters in 1945, Lamar wrote to the Walkers that they took regular two-hour hikes in the hills and along beaches.

For his weekly sojourns to Kailua, Nimitz drove in a big, seven-passenger sedan and changed to swimming gear in a waterfront home, the Damon Property (or 'Prostate Rest'), which the Navy had rented for the use of senior officers between tours of sea duty, but was rarely used by them, because it was too isolated for men who preferred to socialize while they were on shore.[104] The Kailua property was a six-acre parcel owned by Cyril F. "Cy" Damon, a prominent island businessman and President of Bishop

Trust Company, as well as a close friend of the Walkers. His late son Gordon had never heard the property referred to as "Prostate Rest," and had no idea from whence that name came. The property was a sprawling beachfront estate with a three-bedroom house, detached garage and maid's quarters, and paddle tennis court. (The property has since been subdivided into six, separate multi-million-dollar residences.) Gordon also said younger military officers sometimes threw wild parties at the estate.

Nimitz's sojourns consisted mainly of a hike along the beach in bathing trunks—two miles, according to Admiral Spruance, who always went, five miles—according to the recollections of the more tenderfooted officers....[105]

After the hike, Nimitz, Spruance, and Lamar usually swam back part of the way, probably a mile. Kailua beach is in fact about two and a half miles long, so Nimitz's round trip entailed five miles of excellent exercise from walking on soft sand. The less-fit swimmers came ashore exhausted after a quarter of a mile or so.[106]

The July 10, 1944 issue of *Life* magazine noted that Nimitz "devotes a part of each day to exercise of an extremely lively nature for a man of 59[,] and he dines out a maximum of one evening a week."

Describing the wide variety of his exercise regimen, the article concluded that Nimitz's:

> *...enthusiasm for exercise, which amounts to cultism, is perhaps an outlet for interior pressure, all overt signs of which are otherwise missing in his behavior. The Admiral plays a fair game of tennis and has a bounce wall rigged up on the lawn outside his office, so he can practice in spare moments. Next to this device is a pistol target at which, from a wooden platform 20 yards away, he shoots for a few minutes once or twice a week in competition with his flag lieutenant or any caller who may accept a challenge. The pistol shooting takes place, recurrently startling the other denizens of the headquarters, at about*

> 12 o'clock, just after the Admiral's daily staff conference and tends to relieve any feelings of tension engendered thereby. Late in the afternoon the Admiral is ready for more exercise. Having taken one walk of a mile or so before his 7 o'clock breakfast, he may take another, this one of five or six miles to the top of a small mountain, or play horseshoes at his quarters. Once a week he drives 15 miles across the island to a fine beach where he goes for a swim. A Nimitz swim is usually preceded by a three-mile hike along the beach. One of the Admiral's close associates, such as Admiral Spruance, may accompany him into the water. Both as a walker and a swimmer, Admiral Spruance sets a pace and distance that exceed even that of Nimitz.[107]

He "still beats most of his juniors," said another magazine. Comparing Nimitz's war and tennis strategies, he "never hits without figuring in advance where he will place the next shot. Each of his island-by-island thrusts toward Japan has always been part of the next move."[108]

Throughout the war, Nimitz and Chimey Walker, wife of Sandy's nephew Jack Walker, were doubles partners. Jack's autobiography recounted that in the spring of 1942, they were playing in a tournament on O'ahu. The evening of the finals Nimitz called Chimey with bad news. "I am very sorry, Chimey, but I will not be able to participate in the finals tomorrow."

Unfortunately, that meant Chimey and Nimitz would lose by default. He regretted being unable to explain the reason, adding, "later this week you'll know the reason why."

Nimitz later initialed a grim prediction in the *Graybook* that "the whole course of the war in the Pacific may hinge on the developments of the next two or three days."[109] The next morning, June 4, 1942, *Graybook* recorded "the start of what may be the greatest sea battle since Jutland"[110] in World War I. The Battle of Midway had begun, together with a lot of anxiety at Makalapa.

Between our code-broken knowledge of the Japanese invasion fleet and the enemy's ignorance that we were lying in wait, lay infinite possible outcomes, some dire.

Soon, however, Nimitz's tennis partner, Chimey, along with the rest of the world, cheered at America's triumph. "Quite a trade off," Jack Walker concluded. "A tennis tournament default for a victory that turned the tide of the Pacific war." [111] *Graybook* concluded, "This was a great day for the American Navy." [112]

As it was for America as well.

Una's diary often mentions Nimitz calling or showing up for a drive to Kailua or even for drinks and sometimes dinner with no advance warning. Potter explains that the Kailua outings, for example, "came as a surprise because, for security reasons, no pattern was maintained, that is, they rarely came the same day in successive weeks." [113] When summoned, the Walkers dropped whatever they were doing and left with their friend Nimitz.

Unlike many on Nimitz's staff, who vanished whenever Kailua or a hike was mentioned, Una enjoyed the outdoors and exercise and treasured the walks with Nimitz. (An avid horsewoman, Una continued to ride into her nineties.)

In his youth, Sandy was an athlete, playing football in high school and at Harvard. In those days, he played both offensive and defensive positions, with less protective equipment, so, he explained, it was a more brutal game than today. He was so strong that he could pull himself up to a chin bar one-handed. But after contracting tuberculosis in his younger days and recuperating on Waikiki beach, he put on a great deal of weight that he never lost. So, on many of Nimitz's Kailua Beach outings, Sandy would not have walked the entire five-mile roundtrip.

After walking Kailua beach, the Walkers dined with Nimitz at his Makalapa quarters. The dining room was large enough to accommodate a large group. The floors were covered with lauhala woven matting. In the corner of the living room was a card table where four could eat comfortably. The furniture was made of tropical rattan with gracefully curved arms. At every dinner,

Nimitz's staff hand-painted creative nametags for guests such as one with a palm tree and Diamond Head crater in the background. Etiquette dictated that Una's seat was always to Nimitz's right.

Dinner Nametag Hand-Painted by Nimitz's Staff for Una Walker

After dinner, they often enjoyed a movie at a remarkable outdoor theater near Nimitz's quarters. While the back of the theater was covered, most of the audience was exposed to the elements. Una noted that the movie that evening was with Mae West, likely her 1943 musical, *The Heat's On*.

Una's diary was peppered with positive statements about a lovely day, happy dinner, nice dinner, happy fun, lovely swim, and so forth. She was a lady in every sense of the word and an optimist—she believed in the power of positive thinking. In 1982, when she was ninety-five years old, she read the new best-seller, *In Search of Excellence: Lessons from America's Best-Run Companies*,[114] and described the common theme among successful leaders—the ability to motivate people through the power of positive thinking and optimism.

Una wanted to embrace those qualities. She was already an eternal optimist, as was Ginger. I never heard her utter an unkind word about another person (no matter how vile the person), even in private. "If you have nothing nice to say," she instructed, "say nothing."

Una was upbeat, positive and happy, right up to her passing. So, these references in her diary were not Pollyanna-like jottings; they accurately reflected how she felt about those events. That isn't to say she wasn't strong-willed, because she was. She moved mountains, people and events. She was someone to reckon with. She controlled the world around her with grace, persuasion, and feminine mystique. One could hardly say "No" to her. She managed her family and friends, as a symphony conductor directed his orchestra.

Sandy's success and their relationship with the movers and shakers of their day owed a great deal to Una's powerful personality and drive. Through it all, however, she was a positive force for good. Her intentions, and indeed her achievements, were to make the world a better place for everyone. We never fully understood this as grandchildren growing up, when we sometimes rued her control, but I came to appreciate it in my young adulthood. Una was a remarkable Renaissance woman, whom the ten of us are honored to call Grandmother.

On January 10, 1944, Una celebrated Hal Lamar's birthday with dinner including Nimitz, Doc Anderson, Hanko, Sandy, Chimey and Jack Walker. After dinner, they climbed upstairs and played poker and [had] fun. While hands were dealt, smoke filled the poker room. Sandy puffed on a cigar while others, including Nimitz, smoked cigarettes. After-dinner drinks flowed for those with a thirst. When a player won a large hand, Una, who sat regally in the background, clapped her hands with delight and shouted for joy like a young girl. In the last month of the war, she wrote to Nimitz, nostalgically recalling those wonderful evenings upstairs.

"Eight poker players is the perfect number, with seven to play and one [Una] who loves to watch, ever ready, however, to take a hand if she is needed. No time or distance can ever erase the happy memory of those cheery games."

Michael A. Lilly

On January 12, 1944, Una delivered *cypripedium* orchids (considered by Charles Darwin the grandparent of today's exotics) to Nimitz's quarters for a lunch he was hosting. Meanwhile, Nimitz, his deputy Vice Adm. John H. Towers, and Assistant Secretary of Navy Air Artemus L. Gates attended a ceremony at the Walkers' historic Japanese garden. The local newspaper published a photograph of Gates and Nimitz taken that day in the garden.

That evening, the Walkers were back at Nimitz's quarters for dinner with Adm. DeWitt Clinton Ramsey, who was fifty-two and Chief of the Bureau of Aeronautics, Vice Adm. George D. Murray, who was fifty-one and Commander Air Forces Pacific Fleet. Both had been aviation pioneers and were, respectively, the forty-fifth and twenty-second naval officers to complete flight training. (For extraordinary heroism in command of the carrier USS *Saratoga* (CV 3) during the Battle of Guadalcanal in August 1942, President Roosevelt awarded Ramsey the Navy Cross.)

Rounding out the guests was Rear Adm. Forrest P. Sherman, Nimitz's deputy chief of staff. Sherman, who was forty-four, was a handsome man with soft blue eyes and a slightly receding hairline, who was an unabashed advocate for aviators in senior command, as well as his own ambitions. Sherman had established himself a hero as commander of the carrier *Wasp*, sunk off Guadalcanal, and was later lauded for having demonstrated genuine brilliance in tactics and strategy as a principal planner, under Admiral Nimitz.[115] He had a lively personality, and Ginger said he had a spark about him!

While all the guests were close friends or associates of Nimitz's, having the sociable Sandy and Una present ensured lively conversation and a host of amusing stories around the dinner table. "Thank God for the Walkers," Nimitz must have thought during many a dinner at Makalapa. For all their gregariousness in crowds, politicians can be the worst bores or even downright shy one-on-one. Some military officers, having spent most of their lives cloistered around other military men and families, could hardly hold a conversation outside military subjects. Being well-travelled, inquisitive and exceedingly pleasant, Sandy and Una were perfectly able to hold interesting conversations with anyone. They were patient listeners, flattering when needed, and knowledgeable on most any subject. For Nimitz, who was daily besieged with guests from all walks of life and temperament, the Walkers were the most congenial couple to round out his dinner table.

The next day, January 13, 1944, Congress directed the Secretaries of War and Navy to investigate the attack on Pearl Harbor, another of what ultimately became nine separate such investigations.

Meanwhile, Una received a letter from Lamar enclosing photos of a Purple Heart ceremony at the five thousand-bed Aiea Naval Hospital in the hills above Pearl Harbor. Nimitz had pinned Purple Hearts on khaki-uniformed serviceman, all standing at attention outside the hospital. Behind Nimitz is a group of white-uniformed Red Cross volunteers, including Una, who is holding a Purple Heart case and the only white purse.

Admiral Nimitz Awarding Purple Hearts at Aiea Naval Hospital with Una Walker Behind (with white purse), December 22, 1943[116]

Whenever a new group of casualties arrived at Aiea Naval Hospital, Nimitz visited the wards. When told about one young mortally wounded sailor whom the doctors suspected was no more than fifteen years old, Nimitz asked the sailor how old he was.

"Nineteen," was his reply.

"Regardless of your age," said Nimitz, "you're a good sailor, the bravest and best, and we are proud of you." With a smile on his lips, the boy "died shortly afterwards." [117]

On Saturday, January 15th, Sandy was quoted in the paper as saying that many of the problems and shortcomings of maintaining healthy food inventories had been worked out with the cooperation of local food and feed merchants. [118]

Later that day, Nimitz picked up the Walkers and Hanko to walk Kailua beach, followed by a swim. That evening, after dinner at Nimitz's quarters, they watched the lighthearted 1943 Oscar-nominated, *Lassie Come Home,* starring young Roddy McDowall, Donald Crisp and Dame May Witty.

One officer described to Potter how strenuous the Kailua beach walks were. "You lose a layer of skin on the bottoms of your feet [which] are sensitive for two or three days." [119] The last remark in Una's diary that evening, one of only a few to allude to an ailment, admitted she had enjoyed a wonderful day, but suffered a sore toe from the long walk on Kailua beach.

The next day, Una had planned to attend a Texas Round Up, but remained at home all day nursing [her sore] toe. Her toe must have been very painful to miss an event in which Nimitz was the principal figure. At 3:00 p.m., Nimitz was the chief guest of honor at Ala Moana Park, bordering the ocean between Honolulu and Waikiki. He read from a five-page legal size speech, which Una listened to live on radio KGMB.

"He told some forty thousand fellow Texans and guests that, while they were 'thousands of miles away from the Great State we are proud to call home,' the 'gathering proves again that the ties that bind Texans together can be stretched a long way but cannot be broken. It shows that you can take a man out of Texas, but you can't take Texas out of the man."'

Beer flowed freely and the Round Up hurled out of control, as the park was wrecked in a wake of trash and trampled plants. Brig. Gen. S. L. A. Marshall said, "Amid the vast disorder, Nimitz was not only fully at ease, but enjoying himself hugely, laughing, waving to all hands...." [120] (Nimitz was soon to liken its devastation to that unleashed by Allied firepower on Kwajalein Atoll in the western Pacific!)

On Tuesday, January 18th, the Walkers opened their *Honolulu Advertiser* to the following headlines:

Nimitz Declares Fleet Will "Smoke the Japs Out"

"The Japanese," Nimitz was quoted, "are a vicious and resourceful foe," but they were being besieged by the "triple elements of land, sea and air power" of Allied forces.

At 4:00 p.m., Nimitz's personal driver, Henry T. Beach, a survivor of the USS *West Virginia* (BB 48) sunk in the attack on Pearl Harbor, drove Una to Makalapa, from which she and Nimitz trekked up the steep hill to Aiea Naval Hospital—one of Nimitz's favorite hikes that took two hours round trip.[121] The hospital was high in the hills where Nimitz and Una had commanding views of Pearl Harbor—the same views that Ginger and her six flyers had gazed down on the day before the attack. Trails from the hospital snaked through tropical forests to the ridgeline of the Ko'olau Mountains. "Lovely scenery," summed up Una.

Spruance's mighty Fifth Fleet—at three hundred seventy-five ships, larger than today's entire Navy—had been in Pearl Harbor, preparing for *Operation Flintlock* in the Marshall Islands.[122] That Saturday, after Spruance departed for the Marshalls, Una, with a still-smarting toe, joined Nimitz and Doc in Kailua for another walk and swim.

Afterwards, the Walkers hosted dinner in Nu'uanu for Nimitz and a Who's Who of Hawai'i: The Hal Castles and Stanley Kennedys; Mary Lucas Pflueger, heir to vast land holdings in

Hawai'i, one of the wealthiest women in the islands. Pflueger was also active in the Red Cross Canteen Corps, having helped set up a cafeteria in the basement of 'Iolani Palace after the attack, continuously operated by ladies on twelve-hour shifts;[123] Vice Adm. Towers, Nimitz's deputy; Gwen and Charlie Bryant (Ginger's bridge partner the evening before the attack on Pearl Harbor, and Tower's flag lieutenant); Rear Adm. Forrest Sherman—Nimitz's deputy chief of staff; the congenial Vice Adm. Robert Ghormley, who had briefly commanded the naval forces in the south Pacific and the Battle of Guadalcanal in 1942. (After two months of timidity under fire and at the height of hostilities, Nimitz reluctantly replaced his old friend with his own "Patton," the audacious Halsey.* The change radically altered the dynamics of Guadalcanal for the better, becoming Halsey's finest hour. But Ghormley, who was sixty, had been a sore mental struggle, Nimitz lamented to Catherine, "and the decision was not reached until after hours of anguished consideration." [124] Lamar later attributed Ghormley's poor performance to abscessed teeth, which were later removed.[125] By the time of Walker's dinner that evening, three-star Vice Admiral Ghormley was Commandant of the 14th Naval District in Pearl Harbor—a relatively minor administrative position now held by a one-star rear admiral.)

Rounding out the dinner guests was George Wilson Sumner, an American Factors employee who succeeded Sandy as President after the war.[126] During the war, he chaired the Honolulu Police Commission and was likely the source of the Walkers' night travel passes.

(Not mentioned in the genteel Walker home, at least within earshot of ladies, was that the police department issued licenses, commanding a $50,000 under-the-table bribe to the Police Chief,

---

* Nimitz sent King a secret message recommending Ghormley's replacement with Halsey. King responded with the word, "approved." *Graybook*, 902. Assuming command, Halsey told his staff their mission was to "Kill Japs, kill Japs, and keep on killing Japs!" *Nimitz*, 203.

for brothels to operate within the fifteen-square block area of Chinatown during the war.* The brothels were flanked by military medical clinics to help prevent venereal disease from disabling troops; in fact, Hawai'i reportedly had an all-time low for service personnel in any large military area in the United States.[127] Sumner frankly admitted he would not consider closing the brothels, to protect local young ladies from thousands of female-starved servicemen roaming the island "just like animals."[128])

(For a period of three weeks in August 1942, poster-carrying prostitutes picketed the police station and 'Iolani Palace over grievances about onerous regulations.[129] Sandy, who never uttered a profane word in my presence, suffered the ignominy of having to cross that lurid picket line and protest placards twice daily for three weeks while attending to his duties as Food Control Director. Not a word of it was published in the newspapers, and only a few later books mention the subject.)

Whenever the Walkers had such a large number of guests for dinner, Hara, the cook, would say cheerfully, "Just like a restaurant!"

During dinner, the guests gave toasts to one another. Nimitz's grandson Chester Nimitz "Chet" Lay said one of Nimitz's favorites was the old Royal Navy, "Here's to a bloody war or a sickly

---

* Kuris, Ted, *Scarlett Memoirs of a Honolulu Madam*, East West Magazine, Autumn 1985. Betty Jean O'Hara, a Chinatown prostitute and madam during World War II, said the cost to open one of the eighteen brothels included a $50,000 bribe to Police Chief W.A. Gabrielson. That payment was "only for lease and goodwill." On top of that were lease payments, plus up to $100 per prostitute each month to the vice squad. Yet, it was a lucrative business, generating about $25,000 a month to the Madam, a fortune in those days. However, bribery is a two-edged sword. Betty Jean boasted to a police officer during the war "about being able to do what she wanted to, when she wanted to, for she had enough stuff to put the Chief away," and hiked her dress to display her "Gabrielson was here" tattoo at the top of her thigh. (Faria, Chris, *For Real: History of a WWII Honolulu Police Rookie*, Outskirts Press, Inc., 2009, 36.)

season," which irreverently pleaded for promotion as seniors die from battle or disease. They were the "only paths for promotion back then," Chet explained.

With toasts and dinner over, the men crowded together around Sandy's upstairs poker table. Cards were dealt, chips clattered, and circles of cigarette and cigar smoke filled the small room with white haze. A congenial night of fellowship prevailed among some of the most powerful business, community and military leaders in Hawai'i, all under the cheerful eye of Una.

Chapter 7

Nimitz's Refuge from War: Muliwai

THE NEXT MORNING, January 23, the Walkers, with their two adored Scottish Terriers (Dirke and Boykin) and cook Hara, drove over the Pali and along the precipitous Ko'olau Mountains from which shimmering ribbons of waterfalls fell from every crevice. When he reached a particular Monkey Pod tree, Sandy announced, "We're half way to Muliwai!"

They later passed Kualoa Ranch (where part of Jurassic Park and its sequels were filmed fifty years later) and below Battery Cooper, one of many coastal defense gun emplacements in the hills around Oahu. When the USS *Saratoga* (CV 3) was converted from a battle cruiser to an aircraft carrier, its five-inch guns were installed in Battery Cooper. They soon passed Kahana and Punalu'u Valleys, where the Pacific Jungle Combat Center trained soldiers in jungle first-aid and hand-to-hand warfare. Sandy never failed to stop at a little mom-and-pop market in Hau'ula to purchase ice cream and last-minute supplies. Precisely one mile later, they turned right into Muliwai, threading the grass driveway and into its grounds. Sandy backed his wagon into a little parking slot nestled in front of the kitchen, where Hara unloaded provisions and began preparing lunch. Hanko, Hal Lamar and other guests were already there.

That afternoon, after initialing *Graybook* reports of ninety-four tons of bombs dropped on Japanese atolls,[130] Nimitz and Doc Anderson drove to Muliwai from the opposite direction. Driving through fields of sugar cane and pineapple between the Ko'olau and Waianae Mountains, they turned east at Haleiwa, passing Waimea Bay, the now-famous Sunset Beach, the radar unit at Kahuku that detected the incoming Japanese planes on December 7 (which a watch officer had mistakenly thought was an expected group of B-17s from San Francisco), and eventually arrived at Muliwai. Hanko noted that Nimitz often brought groceries that were hard to obtain and beverages almost impossible to obtain.[131]

When guests were expected, Una, with one of her famous floral parasols in hand, waited patiently on a long Koa bench on the Muliwai lanai. As Nimitz's black Buick emerged from the Ironwood hedge driveway, Una exclaimed with delight, "Oh, the admiral is here!" The household immediately gathered to greet Nimitz and his entourage and whisk baggage to rooms.

Excerpt from Una Walker's Diary for January 23, 1944

They changed into sports clothes, then crossed the gracefully arched bridge over Wailele stream and played paddle tennis on the grass court outlined in lime under a bright sun beating down through a cloudless sky. The players perspired copiously in the dry hot weather. Muliwai was in a region of La'ie the Hawaiians called *Malo'o*, meaning, "dry." Indeed, all of Oahu had been unusually parched for several years, with 1944 the driest. Precipitation that year was half its average, about twenty inches total. After tennis, they changed into swim attire, walked the beach, swam in the cool ocean, and had a general happy time.

Ginger Lilly on Muliwai Bridge over Wailele Stream

Nimitz limited his cocktails to two before dinner, usually his signature old-fashioneds. Sandy also brewed, as did his father before him, Okoleha'o (Oke for short), a strong brandy distilled from fermented Ti root. For those brave enough to try (no more than two), he also served "Sandy Tais"—his own Mai Tai recipe—two parts each dark and light Bacardi rum, one part Orange Curacao, one part *Don the Beachcomber* Mai Tai mix over crushed ice in a large, wide-mouth rocks glass, and a dash of lemon or lime juice. Dark Meyers Rum floated on the top. Sandy detested little umbrellas or skewered pineapples added to tropical drinks. "No rubbish," he sternly instructed, "but a straw."

After the sun dropped behind the Ko'olau Mountains, tingeing puffs of clouds with cherry hues, Hara seared Kauai grass-fed steaks over charcoal. Matsuko Goto served the guests at Sandy's long Koa table under the wide eaves just outside the living room. Having dinner at that table was the nearest thing to sitting outdoors. Sandy and Nimitz gave alternate toasts to one another and to inevitable peace. Dessert was partially melted ice cream, scooped with a large spoon ahead of time in a bowl, never hard round balls.

After dinner, they enjoyed one another's company, listened to symphonies broadcast by radio or played on a Victrola record player, and danced and played cribbage or poker at one of several card tables. They also watched the stars come up over the ocean.

"We'd talk about orchids," said Lamar. "We'd talk about mundane things. The war never came into the picture."

Nimitz enjoyed very much his time at Muliwai with close friends who let him get in an aloha shirt and a pair of shorts and talk no business at all. It was very relaxing for him.[132]

At night, they observed blackout. When the blackout restrictions were first imposed, the glass panes of the sliding doors at Muliwai were painted white, as they remain today, so they could sit in the living room with lights on. But it would have been too hot to stay inside for long.

When the doors on two sides of the living room slid away into the walls in the evenings, all lights had to be off. Without lights on a moonless night, Muliwai and its environs were pitch black, except for the marginal glow cast by a riot of stars.

Enhancing the enchantment of Muliwai, Una always brought out her ukulele and sang haunting Hawaiian melodies or popular ditties. Among Una's repertoire were a number of wartime songs such as, *She's a Knockout in the Blackout*:

> *She's a knockout in the blackout.*
> *I only wish that I had seen her in the light.*

We danced 'till the song was over,
Then on she went and disappeared into the night.
I knew her voice was warm and tender,
She had the skin you love to touch.
I wonder had the lights been burning,
Would her face have really mattered very much?
She was delightful though it was frightful,
We waited there for bombs and held each other tight.
She's a knockout in the blackout,
But in the light who knows she might have been a fright.

Ginger said, "Blackouts were romantic."

An officer, George "Beartrap" Triede, had been courting Ginger, until one evening when his Executive Officer, Tony Lilly, accompanied him to Ginger's home, two blocks down from the Walkers'.

Tony's first encounter with Ginger was in the blackout, sitting next to her on a sofa. He could tell she was "a woman of sophistication and humor," but had no idea what she looked like at first. "I was quite taken with her, but [I] couldn't see her because it was blackout. Eventually I had a live date with her and she was beautiful, everything anybody would want in a woman and personality as well." Ginger, who was movie-starlet gorgeous, turned out to be a knockout in the daylight! "So, from then on I pursued her."

By that night, Nimitz had spent so many weekends at Muliwai since his arrival in Hawai'i over two years before, that he and the Walkers had already settled into an easy routine. If the Walkers were merely entertaining Nimitz as a guest, their near-constant companionship might have become a chore.

But their friendship was so close, Nimitz had become not just a good friend, but a surrogate member of the family.

Walker Cottage where Nimitz Stayed While at Muliwai

At Muliwai, everyone turned in early, about 10:00 p.m., with Nimitz walking up the familiar grass path between two verdant berms leading to the cottage on the bluff over the ocean. The cottage had two bedrooms separated by a communal bath. Its rooms were furnished with Koa beds, side tables and desk. Two windows, in addition to a screen door, provided ample ventilation.

    The Walkers normally slept there—Sandy in the room to the left and Una to the right. When Nimitz was in residence, he and his entourage occupied the cottage, while the Walkers slept in the large two-bed room in the main house which was normally assigned to Ginger.[133]

    At Makalapa, Nimitz rarely turned in until after 11:00 p.m., and sometimes after midnight. Worse yet, he suffered chronic insomnia, often rising in the middle of the night to study charts of the western Pacific, wresting with the ever-changing, three-dimensional chessboard of war.

Nimitz at Ease

As he entered the cottage that evening, it dawned on him how tired he really was from the war, the strategy session in San Francisco and so many restless nights in Makalapa. Fortunately, sleep came quickly at Muliwai.

The humid air carried the sweet scent of tropical plants and *ehu kai*—white salt spray—that were mildly intoxicating. A drowsy languor pervaded his room, and a warm glow washed over the admiral. Nimitz never heard of endorphins, but he well knew their effect—a positive sense of well-being from having exercised all afternoon.

Nestled in Sandy's comfortable Koa double bed under an old Hawaiian quilt, Nimitz nodded off, embraced by trade winds wafting through the windows and the soft roar of the Pacific Ocean breaking against the shore below the cottage. Unlike Makalapa, where the toils of war and his room of Pacific war charts forever beckoned, Nimitz had no such distractions at Muliwai where he slept well, until wakened by the morning sun bursting from the horizon.

Nimitz slept so soundly that, perhaps upon awakening, he could not fathom for a moment where he was, or how he came to be there. The rays of the sun shone through the cottage window directly onto his face. From the sound of waves, he could tell he was by the ocean.

Outside came a tapping sound, followed by rustling.

Curious, Nimitz looked through the screen door to find the caretaker, Takeo Higuchi—with a wide planter's hat on his head, Japanese tabis[*] on his feet, dark, loose-fitting, pajama-like shirt, and mid-calf pants—stabbing Kamani leaves with a short, homemade, two-pronged spear and scraping clumps into a shoulder bag. Takeo had emigrated from Japan in the 1930s to labor on sugar plantations, until the Walkers hired him and his "picture bride," who also doubled as a maid.

---

[*] Tabis are Japanese slippers with a divided toe area reminiscent of today's FiveFinger shoes.

Michael A. Lilly

The Higuchis lived in the small cottage by the road and lawn tennis court.

Nimitz no doubt recalled where he was—at peaceful Muliwai and recalled the pleasant evening before. After greeting Takeo, who gave him a wide toothy grin and smiling eyes through spectacles, Nimitz donned floral swim shorts and joined the others for a planned early walk on the beach.

Sandy, upon seeing Nimitz in the morning, always said with a smile in his distinctively rattling voice, "Top o' the morning to you, Chester!"

When Nimitz beat him to the old Irish greeting, Sandy replied, "And the rest of the day to yourself."

Their feet and the paws of Dirke and Boykin were the first that day to leave impressions on sand washed smooth by the night tide. The day was spectacularly beautiful, with clear sunlight and cool trade winds blowing softly from the northeast. The blue Pacific lapped at their feet.

A mixed feeling of peace and exhilaration pervaded the guests. As far as Nimitz looked to the right rose the precipitous Ko'olau Mountains, all that remained of an ancient shield volcano that sheared off in ancient times, crashing into the sea.

Its green ridgeline zigzagged up and down across the sky to the south like a stock market indicator—one of the most arresting views in the world. Nearby at about a thousand-foot elevation, three of the many Army Observation Posts installed in the hills around Oahu maintained constant vigil on the horizon for the enemy.

On the southern horizon was Mokapu Hill on Naval Air Station Kaneohe. From Muliwai, its "hump" and "head" formed the silhouette of a large sea turtle.

Nimitz's View of the Beach from his Cottage at Muliwai[134]

To the right, past the old pier pilings, Nimitz admired a movie-set crescent beach, stretching one-quarter mile and fetching up against a high wall of black lava rock at Pounder's Beach—so called, because the waves broke directly onto the shore, dangerously pounding swimmers onto the sand. In big surf, it was hazardous, with more than one person losing his life to or becoming paralyzed from a broken neck. To the left, the beach curved below Nimitz's cottage to the north for a mile, before reaching a high-lithified dune, called La'ie Point. In heavy surf, swells crashed into and completely over a small rock island just off the Point. During the winter, such as that morning, one often saw pods of humpback whales during annual migrations spouting and cavorting beyond the reef.

The views in all directions were breathtaking. In the early 20th century, a famous Hawai'i painter, D. Howard Hitchcock, was so taken with its vistas that he repeatedly captured them in handsome impressionist paintings. One painting shows Wailele stream, snaking out lazily to the ocean, and a dune with a lone gnarly Ironwood (*Casuarina*) tree struggling against the trade winds where the cottage was later built. When trade winds blew, the tree's needles hissed, like the murmur of a crowd of people whispering.

Nimitz returned from his walk on the beach and swim and had breakfast before leaving. Back at his headquarters by 10:00 a.m., Nimitz tuned into an hour of classical music [that] was beamed out from San Francisco.[135] He turned the sound up quite loud, because he was a little deaf in one ear.[136] While listening to the broadcast, he initialed *Graybook's* good news that "All task groups are proceeding towards their initial stations for [Operation] Flintlock" in the Marshall Islands.[137]

Between January 27th and 29th, Nimitz gathered senior officers of the Pacific Fleet to Pearl Harbor to discuss whether to attack the Marianas, which included Guam and Saipan. The conclusion was to bypass the Marianas for the time being, continue *Operation Flintlock* in the Marshalls, and support MacArthur's march through New Guinea.

In fact, in the last days of January, Spruance's Fifth Fleet overwhelmed the Marshall Islands, destroying all of its Japanese air forces and pulverizing Kwajalein Atoll. Kwajalein, the largest atoll in the world and a territory of the Japanese Empire for some twenty-five years, had fallen. The positive news from the front was a relief to Nimitz, for there had likely been a lot of nail-biting at CinCPac headquarters.[138]

January 29th marked a momentous occasion on the East Coast. The battleship, USS *Missouri* (BB 63) (which solidified its place in history the following year, when the Instrument of Surrender was signed on its 0-1 deck, below Hanko's gaze from its bridge), was launched from Brooklyn Naval Yard. Missouri Senator Harry Truman's daughter Margaret was the ship's "sponsor," breaking a bottle of champagne against its bow. "Overhead the winter clouds were dark, but the moment the great stern began to float, the sun came out." [139] That afternoon, Nimitz called on the Walkers on his way to a dinner.

After the strategy session ended that afternoon and with Kwajalein still being pounded into submission, Nimitz, along with Doc and Lamar, drove the Walkers to Muliwai. Ginger and her two daughters, Maile and Sheila, arrived separately. They had a swim in the ocean and dinner and all spent [the] [night]. On one such evening at the poker table, an ugly six-inch centipede dropped from a ceiling crossbeam, landing on Sandy's arm. The poker players were shocked, knowing that its bite felt like a jolt of electricity that caused immediate swelling. Though bitten, Sandy just laughed and swept the insect away with his other hand. "I raised bees as a child," explained Sandy, "and was stung so many times I don't even feel it anymore." Everyone was amazed that he was hardly fazed by the bite, as he reached for his next hand of cards.

On a moonless evening at Muliwai earlier in the war, Sandy pointed out to Nimitz a unique cluster of stars in the shape of a small fist, called the Pleiades or "Seven Sisters." At their apex, the *Na huihui o makali'i* (cluster of little eyes) hover directly over O'ahu, providing a beacon by which the Polynesian voyagers navigated to the islands from the south Pacific in outrigger canoes over a millennia before. Being a navigator himself, Nimitz would have found their connection to the islands and its indigenous peoples particularly fascinating.

Retiring that night in what had become Nimitz's refuge from war, the admiral slept well until awakened, rejuvenated, by the rising sun and the sound of Takeo stabbing Kamani leaves. He joined the Walkers and their terriers for a beach walk and swim before enjoying a kidney breakfast, cooked by Hara. Nimitz left right after for Makalapa where he received regular reports of Spruance's successful assault on the Marshalls. The last entry that day in Nimitz's *Graybook* read, "There have been no reports, so far, of any enemy air attacks or submarine attacks on our forces." [140]

That evening Nimitz's driver, Beach, arrived at Nu'uanu with Hal and Doc to drive the Walkers and Hanko to Makalapa for dinner. Guests included Admiral Halsey, the Hal Castles, and Mary

Pflueger. With such a dynamic group, there would have been no end of stimulating conversation. Hal Castle was a rugged, pioneering character who built Kaneohe Ranch into a sprawling enterprise. As a young man, he and his young children wore cowboy gear, while he filmed an entertaining silent western about a gang of thieves. Pflueger was outgoing and loved a good yarn, the more risqué the better.

Halsey, of course, was boisterous and gregarious—in MacArthur's words, "blunt, outspoken, dynamic" [141]—and just plain fun at any gathering. One can well imagine him entertaining Mary Pflueger with ribald stories. In addition to animated conversation, the guests would have enjoyed a splendid meal. Nimitz's excellent steward, Ramirez, got the best cut of meat, filet mignon being a favorite. He had a garden in which he raised fresh vegetables and salad greens for the Admiral's table. For dessert he served tropical fruits, pineapple, avocado, papaya, and Chinese gooseberries…and ice cream. One of Nimitz's favorites was avocado ice cream! [142]

After dinner, they strolled over to the outdoor theater to watch the 1943 movie, *Destination Tokyo*. A look-alike Admiral King transmitted sealed orders to Cary Grant, commanding officer of the fictional submarine USS *Copperfin,* to negotiate the minefields of Tokyo Bay and offload a landing party to obtain vital intelligence for the upcoming *Doolittle Raid*. Nimitz was amused to watch Grant play a part Nimitz had served when he was a submarine commanding officer.

To be legally out after curfew at 6:00 p.m., the Walkers were regularly issued Temporary Night Passes, allowing them to travel on a given day only from Makalapa to their residence in Nu'uanu. (Headlights were taped so only a sliver of light showed which barely lit the road, but helped warn others you were coming.) "It wasn't dangerous," Una recalled, "because there were very few cars on the road at night."

Hanko wrote that, while the Walkers needed a pass, "Nimitz could travel after curfew hours with impunity." [143]

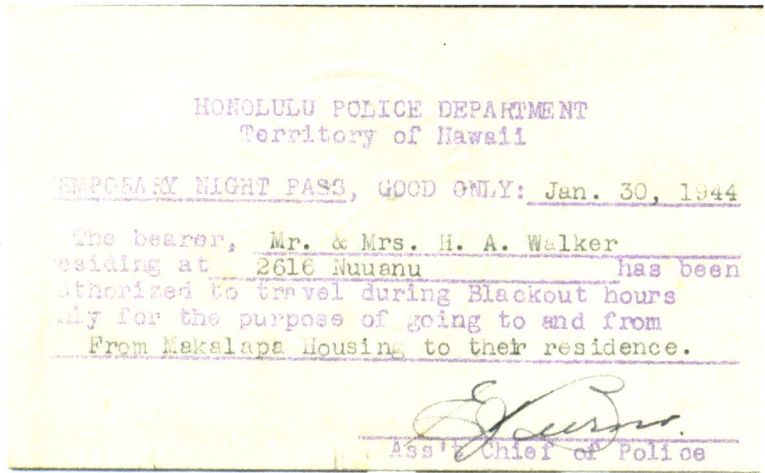

Night Pass for the Walkers, January 30, 1944

The last day of January, when Marines landed on Kwajalein Atoll without opposition, was the first time Japanese territory was invaded by American forces. Nimitz immediately assumed the title, Military Governor of the Marshall Islands, under which he issued Proclamation No. 1, establishing a Military Government "to preserve law and order and provide for the safety and welfare both of my forces" and the Marshall people.

With the amphibious landings at Kwajalein in mind, Nimitz gave the Walkers a frame with two pictures of similar landings. One was a painting of an ancient Persian ship offloading elephants and troops. The other was a photo of an LST with armed troops spewing from its bow. The picture demonstrated that modern amphibious operations had its roots in ancient history. The frame was hung on the wall by the Muliwai front door where Nimitz could admire it every weekend.

Michael A. Lilly

Chapter 8

Kwajalein, Truk & "Umlaut!"

ON FEBRUARY 3ʳᴰ, the Walkers joined Nimitz for a walk and nice swim at Kailua. All reports from the western Pacific were positive, with the worst casualty being a bad collision between battleships, the USS *Washington* (BB 47) and USS *Indiana* (BB 58).

The next day, *Graybook* reported, "The capture of Kwajalein, Burton, and Blankenship Islands…was completed today." [144] Una's diary recorded that Nimitz and Doc left for Kwajalein on a B-24 Liberator for a six-day tour.

The atoll was literally flattened by bombs, shells and napalm with nary a leaf remaining on a tree. A *Time* magazine correspondent said the bombardment was "like pouring hot water on a column of ants." [145]

No sooner had he landed at about noon, Nimitz surveyed Kwajalein with Spruance, strolling past the detritus of war—bombshell holes, green jeeps, pillboxes, trucks, and stands of shredded coconut trees, like tall fingers pointing to the sky.

When asked his thoughts, Nimitz looked around the surreal wasteland and replied, "It's the worst scene of devastation I have ever witnessed—except for the Texas picnic." [146]

Admirals Nimitz and Spruance on Kwajalein, February 5, 1944

Michael A. Lilly

Admirals Nimitz and Spruance on Kwajalein, February 5, 1944

The extent of damage was readily evident in photographs Nimitz gave the Walkers, including one autographed by Nimitz and Spruance and inscribed, "Two Full Admirals—Full of Conversation" and dated, "Kwajalein, 5 Feb."

Nimitz next shifted his bull's-eye to Eniwetok and Truk, although his *Graybook* acknowledged, "No target date has been set for either as yet." [147]

Nimitz returned to Pearl Harbor on February 9th. He and the Walkers awoke the next morning to a *Honolulu Advertiser* editorial giving its full support to Nimitz under the banner, The Right Road. "Nimitz takes the long view," it explained. "His objective is the island of Honshu. He will probably get there long before the most optimistic commentator." [148]

In orders dated February 12th, Secretary of the Navy Frank Knox directed retired Adm. Thomas C. Hart, who was then sixty-six, to conduct an inquiry into the attack on Pearl Harbor. At the time of Pearl Harbor, Hart had been the Commander in Chief of the Navy's Asiatic Fleet based in the Philippines. He wisely dispatched his fleet to sea before the Japanese attack. With his shore facilities in shambles, he ordered that the fleet abandon the Philippines. Hart retired the following July, but he was recalled in 1944 to conduct the Hart Inquiry and preserve important evidence and testimony, before it was lost to the exigencies of war. He interviewed forty witnesses in Washington D.C., Pearl Harbor and the South Pacific through June 15th.

After interviews in D.C., Hart would soon fly to Hawai'i to reconvene his inquiries there, where he would also rendezvous with the Walkers and Nimitz at Muliwai.

Una enjoyed a short swim with Nimitz in Kailua, followed by dinner at Makalapa with Under Secretary of the Navy as guest of honor. Forrestal, fifty-two, was a brilliant and meticulous man, voted by his Princeton senior class as most likely to succeed; and, although he did not graduate, he did succeed—soon to be the Secretary of the Navy and later the first Secretary of Defense. He advocated physical fitness as much as Nimitz and still carried a slightly-smashed nose from years of amateur boxing. However, unlike many public officials, he was a modest executive with a desire for anonymity,[149] and painfully shy, avoiding public exposure like the plague. Potter, in *Nimitz*, summed up that, "Forrestal could never be fully at ease with Nimitz because, half-buried in his consciousness, there was a neurotic streak that was hostile to authority, particularly as symbolized by high military rank." [150]

Nimitz included the loquacious Walkers to ensure lively conversation around the introverted Forrestal.

The next day, Sunday, February 13th, the Walkers hosted a lunch at Muliwai honoring Forrestal. Guests included Nimitz, Gen. Robert C. Richardson, Jr., Commanding General of Army forces in the Pacific and Military Governor until June 1, 1943, when martial law was abolished. Capt. (soon, Commodore) Worrall Reed Carter, Commander Service Squadron 10 in Pearl Harbor, and Rear Admiral Sherman, Nimitz's Deputy Chief of Staff. Also present were Hanko, Ginger and her two daughters Maile and Sheila.

Lunch was buffet-style at the long Koa dinner table. Tamale Pie and rice were scooped onto wooden plates, along with baked bananas, papayas, and homemade Mango Chutney (in the summers, there were lychees and sliced mangoes). Nimitz may have brought his personal Cactus Fruit Jelly from his mother's Texas recipe, which the Walkers called by its Hawaiian name, *Panini* Jelly. Glasses of iced tea with sprigs of mint and cups for coffee were lined up on a tray at the end of the table. Beer and mai tais were available to those wanting something stiffer. Guests ate at card tables or sprawled on large woven *hala* mats rolled out on the lawns under the shade of Kamani trees. Most guests wore bathing attire or shorts, but Secretary of the Navy Frank Knox perspired in pin-striped suit and tie. Some senior officers wore uniforms. Unless she was swimming, Una sported a floral dress and flats. Forrestal likely arrived in more formal gear, but, in the relaxed atmosphere of Muliwai, soon shed his coat and tie.

Secretary of the Navy Frank Knox with Una Walker at Muliwai, 1942[151]

The February issue of the *United States News* reported that the "Stage is now being set in the Pacific for the first decisive naval struggle in the war. One stake in that coming test is to be Truk, Japan's main base in the Carolina Islands."

The article went on to point out the value of taking Truk:

> *If Truk falls into American hands, this country will have a strong naval base 2,100 miles from Tokyo. The Americans, if they get Truk, will have taken a long step back toward the Philippines. If Truk should fall, there would be no assurance that the Japanese could hold other key bases in the Palau Islands, the Marianas, or perhaps even in the Bonins, which are within convenient bombing range of all of industrial Japan.*

"Dog Day [D-Day] for the assault" on Eniwetok, *Graybook* recorded, was set for February 16th HWT and Truk "D minus 1." Right on schedule, *Graybook* noted, "Carrier Task Forces hit Truk."

Una's diary echoed that the Attack on Truk had begun.[152] Admiral King had advocated bypassing the island. Truk's formidable fortifications were deemed so invincible that the atoll was known as the Gibraltar of the Pacific.[153]

Nevertheless, Nimitz insisted on taking it. Truk was to Japan what Pearl Harbor had been to the United States, so its fall would pay huge dividends. *Operation Hailstone* was a massive air and naval strike by Spruance's armada, the largest assembled in history, which pulverized the island and destroyed fifteen Japanese warships, numerous smaller ships and merchants, and two hundred seventy aircraft.

Nimitz hung on every word transmitted from the Western Pacific as the victorious battle unfolded. Nimitz's gambit won, with Japan's major forces leaving the fortified island base in just two days. The remaining enemy garrison hung on for some months, but Truk no longer was a serious military threat.

Nimitz announced in a dispatch widely published that "the Pacific Fleet has returned at Truk the visit made by the Japanese fleet at Pearl Harbor on December 7, 1941, and effected a partial settlement of the debt." [154]

In response, two of Nimitz's daughters Kate and Nancy sent

congratulations in humorous rhyme:

> *Like Carrie Nation guzzling booze,*
> *When man runs over Truk, that's news.**

With the battle of Truk raging and Congress confirming Spruance's promotion to four-star Admiral, Una hosted a dinner at Nu'uanu for eighteen people, including Nimitz and his staff, with nothing but good news on the war front in their minds, if not on their lips. Nimitz had little sleep during the assault, but the victory surely lifted a weight from his shoulders.

The next day King threw water on Nimitz's reverie over Truk in a long letter chastising him against talking to the press, whose interests were solely to sell papers. Recent statements by Nimitz left no doubt in the minds of the enemy of future war objectives.[155]

Ironically, Nimitz never liked newsmen[156] and avoided public announcements, leaving such matters to his more outgoing, and thereby famous, subordinates, such as Halsey. (Later, when Nimitz was Chief of Naval Operations and put up in a posh out-of-town hotel, he exchanged his suite with his aide's smaller room to avoid incessant phone calls from the press.)[157] Nimitz may have been chastened by King's message, but because of his handsomeness, folksy, aw-shucks personality and wit, he was slowly becoming one of the most quoted, photographed, and written-about military leaders of the war. King, who was frequently in newspapers, but not nearly as photogenic or approachable, may have been a little bit jealous of his photogenic subordinate.

Nimitz was, however, justifiably careful to keep war information secret. The day after the Battle of Midway, the *Chicago Tribune* published a story, repeated by other papers, that all but

---

* As related to the author by Chet Lay, Nimitz's grandson, who said, "The press wanted to print it but discovered that Carrie Nation had living relatives who apparently were" as fastidious as Carrie, "...so decided not to. Quel Dommage!"

revealed that Nimitz's command had broken the Japanese code. Fortunately, it appeared that the Japanese never read the story! Nimitz wisely withheld confidential information from even close associates and family. When his daughters Kate and Nancy were still living in an apartment building in Washington D.C., a curious neighbor and notorious gossip began pestering them for inside war information.

She was convinced that Nimitz's two daughters were getting "the real scoop," which, of course, they were not. After becoming exasperated by her endless questions, Kate and Nancy finally told her that they had a manservant—a Prisoner of War from the Eastern Front—named, Umlaut. They explained that Nimitz had sent Umlaut as a gift to do the girls' cooking, cleaning and errands. The neighbor woman was duly impressed and convinced the story was true, never mind that Nimitz had nothing to do with the European Theater.

Several weeks later, the neighbor again cornered Kate and Nancy, asking, "Say, you only have a two-bedroom apartment. Where does Umlaut sleep?"

"In the broom closet," Nancy replied.

"Not possible," the neighbor shot back. "It's only a foot deep!"

"Well," Nancy said, "he's very thin and can sleep standing up."

After a moment, the neighbor's face turned from questioning surprise to somber reality, finally realizing she had been had. She stormed off in a huff, never to bother them again.[158]

Saturday, February 19th, was Sandy's fifty-ninth birthday.* Despite the enormous demands of command, and while his forces pulverized Eniwetok, Nimitz took the time to send Sandy a birthday card, wishing him "health and happiness always"; he later hosted a birthday dinner for the Walkers, necessitating a night pass.

---

* Nimitz was five days younger than Sandy.

Birthday card from Admiral Nimitz to Sandy Walker, February 19, 1944

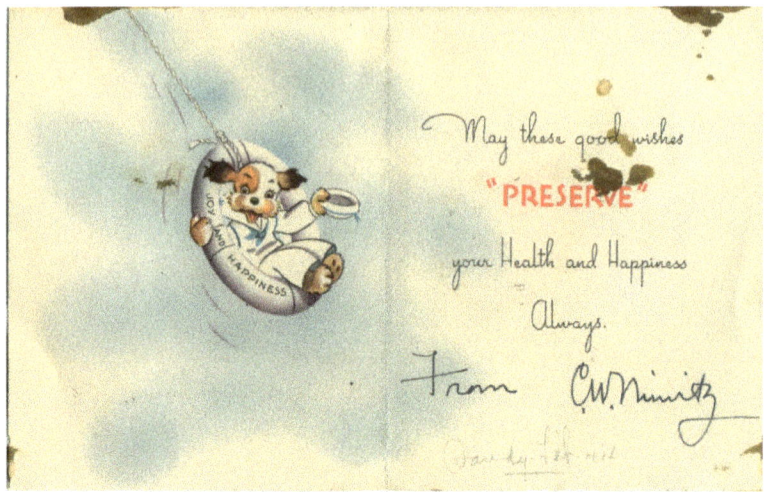

Nimitz, Lamar, and Doc drove the Walkers for a swim at Kailua. That evening, Nimitz gave a surprise birthday dinner for Sandy with a number of guests including Ginger.

But it was no surprise to Sandy.

The day before, Sandy wrote to his daughter Ann on the East Coast, that the "Admiral is giving me a birthday dinner—a surprise, only, you know me, it is not a surprise as I already know it. The twenty-forth is his [Nimitz's] birthday, and we are giving him a dinner—no surprise though."

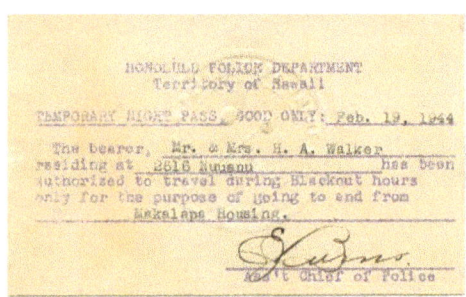

Night Pass for the Walkers to attend a Birthday Party for Sandy at Nimitz's Makalapa Quarters, February 19, 1944

Nimitz at Ease

Again, the Walkers received a travel pass. The next morning, with battles still raging in the western Pacific, Una met Nimitz and Doc at Makalapa and drove to Nimitz Recreational Park in Pearl Harbor. From there, they drove to the home of the stout and gregarious Hans L'Orange for a swim, but [a] very hectic luncheon!

Hans L'Orange was the manager of O'ahu Sugar Co.'s massive plantation based in Waipahu, where he often threw lavish parties of barbecued steaks and pork for naval officers at his manager's house. Guests frolicked in a large swimming pool—in reality, a massive concrete tank—by the house where Walker grandchildren later took swimming lessons.

The plantation was a subsidiary of Sandy's American Factors. Over a period of several days in 1940, L'Orange's plantation workers built the Walkers' tennis court where Nimitz played throughout the war. On the day of Pearl Harbor, realizing they were under attack by the Japanese, L'Orange phoned Civil Defense Headquarters in Honolulu, which set off the first air raid alarms of World War II.

On February 22nd Eniwetok was finally liberated. A relieved native, who had been forced from his home to perform slave labor for the Japanese, said, "Sometimes war is a good thing." [159] The following day, Spruance's carriers launched attacks on the Marianas, including Guam and Saipan.

The next day, Nimitz and Doc drove Una to tour the Nu'uanu Branch of the Red Cross followed by lunch on the back lanai of the Walkers' Nu'uanu home. In addition to a light main course, Una served guests a salad of pealed pomelo (Chinese grapefruit), avocado, and lettuce nestled in crescent-shaped glass plates and dabbled with tangy vinaigrette dressing.

Michael A. Lilly

Excerpt from Una Walker's Diary for February 24, 1944 Regarding the Walker's Birthday Party for Nimitz.

On Thursday, February 24th, while Spruance continued operations against Saipan, Tinian and Guam, Nimitz turned fifty-nine. The *Honolulu Advertiser* reported that he "quietly had his own little celebration." As Una's diary reflected, his birthday was neither little nor quiet—he celebrated it at the Walkers' home, where they played tennis[*] and pitched horseshoes. In a foursome at tennis, Nimitz and Una beat Vice Adm. Charles A. Lockwood and his wife Betty. Lockwood, Commander of the Pacific Submarine Forces, met every submarine on its return from patrol and was so adored by ordinary submarine sailors that he was known affectionately as

---

[*] The Walkers' tennis court and covered gazebo were featured in a 1981 *Magnum, P.I.* television episode, "The Woman on the Beach."

Prince Charlie.

Because Nimitz loved the game, Sandy installed horseshoe courts at Muliwai and in town. In a birthday foursome, Nimitz and Una beat Sandy and Herman von Holt. The win was likely, because Nimitz was extremely accomplished in pitching horseshoes. That night, they enjoyed a very gay dinner and presents for Nimitz. An entertainer furnished music while everyone drank plenty! The birthday party was topped off with their usual game of late-night poker in the smoke-filled second floor room.

The last weekend of February was spent at Muliwai. Nimitz, Hal and Nimitz's flag secretary, Capt. Preston Mercer, arrived Saturday afternoon and were greeted by Una, waiting patiently at the Muliwai portico with flowered parasol in hand. After settling in and changing into sports gear, the guests crossed the arched bridge over Wailele stream and played a foursome of paddle tennis on the grass court. Afterwards, they passed through the barbed wire strands to swim in the cool Pacific, with armed army guards watching longingly from their hot corrugated iron command post.

Although the climate remained unseasonably dry, Una recorded that stormy weather blew in off the ocean that evening. Hara's Kauai steak dinner or fish chowder was followed by classical music and the usual game of poker, while rain poured down outside. Una described it as happy fun and, indeed, it was always especially cozy at Muliwai during a rainstorm. That was one of the few nights during the war that Nimitz became drenched, as he trudged against fierce squalls to the cottage on the bluff. Nestled in his cottage bed, he nodded off, while raindrops beat a tattoo against the roof and streamed off eaves into the foliage.

By morning, the storm was gone, and the sun awoke Nimitz at 6:04 a.m. With the rain the night before, Wailele stream broke through the sandbar. The beach walkers found a raging torrent blocking their way to Pounders and a broad bloom of brown silt spread out in the ocean like a *Rorschach* blot. After a swim and breakfast, Nimitz and Lamar went home!

Back at Makalapa, Nimitz was relieved to learn the Marshall

Islands were all but secure, representing a strategic and tactical victory for the Navy. From the Marshalls, the Allies were free to assault the Caroline and Marianas islands. With the loss of Kwajalein and Eniwetok Atoll, and Allied raids on Truk, Saipan and Tinian, *Life* magazine reported, "February was the blackest month in the history of the Japanese Empire." [160]

The situation was so dire that the Japanese Prime Minister, General Hideki Tojo, with the approval of Emperor Hirohito, fired his army and navy chiefs—Field Marshal Hajime Sugiyama and Admiral Osami Nogano. Five months later after the fall of Saipan, Tojo, who some called the Hitler of Japan,[161] would resign.

Meanwhile, in Nu'uanu, with the frenetic pace of lunches, dinners, hikes, swimming and late-night parties, Una came down with a bad cold, which she noted boldly in her diary. Una loathed admitting to illness or any human frailty, so she must have been quite ill to note it in her diary.

Chapter 9

A Stressful Brisbane Trip

MARCH WAS UNA'S favorite month in her yard. "I plant my gardens to peak in March," she told me, "so all the many orchids bloom together in profusion." So it was that month. Hundreds of *dendrobiums,* streaming in long sprays from the trunks of tall tree ferns lining the curved driveway, were in full bloom, and along with pikake and plumeria, filled the air with a perfumed fragrance enhanced by the sultry tropical air. Dozens of *Cattleya* orchids—pink, yellow, lavender, and white—were abloom in myriad crevices of ancient trees. Filtered sunlight dazzled innumerable other orchids in every direction one looked, reflecting the colors of the rainbow.

"You hear about the rare 'black orchid'," mused Una. "but there never has been one. One of my purple *Cattleyas* may look black from far away, but it's only an illusion."

The Walkers were having an unusually quiet evening at home alone on the first day of March, when the doorbell chimed. As Nimitz was wont to schedule events at the last minute for security reasons, his driver, Beach, unexpectedly showed up at 6:15 p.m. with an invitation to dine with Nimitz at Makalapa. Telling Hara that dinner was off, the Walkers departed with Beach. At Makalapa, only Nimitz, Lamar, Doc, Soc McMorris, and the Walkers were present. After a delightful dinner among now-close friends, they danced to Straus's waltzes, all behind blackout curtains covering every window. Nimitz wanted to spend that evening with the Walkers, because he and members of his staff were leaving for Washington the next day and would not return for several days. After poker, Beach drove them home at midnight.

The next afternoon, the Walkers bid Aloha to Adm & Hal & Mercer & Sherman, who were off on long plane rides to Washington D.C. to "plan strategy for getting Allied forces to the Luzon-Formosa-China triangle." [162]

Nimitz and King wanted to bypass the Philippines, while MacArthur planned to make good on his promise to that country that he would "return." No final decision had been made on the subject, nor could they, because MacArthur had snubbed an invitation to attend the conference to resolve the impasse. During the trip, Nimitz attended his daughter Catherine's marriage to Cdr. James T. Lay, Jr. Nimitz also appeared on the March 6, 1944, cover of *Life* magazine.

In a meeting, the President asked Nimitz why, after his successful raid on Truk, he decided to raid Tinian and Saipan, two islands near the Japanese homeland. Drawing on his joke about the hypochondriac who woke up after an appendectomy to find his tonsils removed as well, Nimitz replied, "You, see, Mr. President, that was the way it was. We just hit Tinian and Saipan for an encore." [163]

On one of his return flights crossing the continent from D.C., Nimitz played one of his practical jokes. The plane was filled with staff and reporters while he occupied a cabin in the back. With passengers slumbering in the early hours of the morning, the lights suddenly came on as Nimitz emerged from his cabin and announced: "All please rise. Now bow your heads in reverent silence. We are passing over the birthplace of a famous naval officer."

Looking out, the sleepy passengers figured out they were flying over the C-in-C's hometown—Fredericksburg, Texas! [164]

Another practical joke happened during his train ride from Chicago to Los Angeles after the attack on Pearl Harbor. While Nimitz was in the bathroom as the train approached a station, the porter locked the door. "The lock," he wrote his wife Catherine, "is designed to let the person inside open the lock—but this time it wouldn't work [and] I was locked in."

He repeatedly pressed a bell to summon the porter for several minutes, until the porter finally arrived to release him. "He was sarcastic about the bell [and] announced the door could be opened from inside."

When the porter offered to demonstrate how the lock worked, Nimitz locked him in the bathroom where he stayed for some time "until I unlocked the door. He was convinced that I had a good reason to be vexed." Lamar was "highly amused when I told him about it." [165]

On Wednesday, March 15th, Una recorded that Nimitz "arrived [in Pearl Harbor] from Wash." The trip to and from D.C. was grueling. The Coronado Flying Boat took at least thirty-four hours in the air each way—today, the same trip takes ten hours nonstop! On landing, Nimitz was informed that "Before dawn that morning eleven B-24s from Kwajalein, carrying out the JCS* order to neutralize Truk, had pounded the base with sixty-six 500-pound bombs, settling ablaze hangars, ammunition dumps, and oil-storage tanks." [166]

Also awaiting him was an invitation from MacArthur to visit him in Brisbane, Australia, which he graciously, if warily, accepted.

Sandy was still busy managing food distribution in the islands and explained in a letter to daughter Ann on March 17th that he "would love to be at your graduation" from Ethel Walker School in Connecticut that summer, "but I can't leave my job of feeding this Territory which as you know is my war job. Anyway, you will

---

* JCS stands for Joint Chiefs of Staff.

know I will be with you every second in spirit."

On March 20th Nimitz was invited to dinner in Nu'uanu and arrived with Lamar, early enough for a game of horseshoes with Sandy and Hanko. Ginger and Una watched from the sidelines. Nimitz was adept at the game in which the winner either scored a "ringer," with the two ends of a horseshoe enveloping a stake, or was the closest to the stake. That afternoon Sandy not only scored a ringer, but also a "Double Ringer"—two horseshoes hugging the stake. Sandy had made a brass plaque in a wooden drink tray, entitled "Sandy Walker's Horse Shoe Court," on which he engraved the "Roll of Double Ringers." (Never wanting to better his guests at any game, Sandy was mortified at personally winning the first "Double Ringer" award on his own plaque.) Afterward, Una served pork roast for dinner before an hour of poker.

Sandy Walker's Horse Shoe Court "Roll of Double Ringers"

Nimitz at Ease

At Lamar's request, for the trip to Australia Sandy and Una provided Nimitz with a cache of rare orchids kept fresh by inserting their stems through rubber gaskets into little glass tubes of water.[167] Nimitz was grateful and phoned [to say] good-bye, before leaving by seaplane to meet with MacArthur. The trip took two days of exhausting island hopping, refueling stops and aborted take offs.

Nimitz delivered his gifts from Hawai'i. MacArthur and his wife were delighted with the magnificent display of orchids the Walkers had gathered for Nimitz.[168]

MacArthur was brilliant, sixty-four years old, charismatic and conceited. Tall, with a strong baritone voice, the General was used to getting his way, whether by bullying or otherwise. *Life* magazine described him as having "an ebullient sense of ego," and taking "a direct hand in almost everything that happens in this theater and much that happens elsewhere."[169]

James Forrestal later said MacArthur "had a compelling and rather supercilious charm" and "a high degree of professional ability, mortgaged, however, to his sensitivity and vanity."[170] While Nimitz's messages to MacArthur read in the third person, "CINCPOA to CINCSOWESPAC," MacArthur's read, "MACARTHUR to CINCPOA." Never commanding more than a fraction of Nimitz's forces during the war, MacArthur's attempts to expand his authority and troops under his command were repeatedly rebuffed.

Nimitz, the patrician gentleman, was his opposite. "While MacArthur is a star general, Nimitz is the maker of star admirals, with the result that several of his seagoing subordinates...are probably better known to the public" than Nimitz.[171]

The meeting was collegial until Nimitz revealed that the Joint Chiefs of Staff wanted them to draw up alternate plans to bypass the Philippines. MacArthur "blew up and made an oration of some length on the impossibility of bypassing the Philippines" in the war.[172]

Michael A. Lilly

MacArthur & Nimitz in Brisbane, March 27, 1944[173]

Meanwhile, despite their fundamental dispute, the Navy disingenuously announced that their "Plans were completely integrated so that a maximum of cooperative effort might be exercised against the enemy." [174]

Nimitz, the consummate gentleman, was taken aback, though not completely surprised, by MacArthur's abrasive reaction. Without reaching an agreement about the Philippines, Nimitz departed Brisbane on March 27th, the same day that Admiral Hart arrived to take testimony from witnesses in Hawai'i on the Pearl Harbor attack.

Nimitz's return to Hawai'i took another grueling two days, landing on March 29th. Perhaps with one of his many long ocean flights in mind, Nimitz said the main obstacle in the war was not the Japanese, but "the size of the Pacific Ocean." [175]

Having suffered back-to-back prolonged plane trips, endured MacArthur's blow up, and dealt with innumerable challenging war details, Nimitz was exhausted. He needed time away from his office and eternal responsibilities. Their friendship had become so close that Nimitz was comfortable calling the Walkers to ask if he could come over, alone, for dinner. They dropped whatever plans they had.

Nimitz drove to Nu'uanu by himself. Contrary to form, he even left his ever-present flag lieutenant, Lamar, at home. As if carrying a great weight, the weary admiral climbed the granite steps to the Walkers' front door with more difficulty than usual.

Sandy answered the doorbell with his characteristically refreshing wide grin and accompanied Nimitz to their back lanai, where Una greeted him warmly. Hara the cook was dispatched to his quarters above the Carriage house while Sandy fixed [a] fine dinner, cooking over his commercial-sized gas stove. They ate on the back lanai, after which they "played crib."

The three friends enjoyed one another's company, counting cards and advancing pegs, while cool trade winds blew through the trees carrying sweet scents of spring flowers. Nimitz needed quiet time away with close friends to recharge his batteries and wind down from war stresses.

Nimitz may even have let his hair down and confided some of his war dilemmas, including his unsettling experience with MacArthur, to the Walkers. Sandy was a perfect confidante, for he was an easy listener and never divulged a secret. Sandy often said, and surely did to Nimitz, "Sometimes, it is better to follow your heart and not your head."

Nimitz was, indeed, a master at listening to his inner voice in the selection of subordinates, outthinking opponents, and crafting strategies that repeatedly crushed the enemy everywhere in the Pacific.

Returning to Makalapa late that evening somewhat refreshed, Nimitz initialed the *Graybook* in red, next to a handwritten notation, "Adm Nimitz & staff returned Pearl." He was pleased that raids against enemy positions in the Marshalls were proceeding well and torpedoes from the submarine USS *Tunny* (SS 282) damaged the Japanese super-battleship, *Musashi*, forcing its return to Palau for repairs.

The last day of March, while forty-two tons of bombs were being dropped on Truk, the Republic of Ecuador conferred an honorary doctorate on Nimitz, one of an endless list of such awards he would receive over the years.

Chapter 10

The Hart Inquiry and Admirals at Muliwai

THE FIRST DAY of April, a Saturday, with the Marshall Island's Bikini Atoll finally liberated from thirty years of Japanese occupation, the Walkers enjoyed a long walk & swim at Kailua with Nimitz and Lt. Gen. Alexander A. Vandegrift.

On January 1st that year, Vandegrift, who was fifty-seven, had become the Marine Corps' 18th Commandant, headquartered in Washington D.C. Two years before, he was the hero of Guadalcanal, the most prolonged, bitterly-fought, and precarious battle of the Pacific, rivaling Okinawa. Husky and bald as a grapefruit with a "bullet head" and penetrating eyes—*Daddy Warbucks* in khaki—Vandergrift successfully defended Guadalcanal with meager forces against successive waves of suicidal Japanese attackers, paying a dreadful cost in blood, for which he was awarded the Medal of Honor and Navy Cross. Sandy and he shared similar political and personal attributes, making them kindred spirits.

While Nimitz, Vandegrift and the Walkers were walking Kailua Beach, Admiral Hart was taking the testimony of Soc McMorris, who was the Pacific Fleet War Plans Officer under

Kimmel at the time of Pearl Harbor. When McMorris was asked whether a surprise attack was considered a possibility, he replied "Probably not. At least, I...did not hold such a view with respect to the Hawaiian Area, although I did consider such an act possible in the Philippines or even against Midway or Wake."

The examination concluded at 5:35 p.m., and shortly thereafter Hart was at Nimitz's quarters dining with Nimitz and the Walkers.

The next morning, Monday, April 3rd, Sandy and Una drove to Muliwai with Ginger and her daughters.

On that day, Hart was examining Vice Adm. Richmond Kelly "Terrible" Turner, Commander, Amphibious Force, South Pacific, who was in town. On the day of the Pearl Harbor attack, Turner, who was 58 and whose round glasses and bald scalp gave him a disarmingly professorial appearance, had been the War Plans Officer for Adm. Harold Raynsford Stark, Chief of Naval Operations in Washington D.C.

Turner considered himself one of Stark's principal advisers. He was also, perhaps, Stark's greatest apologist. Turner admitted that Stark had apprehensions of a surprise air attack [by the Japanese] on Oahu. Indeed, contrary to Soc's testimony, he said that the "attack of December 7th came as no surprise whatsoever to me, nor to the Chief of Naval Operations."

When Turner was asked if the CNO had warned Kimmel of his apprehensions that the Japanese would launch a surprise attack, he responded that they had not, but did not think they needed to:

> A. There was no specific warning sent out against attack on the Fleet here at the time the war warnings were dispatched. The only measures that we estimated specifically the Japanese would take were the general forms of his major attack, which was on Malay, the Philippines, and possibly Borneo, initially. That is, it was the major movement with which we were concerned in the Department. It was against policy—rightly so, I

> believe—to be too specific in details as to tactical matters. The idea was that we would give the Commanders-in-Chief general tasks, provide them with full information, and assign to them forces adequate for executing those tasks. We looked to the officers in the field to decide all tactical matters and methods. We did not wish to hamper them with detailed instructions concerning matters within their own fields of action. This was particularly important in the case of the Pacific and Asiatic Commands, which are so far distant from Washington that the officers there can never be adequately advised as to events and conditions.[176]

What Turner and the CNO Stark had done was send all commands a warning on November 27, 1941.

> Consider this dispatch a war warning...Japan is expected to make an aggressive move within the next few days...You will execute a defensive deployment...

In his post-war testimony before a Congressional inquiry, Turner said the Pacific Fleet could have been kept at sea after the war warning.*

The previous Friday, then-Captain Layton, Kimmel's intelligence officer, had testified that after receiving the war warning, he "presumed that they were going into full condition of readiness, including the emplacement of anti-aircraft and other mobile weapons around Pearl Harbor and other important points on Oahu."

---

* If Kimmel, in fact, knew the Japanese were going to attack Pearl Harbor, he no doubt would have ordered the ships to sea; but it would have presented a "Hobson's Choice." Nimitz later said that, if the fleet had been at sea and sunk by the Japanese, there could have been twenty thousand casualties instead of one-tenth that amount.

Michael A. Lilly

He had been so concerned, however, about the lack of information emanating from Washington in the days leading up to the attack that he "remained at our telephones throughout the week-end" in case anything important came through. Nothing, of course, did until long after the attack.

Hart adjourned Turner's testimony at 12:03 p.m., until the next morning. After lunch, Nimitz, Mercer and Hart climbed into the black flag Buick at 1:30 p.m., heading for Muliwai. Una's diary recorded that at 2:30 p.m., the Buick emerged onto the wide Muliwai lawn to Una's shouts of delight. "Adm N & Hart & Mercer arrived for sun, swim and dinner" and a "nice time."

It was Hart's first and only time at Muliwai, which was always a pleasant surprise for people to find that such a peaceful oasis existed. Not a mention of Hart's inquiries into Pearl Harbor escaped his lips while relaxing at Muliwai.

Ginger and her daughters were present. Nimitz had become so fond of Maile and Sheila that he nicknamed them the "Gremlins." Maile was "Major Gremlin" and Sheila "Minor Gremlin." Whimsical photographs were taken of everyone in bathing suits on the beach side of the house. One photo shows the men with Maile, Sheila and Ginger.

In another, Maile was upside down on Nimitz's back, as he carried her around Muliwai.

(Left-to-Right) Captain Mercer, Admiral Hart with Sheila, Nimitz with Maile and Ginger, Muliwai, La'ie, April 3, 1944

(Left-to-Right) Maile, Nimitz and Sheila, Muliwai, April 3, 1944

Michael A. Lilly

When she was shown these photos, Sheila remarked that Nimitz was a handsome bloke. "Every weekend," she recalled, "I rode home with Nimitz, sitting on his lap in the back seat, just the two of us. Usually I would get nauseated, as we rode up the old, twisty-turny road over the Pali, and he'd have to stop the car because I got sick. Nimitz held me as I bent over and threw up beside the car. That old road took forever!"

Imagine! America's most famous admiral consoling then four-year-old *Minor Gremlin*, as she lost her breakfast!

After photographs, everyone enjoyed a splendid swim in the blue Pacific, followed by dinner, classical music and poker. As mentioned earlier, a tropical Muliwai evening was never complete without Una bringing out her ukulele for a song or two. Among her usual repertoire were the lighthearted, "Coconut Willie" and "Princess Pupule* Has Plenty Papaya," as well as Johnny Noble's romantic, "It's Heaven in Hawai`i." Her favorite war song was Alex Anderson's popular ditty, "They Can't Take Ni'ihau No-how!" recounting sheep-herder Ben Kanahele's heroic battle with a Japanese pilot (who had crash-landed on the small Hawaiian island of Ni'ihau after hitting Pearl Harbor), which she sung in perfect harmony to the pleasant notes emanating from her ukulele:

> *On the tiny isle of Ni'ihau, no one knew a war was on.*
> *Till a Japanese flier decided to retire and landed with a machine gun.*
> *Then Big Ben Kanahele laid aside his ukulele*
> *And told the aviator he would throw him in the crater if he didn't get the heck right out.*
> *But the Jap shot Ben in the shoulder, in the hip and in the groin.*
> *Kanahele took a swallow and tightened up his malo and then he girded up his other loin.*
> *Ben Kanahele grabbed the Jap around the belly and*

---

* *Pupule* is Hawaiian for "crazy."

> *threw him down against a stone wall.*
> *Then Mrs. Kanahele took a rock and made a jelly of his head till he was dead and that was all.*
> *Oh, they couldn't take Ni'ihau no-how with the Ben Kanahele's around.*
> *The Jap was a sap to think it a snap when he set his airplane down.*
> *They couldn't take Ni'ihau no-how when Ben Kanahele said pau.**
> *He made a grand slam for his Uncle Sam and they couldn't take Ni'ihau no-how!*

Gracefully strumming her ukulele, Una's melodic voice with perfect pitch echoed in the dark with the humid trade winds blowing in from the sea and rustling the leaves of trees. Hart's inquiry must have seemed oceans away as he enjoyed the lively songs, while lying on the *hikie* (Hawaiian sofa bed) and basking in the languid beauty of Muliwai. Growing up in Michigan and spending a long career in the Navy, Hart had never experienced anything like that magical evening on the north shore of O'ahu.

They likely discussed an article appearing in the morning paper about Sandy's annual report to the stockholders of American Factors. He praised the contributions of students "in all our plantation communities" for "turning out for part-time agricultural work," which "played a most important part" in the production of sugar.[177] He lamented, however, that the war prevented capital improvements and repairs, which "cannot be undertaken until peace-time conditions again prevail."

Since taking the helm of American Factors a decade before and successfully lobbying Congress for sugar legislation, Sandy was an unabashed advocate for the sugar business in Hawai'i. "Did you know," he surprised Nimitz, as he did most everyone he met, "it cost more to offload a pound of sugar at the New Jersey docks than

---

* "Pau" is Hawaiian for "stop."

it does to ship that pound of sugar all the way from Hawai'i, though the Panama Canal, to New Jersey? Such is the expense that stevedores add to the price of sugar in the marketplace."

He also advised that, whenever one found little bags of C&H sugar at one's table in a restaurant, "Use one in your coffee, but break a second one in half for the industry," instructed Sandy.

Everyone was very sleepy before turning in to the pleasant sound of giant tropical cane toads (*bufo marinus*) warbling their melodious mating calls. Sandy explained to Nimitz that the toad was brought to Hawai'i from Puerto Rico a decade before in two suitcases by the Chief Entomologist of his Hawaiian Sugar Planters Association to fight sugar pests and noxious insects. The toad population soon multiplied, and they were everywhere, voraciously munching on centipedes, mosquitoes and spiders. Sheila recalled that there were so many toads on the road to Muliwai you would "hear them being squashed under our car tires—kpuckity, puckity, squish, squash—lots and lots of them!"

Nestled in Sandy's Koa bed with visions of the most pleasing afternoon of exercise, a splendid steak dinner and Hawaiian songs, banished all thoughts of war in the western Pacific from the far reaches of Nimitz's mind, as he fell into the most contented oblivion.

After a restful sleep and morning beach walk and swim, Nimitz, Mercer and Hart left very early. Nimitz initialed *Graybook's* reports of air strikes against Truk, enemy-occupied atolls of the Marshalls, Ponape and Wewak in New Guinea.[178]

Hart resumed his examination of Admiral Turner at precisely 8:15 a.m. on April 4th. Turner had earlier testified that he had drafted the war warning of November 27th. The CNO expected commands to undertake war scouting measures, deployment of submarines, carriers put to sea, with their protective vessels, and a high degree of readiness by ships, defensive troops, and anti-aircraft. However, when he was asked whether any other repeated warnings were sent to Kimmel after late November, Turner replied, "I recall no official dispatches or official letters which gave repeated warnings."

As to the vulnerability of Pearl Harbor ships to aerial torpedoes, Turner said, "The Bureau of Ordnance sent out a letter…stating rather categorically that, in their opinion, the water in Pearl Harbor was too shallow to permit the dropping of torpedoes and, unquestionably, that influenced the authorities here in determining not to use nets."

However, Turner never accepted that opinion and saw no reason whatsoever why torpedoes cannot be made to drop in shallow water. He did not share his contradictory opinion with the Navy leaders in Pearl Harbor, who were as shocked as everyone else that the Japanese developed a torpedo that could sink ships in shallow waters.

A subordinate of Turner's described him as "forceful, pigheaded, and so violent in his arguments that other officers of all services backed down, rather than quarrel with him." [179] Reading Turner's firm responses to Hart's questions, what emerges, in the author's opinion, is a man with those very qualities—a "macho" man, who formed strong, firmly-held opinions with no ambiguities: a sometimes-toxic combination.

On Thursday, April 6th, Spruance's naval forces attacked Palau, Woleai and Yap, and entered Majuro lagoon in the Marshalls. Sandy's letter that afternoon to daughter Ann reported that Ingraham Stainback, Territorial Governor since June 1942, had reappointed him Chairman of the Board of Leper Hospitals and Settlements "for another four years, which will make sixteen years, and then I think I will have done my duty and can retire."

In addition to running American Factors, he was still in charge of food control, which took a lot of time to see that everyone here gets something to eat.

Ann responded, "Really Daddy, you are turning into a Joan of Arc. [Sixteen] years on the Leprosy Board ought to entitle you to at least a small halo."

That evening Sandy and Una hosted a large gathering at Nu'uanu. Nimitz and Lamar arrived early for horseshoes and tennis with Hanko and Una. This time Hanko won the game with a Double Ringer, becoming the second winner after his father inscribed on Sandy's brass plaque. Una noted that it was a cheery afternoon in garden and horseshoes, although she and Sandy would have preferred the Admiral to have won a place on the Double Ringer plaque. In addition to Nimitz and Lamar, the large crowd for dinner that evening included General Richardson, Soc, Doc, the Hal Castles, and Ginger. After dinner, they played charades, followed by the ubiquitous poker game upstairs.

It may have been that evening described by Tony Lilly in his memoirs, *A Sailor's Life*. He had been dating Ginger whenever his ship was in port. Ginger was suddenly summoned to Una's home to round out the poker table with Nimitz. According to Tony, "She promised to duck out as soon as she could and left me in her living room with the girls tucked in the next room. They [the Gremlins] plotted some fun—probably, Maile was chief plotter—and they raced into the room giggling, and Sheila pulled her nightgown over her head." Tony was mortified, writing "Scared me to death."

Una's diary recorded the next day that Nimitz, Sherman and Lamar departed by seaplane for the twenty-three hundred miles to "Majuro" in the Marshall Islands. On the way, he had the usual Nimitz plane trouble. The staff plane had to turn back with engine trouble, but shortly after landing they were off again in a PB-2-Y (Coronado Flying Boat).[180] The purpose of the trip was to discuss the upcoming naval operations at Hollandia, New Guinea.

That Sunday was Easter, so Nimitz was not in residence. The previous year, he had hosted an Easter egg hunt at his quarters, inviting all his Honolulu civilian friends to bring their children. My cousin Johnny Walker, son of Nimitz's occasional tennis doubles partner, Chimey Walker, recalled a humorous experience when, as a young lad, he had attended that event. Johnny, along with other children carrying baskets, scurried around the lawns picking up colored eggs, while parents watched from the sidelines. Johnny suddenly needed to use the bathroom, so he entered the main house where he threaded himself around, until he located a small water closet with toilet and sink. Then Johnny learned a lesson in Nimitz's wry sense of humor—this time regarding his warrior enemies. In the bathroom were three rolls of toilet paper on which faces were printed. One was of Emperor Hirohito, another of Hitler and the last Mussolini. (Johnny kept several sheets of each for years, before they finally disappeared.)

After Nimitz returned to Honolulu, he played tennis in a foursome at the Walker's. Una and Nimitz beat Hanko and George Sumner's daughter Evanita. That night they had dinner at the Samuel Renny Damon's estate on a hill in Moanalua with commanding 360-degree views. To the west was the Pacific Ocean, to the north O'ahu's Salt Lake, to the east Diamond Head, and part way up the Ko'olau Mountains was the future Tripler Hospital under construction. The Damon and the Walker families had been close friends and associates for generations. (In the 19th century, Sandy's and Samuel's fathers had served together as members of King Kalakaua's Privy Council.) Damon's wife was Vice President of the Hawai'i Red Cross Production Committee, established in June 1940, to begin preparation for the expected war with Japan.

Two days later, Nimitz and Lamar drove Una to Muliwai. Sandy, Hanko, Hara and the terriers arrived separately. During the course of the war, Hara must have served over a hundred meals for Nimitz and other military and political leaders. Hanko commented on the irony that Hara, a Japanese national, could have poisoned Nimitz and the leaders of the war against Japan:

> *One interesting sidelight to these dinners was that our cook was a Japanese national named Hara…It is an interesting footnote to history that if Hara should have wished on many occasions, he could have poisoned our dinner table of almost the entire high command of the Pacific. The funny thing was that nobody ever thought about it until after the war was over.*
>
> *Nimitz regularly used to enter the kitchen after dinner and compliment Hara on his fine meals. What a*

paradox that was. The loyal but totally honorable Japanese national in our kitchen and the Commander in Chief, Pacific, at our dining room table.[181]

While the government planned mass internment of Japanese in the islands, as happened on the U.S. homeland and, indeed, Secretary of the Navy Knox proposed it,[182] it never came to pass, in part because of the intercession of Sandy, the only *kama'aina* member of the Military and Civilian Governor's staffs. In 1985, a Buddhist monk named Sensei Steven Tanouye told me, "You and your family have great aloha, Mike. During the war, there were plans to ship out the Japanese in Hawai'i into labor camps, just like on the mainland. Your grandfather testified in favor of my father, and we were not interned."

Sandy, having grown up with Japanese all his life and knowing they were loyal, opposed the idea. He helped convince his friend and Military Governor Emmons to the same view. Nimitz had a similar belief in the loyalty of the Japanese, perhaps in part from Sandy's influence. Accordingly, there was no wholesale internment in Hawai'i. Only a relative handful of Japanese with direct ties to Japan or recent arrivals, representing about one percent of their island population, were actually interned.

At Muliwai on the evening of April 14th, they enjoyed a delightful evening and dinner of Hara's "Kauai steaks," as Hal Lamar later reminisced in a newspaper article:

> *Lamar said Nimitz's favorite local friends were Alexander and Una Walker in Nuuanu. Walker was head of American Factors (now Amfac).*
>
> *"Once a week, we went to their country place at La'ie [Muliwai] for steaks and classical music, or they came here [Makalapa]," said Lamar.*[183]

Potter writes that Nimitz often played classical music after dinner "to the acute boredom of some of his guests."[184] Not so with the

Walkers, who were lifelong members of the Honolulu Symphony and loved classical music as much as Nimitz.

One such evening, with a symphony playing in the background, would have provided an opportune moment for Sandy to relate one of his humorous stories while attending Harvard—one that would have appealed to Admiral Nimitz.

"My fraternity brother's father owned the vaudeville and opera houses," Sandy said. "One night, our fraternity booked the entire front row of the opera. Unlike vaudeville, the audience was rigidly formal—both in attire and attitude. We were in tuxedos, white gloves, carried umbrellas, and primed for some fraternity antics.

"The leading lady—an enormous woman with a monstrous chest—commanded the edge of the stage, as she did every night, for her booming aria. We were just a few feet below her. When she reached the crescendo of her aria—as her voice hit the highest and loudest note—our entire front row opened umbrellas over our heads to protect us from her spittle. The singing came to an abrupt halt, while we and our offending umbrellas were thrown out of the opera under the furious glare of the diva."

Throughout Sandy's tale, and all his other ones, a huge grin covered the broad expanse of his face under sparkling eyes. And his chuckling humor was so infectious that everyone laughed with him.

The next morning, after walking the beach, everyone left early. At his headquarters, Nimitz learned that the western Pacific was unusually quiet. Sandy and Una were back in Nu'uanu in time for lunch. But at 1:30 p.m., Nimitz picked them up, and drove back over the Pali to walk Kailua Beach with Admiral Spruance and Gen. Holland 'Howling Mad' Smith.[*] Una, who enjoyed a long walk, described it as lovely exercise. After returning home over the Pali, Nimitz drove the Walkers to Makalapa that evening for a fine dinner and dance at the submarine base with Vice Admiral Lockwood. Late that evening, Nimitz drove the exhausted and

---

[*] Smith was head of the V Amphibious Corps until August 1944 when he assumed command of the Fleet Marine Force, Pacific.

happy Walkers home. The time spent in cars alone that day—from Muliwai to town to Kailua to Makalapa to Nuʻuanu—consumed at least three hours.

Nimitz and his Commanders in the Western Pacific: Rear Adm. Richard Turner, Adm. Raymond Spruance, Nimitz, Brig. Gen. Henry Holmes, Lt. Gen. Robert Richardson, Maj. Gen. Ralph Smith, Maj. Gen. Holland "Howling Mad" Smith, and Rear Adm. Charles "Soc" McMorris[185]

The last two weeks of April, while the Navy continued pounding Truk, neutralizing enemy forces on outlying Marshall atolls, and destroying the Japanese base at Hollandia, New Guinea, Nimitz and the Walkers were together nearly every day for a whirlwind round of endless social activities. They played tennis and horseshoes, drove together to various dinners hosted by the George Sumners, Hal Castles, and other civilian friends of the Walkers, hiked and swam at Kailua, and spent the weekend at Muliwai. Nimitz initialed *Graybook*'s warning that Japanese "raids in force" on Midway and Oahu "continue possible but not probable." [186]

On April 18th, the Walkers, Nimitz, Ginger and several friends had a cheery evening and dinner at the home of Herman von Holt and his wife Betty. The von Holts were a prominent local family. Herman, a third generation of the von Holt family in Hawai`i, was a successful businessman and longtime executive secretary of the sprawling Campbell Estate land trust. His wife Betty, was the energetic chairman of the Red Cross' Volunteer Special Services, encompassing several thousand workers. [187]

While Nimitz lamented allied casualties in the western Pacific, he celebrated one death that evening. The year before, Nimitz's code breakers had discovered the itinerary of his Japanese counterpart—the Commander in Chief of the Imperial Japanese Combined Fleet and architect of the attack on Pearl Harbor, Admiral Isoroku Yamamoto. Having obtained approval from President Roosevelt, Nimitz authorized Yamamoto's assassination. His plane was shot down near New Guinea on April 18, 1943. Yamamoto's death was a huge blow to the Japanese war effort and a partial repayment for Pearl Harbor.

That last weekend of April, Una pointed out to Nimitz, as she did every year, that their Plover was no longer in residence. Until late April every year, a lone *Kōlea* (Pacific Golden Plover) darted around the Muliwai lawns, sharply bobbing and ducking its head at every stop. When a car entered the property, the Plover took wing with a piercing screech, and circled around and landed across the stream by the paddle tennis court or on the roof of the house. (As spring neared, male plovers slowly donned "tuxedos," turning colors from light brown to nearly black and white.) Near the end of every April, a primeval urge overcame the species. Plovers abruptly abandoned their solitary natures and gathered in flocks until, responding to some unheard command, they took to the air in unison, flying some twenty-five hundred miles or so without rest, until they reached their Alaskan nesting grounds. They did not return until late August, usually to the same property they left in April. For many years, a one-legged Plover, nicknamed Oscar, returned every August to the Walkers' Nu'uanu property.

On April 26, while *Graybook* reported that B-24s dropped thirty-seven tons of fragmentation bombs on Truk Island,[188] Sandy, Nimitz, Walter Dillingham, and Hawai'i Governor Ingram Stainback flew to Maui for [a] decoration and tour. Dillingham was a successful businessman, whose many achievements included clearing the entrance to Pearl Harbor, building its first dry-dock, dredging the Ala Wai Canal in the 1920s and filling Waikiki's swamps, thereby making Waikiki's development possible.[189] One writer called him, "Perhaps the most powerful man in Hawaii during the 1920s."[190] In 1929, *Time* magazine described Dillingham the "No. 1 Tycoon of the Islands." During the war, he served under Sandy at 'Iolani Palace as the volunteer Territorial Director of Food Production.

That evening, the Walkers were back in Nu'uanu hosting a dinner for a group of distinguished guests, including Gen. William J. "Wild Bill" Donovan, Admirals Nimitz and Spruance, Rear Adm. Lloyd J. Wiltse and local business leaders. Donovan, sixty-one, was head of the Office of Strategic Services (OSS), predecessor of the CIA, during World War II and a decorated World War I hero (Medal of Honor). Wiltse, at fifty-three, was also a war hero credited with saving his cruiser USS *Detroit* (CL 8) from damage during Pearl Harbor and was later awarded the Navy Cross for action in October 1944 as Commander, Task Group 30.3, repulsing Japanese air attacks while towing two damaged cruisers from enemy waters. (This was another of the many fascinating Walker/Nimitz evenings one might have sacrificed an eyetooth to attend.)

On April 28th, an urgent radio message to all Navy ships and commands bore sad news that the Secretary of the Navy, Frank Knox, had passed away after a heart attack. He was only seventy years old. Knox, who had served as a Rough Rider under Theodore Roosevelt at San Juan Hill in 1898, was buried on May Day at the

Arlington National Cemetery. The ceremony was "Washington's most impressive official funeral since the death of William Howard Taft in 1930." [191] In a tribute, Admiral King said Knox had left the nation "secure in the knowledge that his energy and farsighted vision have been responsible…that we are so far advanced on the road to victory." [192] Roosevelt promptly appointed Knox's immediate subordinate, James Forrestal, then fifty-two, to succeed him.

On April 29th, while Nimitz and the Walkers enjoyed a walk and swim at Kailua, Hart was in Washington, D.C., taking the explosive testimony of Capt. L.F. Safford, often called the "Father of Naval Cryptology." In December 1941, he was the senior officer responsible for Navy communications intelligence in D.C. In a phenomenal revelation, Safford testified that on December 7th, they had "positive information … that the Japanese declaration of war would be presented to the Secretary of State at 1:00 p.m. (Washington time) that date. One o'clock p.m. Washington time was sunrise in Hawai'i and approximately midnight in the Philippines. This," he concluded "indicated a surprise raid on Pearl Harbor in about three hours." He had sent this warning to Secretary of the Navy Knox.

When asked whether that critical information was transmitted to the 14th Naval District in Pearl Harbor, he said, "No, Sir." As to whether the 14th Naval District had intelligence material from which it could have drawn the same conclusion, he answered in the negative. "They could not possibly have gained this information." *
As to why he did not transmit that information directly to Pearl

---

* Perhaps with a tinge of guilt, Safford revealed to Kimmel's attorneys in January 1944 that he learned that critical intelligence information had not been forwarded to the Pacific command. *A Matter of Honor*, 304. Some of Safford's testimony to Hart that revealed pre-Pearl Harbor decrypts of Japanese messages was planned by Kimmel's attorneys, with Safford's help, as a way to both defend Kimmel and protect national security, while the war was still being fought. *Id.*, 306.

Harbor, he said he had no authority to do so—that it was solely within the province of the Office of Naval Intelligence under the Chief of Naval Operations.

In fact, the Washington hierarchy was well aware that war was imminent. Stark had asked Army Chief of Staff Marshall to send a telegram to that effect to the Navy in Hawai'i. He did, but it went by slow boat and was received by Kimmel "Eight hours after the start of the attack." The failure of Secretary Knox and the CNO, Stark, to timely transmit the telegram, including Safford's expectation of an imminent attack[193] on Pearl Harbor, was among the worst intelligence failures in military history.*

---

* Knox was less than truthful with the American people when, after flying to Hawai'i on December 15, 1941, he disingenuously reported to the nation that the "United States services were not on the alert against the surprise air attack on Hawaii. This fact calls for a formal investigation, which will be initiated immediately by the President." (*New York Times*, December 16, 1941.)

Nimitz at Ease

Chapter 11

An L.S.T. Tragedy in Paradise

ON MAY 2ND Nimitz issued *Communiqué No. 44,* which publicly announced that "Powerful naval task forces of the Pacific Fleet...have completed further attacks against the enemy bases in the Central Pacific following their operations in support of the Hollandia-Humboldt Bay occupation."

Graybook noted that over fifty tons of bombs were dropped on Truk and three tons on Ponape.[194] Nimitz called the Walkers to "Say, Hello," followed by the arrival of Spruance, who drove them to the Walter Dillingham's for dinner. Dillingham had built their magnificent pink mansion at the base of Diamond Head in 1921, replicating the brick and tile villa where he and his wife had honeymooned in Italy. He called it "La Pietra"—meaning "gem." Una recorded that they had dinner, dancing [and] what not!

Early the next morning, Una and Hanko drove to Makalapa at the early hour of 6:40 a.m. for a walk with Nimitz and Spruance, after which they breakfasted on scrambled eggs, bacon, toast and a ripe papaya with a wedge of lime.

The next day, Nimitz, Sherman and staff flew to San Francisco for meetings with Admirals King and Halsey to discuss the cross-channel invasion of Normandy, planned for June 1944, the invasion of China, and Pacific war policies.[195] They decided that Nimitz's flag secretary, Captain Mercer, whom Nimitz had awarded a Legion of Merit for exceptionally meritorious conduct for service in his command, would get a sea command. During this meeting, Nimitz also urged the end of segregation of blacks in the Navy. Nimitz and King also again discussed bypassing the Philippines in favor or Formosa, but based on Nimitz's recent trip to Brisbane, he expected angry opposition from MacArthur.

When planning operations, Nimitz applied a three-way test listed on a card. Is the proposed operation likely to succeed? What might be the consequences of failure? Is it in the realm of practicability in terms of materiel and supplies?[196] The answers determined whether Nimitz favored the operation, which in this case favored Formosa over the Philippines.

King awarded Nimitz the *Distinguished Service Medal* for "His brilliant leadership" which "enabled units of his command to defeat the enemy in the Coral Sea, off Midway, and in the Solomon Islands, and to capture and occupy the Gilbert and Marshall Islands."

Nimitz was equally proud to learn on May 7th that his son Cdr. Chester W. Nimitz, Jr. was awarded the Navy Cross for extraordinary heroism as a submarine skipper in skillfully directing his vessel in a series of successful torpedo and gun attacks on Japanese men of war and escorted merchant shipping.

Una and *Graybook* recorded Nimitz's return on May 8th. The following day, the Walkers had dinner with Nimitz, Spruance and Soc at Makalapa.

Una's painted place card pictured an outrigger canoe and thatched roof hut with coconut tree on a peaceful tropical island. After dinner, they strolled over to the outdoor theater. With a brilliant, tropical, full moon rising behind them over the Ko'olau Mountains, they enjoyed the 1944 comedy, *The Miracle of Morgan's Creek,* starring Eddie Bracken and Betty Hutton. The movie portrayed a woman who woke up, after entertaining troops, married to a stranger and—pregnant!

Dinner Nametag Hand-Painted by Nimitz's Staff for Una Walker

On May 10th Nimitz initialed a report that six hundred twenty-one emaciated prisoners of war were liberated on Hollandia, the first mention in *Graybook* of Allied POWs being freed.[197] The brutality by which Allied prisoners were treated, in violation of the Geneva Convention, deeply saddened Nimitz. While Japanese prisoners were generally handled honorably, not so Allied POWs of which nearly thirty percent perished in the hands of their ruthless captors.

When Nimitz arrived at the Walker's that evening, his friends had no inkling of the painful knowledge he shouldered, about how badly Allied POWs had been treated. Yet, their conviviality and friendship helped him cope with his anguish. Guests included Sandy's best friend Paul Fagan, Midi Midkiff, Ginger, Hanko, Doc, and Lamar. After dinner, they walked upstairs to Sandy's sitting room where they played poker until 11.30! Nimitz, Una noted, won $18. Una, of course, shouted with delight every time a big hand was won.

On Thursday, May 11th, Nimitz and every flag and general officer on Oahu participated in a celebration at Schofield Barracks of the one-year anniversary of the liberation of Attu. "I wish every American could have the opportunity of seeing the Seventh Army Division this morning," the next morning's *Honolulu Advertiser* quoted Nimitz. "I consider it a great honor and a high privilege to have been invited to participate in this review."

That evening, Nimitz drove the Walkers for dinner at the von Holt's to celebrate Admiral Lockwood's birthday. The liberation of Attu was discussed over dinner. Afterwards, they danced all evening.

The following weekend, Nimitz and the Walkers enjoyed a swim at Kailua. Una wore a new brown and yellow bathsuit, and Nimitz and Lamar were in yellow shorts. That evening they drove to Muliwai for the night. With the sun setting, they had fun dancing to the stars before retiring.

On May 12th came the news that the Soviet Union had finally freed Crimea from the German army. With the Soviets in the news, Sandy may have taken the occasion that evening to tell Nimitz one of his favorite anecdotes from his Red Cross service at the end of World War I, when he operated an anti-typhus relief train from Vladivostok across Siberia to the Ural Mountains and back.[*] The

---

[*] A. L. Castle, a lifelong, close friend of Sandy's, was appointed General Field Director of the Red Cross for the Territory of Hawai'i on April 28, 1918. With Castle's assistance, Sandy joined the American Red Cross. In the fall of 1918, Castle, Sandy, and more than a dozen Hawai'i Red Cross volunteers travelled to Vladivostok to fight outbreaks of typhus among refugees of the Russian Revolution. Sandy ran a train across the vast reaches of Siberia, sometimes travelling over three thousand miles to the eastern slopes of the Ural Mountains, to bring refugees back to Vladivostok. No sooner would he disembark his refugees, but back he would go, across the Siberian steppes, to fetch his next group. On March 15, 1919, Sandy wrote Una from Vladivostok:

> *Dear Uni, Just a note to let you know I am back. I got in at two this morning and will go right out again in a couple of days ...It was a very hard trip and I have been*

starving refugees fleeing the Bolsheviks, whom he had retrieved, were lice-ridden, starved and filthy.

"When I picked up the refugees," Sandy said, "I at first had to get rid of their *ukus*—body lice. I had them disinfected with kerosene in a railroad car specially designed for that purpose.

"However, I'd no sooner delouse them, but find the refugees crawling with vermin again. Where [were] the lice coming from? I didn't want them on my train."

Sandy's investigation discovered the most astonishing fact. "What I learned," Sandy continued with the widest grin, "was that those refugees had spent their entire lives covered with body lice, which only left a body after death. To them, if someone lost their body lice, they would die. I discovered a man on my train was hoarding lice in matchboxes, which he sold to refugees, who put them back on their bodies. Imagine that! To those refugees, it was normal to have body lice crawling all over them. They had never known a day without the critters."

On Sunday they wakened at Muli at 6.30 [a.m.], just seven minutes after the sun burst over the eastern horizon. It was Mother's Day, and Nimitz had brought Una a Makalapa Cake, baked by his flag chef. Una noted, "Everybody [was] so nice to me!"

Together with the Walkers' terriers, Dirke and Boykin, they ventured through the barbed wire and past the guards for a long walk on the pristine beach, and swim. Gazing at the long line of mountains stretching to the south, Una never ceased amazement of their ever-changing hues, sometimes disappearing altogether in rain clouds. After breakfast, Nimitz and his group departed at 10:00

---

unable to shake my cold but don't say it to anyone.

His Siberian experience ended the following summer, when he escorted a shipload of Czechoslovakian refugees from Vladivostok around the world, repatriating them in Eastern Europe! Sandy often told many humorous stories of his Siberian adventure, which he would have related to Nimitz.

a.m. Back at headquarters, Nimitz initialed *Graybook's* pleasing report of the sinking of five Japanese ships by submarines *Sturgeon*, *Bonefish*, and *Ray*.[198]

Nimitz and the Walkers were together again, including Hanko, for dinner and a movie that evening at Makalapa. With exhaustion from exercise and partying, Una's diary noted that, during the movie, Hanko and the Walkers all fell *moe* (asleep).

Una, Ginger and the Gremlins remained at Muliwai until the next morning. No sooner did they arrive home, but Nimitz, Doc and Lamar drove them back over the Pali for a hike and swim along Kailua beach. That evening, they had dinner in Nu'uanu with a large group of the Walkers' local friends, followed by a game of poker upstairs.

On one such evening Nimitz pressed on his fleet surgeon, Doc Anderson, an extra-strong, and fairly old cigar, one of Winston Churchill's, given to Nimitz by Roosevelt. Nimitz smiled as he watched Doc puff on the cigar, but the "Poor medico finally gave up and excused himself, claiming it was too hot for him indoors." Doc later admitted he was so woozy he nearly didn't make it out the door.[199]

The next morning, May 21st, Nimitz's driver, Beach, called for them and drove to Nimitz's Beach for [the] marine Guard Picnic. Nimitz Beach was at Naval Air Station Barbers Point. They had lunch and a swim and returned to Makalapa to pitch horseshoes and shoot pistols at Nimitz's target range.

Depending on one's source, Nimitz's shooting gallery was the brainchild of either fleet surgeon, Dr. Gendreau, or his successor, Doc Anderson, who recommended target practice for relaxation, because in shooting a pistol one can think of nothing else but pulling the trigger.*

---

* Potter attributes the target range to Gendreau. *Nimitz*, 176. Hal Lamar said it was Doc Anderson. Interview with Hal Lamar, 32; *I Saw Stars*, 11. Edwin P. Hoyt, in *How They Won the War in the Pacific*, 395-96, concurs with Lamar.

Lamar wrote that they had consulted with specialists in Washington, who recommended a shooting gallery as an excellent cure for nervousness.[200] The gallery seemed to work, in more than one way. The newspaper correspondents, seeing Nimitz on his shooting range, jumped to the happy if erroneous conclusion that everything must be fine if the "old man" could play with his popguns.[201]

Of course, his target practice was for relaxation and not from happy war news. By the time of the surrender, Lamar estimated, "We must have fired at least half a million shots!"[202]

Festivities came to a halt when, at precisely 3:18 p.m., loud explosions emanated from the far side of Pearl Harbor.[203] A mortar round aboard a Landing Ship Tank (LST) at a West Loch staging area detonated, quickly spreading a chain reaction of fires and more explosions. One LST in flames drifted away, threatening twenty-eight others, reminiscent of fire ships used during the days of wooden ships to destroy enemy ships at anchor. Fires ignited fuel and set off ammunition. Six LSTs sank. Some one hundred twenty-seven men perished, and hundreds were hospitalized.[204] The explosions reverberated throughout Pearl Harbor, with many fearing it was a renewed Japanese attack or earthquake.

Because of the "L.S.T. tragedy," wrote Una, they cancelled a planned post-dinner cruise around Pearl Harbor aboard Nimitz's dark blue admiral's barge. Instead, they "rested with [a] private dinner with Adm. [and] Doc [and] Hal" at Makalapa. While they dined, the LSTs continued to explode and burn to the waterline. Nimitz was given updates on efforts to contain the disaster across the harbor.

The last explosion occurred at 10:30 p.m. (Because of concerns for security, the Navy ordered that the incident and its investigation be marked Top Secret and very little was released publicly.)* Before returning home, Nimitz and the Walkers made plans for a long and spectacular hike three days later.

Dinner Nametag Hand-Painted by Nimitz's Staff for Una Walker

On May 24th, Una, Nimitz, Spruance and the von Holts drove to Palehua where they "walked many, happy miles" high in the Waianae Mountains. Palehua is a dry region above today's Makakilo. A switchback trail snaked through forests of bamboo, Strawberry Guava, ferns, Ohia, and Ironwood and outcroppings of basaltic rock. Nearing the top, they entered a rock tunnel, beyond which they traversed a narrow, precipitous ridge of red hardpan— the red from oxidized volcanic iron. The higher they walked, the less the vegetation. At the summit, Palikea, they reached an elevation of over three thousand feet. There, they enjoyed birthday supper and cake on [the] mountain and exquisite vistas across the

---

* The rusting hulk of one LST is still visible today in West Loch. Some munitions from the LSTs were dredged from the bottom of the harbor and detonated by the Navy in October 2013.

mountains to the west and Diamond Head to the southeast. (Una does not indicate whose birthday, but it was a "happy outing.") The trail varies from five to seven miles and takes between five and seven hours to complete—a strenuous, but rewarding, hike.

Meanwhile, during the mid-May period, Nimitz and his Pacific Command were deeply involved in the planning and rehearsal for the upcoming Marianas campaign. The assaults on the islands of Guam, Saipan and Tinian would be carried out by an unholy alliance of marines and army soldiers fighting side-by-side under General Smith. That prescription for in-fighting and rivalry reminded Nimitz of "the first amphibious operation—conducted by Noah! When they were unloading from the Ark, he saw a pair of cats come out, followed by six kittens. 'What's this?' he asked. 'Ha, ha,' said the tabby cat, 'and all the time you thought we were fighting.'" [205]

The weekend of May 26-28th was another whirlwind of social and physical activities. On Friday, Nimitz and Lamar drove the Walkers to Edie Podmore's Kahala home for a "very cheery" dinner. Saturday morning, everyone went to Muliwai.

Una, Nimitz and Doc had a long walk across Kamehameha Highway along a levee above the normally dry Wailele streambed, through the vast Kahuku Sugar Plantation fields of green sugarcane and into the verdant mountains beyond. Occasional squirrel-like, brown mongoose scurried across their path. The critters briefly stopped to surreptitiously stare at the hikers before slinking into the foliage. During their hikes in the fall and winter, a solitary Plover commanded a position every hundred yards or so on the levee, but most in the species had departed for Alaskan nesting grounds the month before.

Once in the woodland, the hikers would have taken one of several trails into the mountains or circumnavigated the woodland behind the white La'ie Mormon Temple completed in 1919. In the forests, they heard the rich and harmonious warbles, whistles and clicks of the White-rumped Shama Thrushes, calling from limbs of trees. (The Shama, a recently-introduced, robin-like bird with blue coat and orange chest, had the most beautiful song of any bird in Hawai'i.)

By the time the trio returned to Muliwai, they had walked some five miles or so and were pleasantly tired, dusty, and damp from perspiration. They donned swimsuits and plunged into the ocean for a cooling swim. That evening they had cocktails and dinner, followed by dancing and the obligatory poker. Una summed the day up as "good, happy fun."

Nimitz again retired to the familiar Koa bed with a sense of well-being from the exercise and fellowship. During the few times that Nimitz awoke in the middle of the night, he was treated to peaceful solitude, broken only by the sound of surf, wind, and occasional roaring, rain squalls.

On a moonless night, the sky was littered with millions of brilliant stars unspoiled by light pollution. They were so bright and seemed so close, it appeared as though he could reach out and touch them. The serenity was reminiscent of Nimitz's childhood home in Texas. Settling back against his pillow with the caressing trade winds patting against his face, Nimitz was soon fast asleep without a thought of beckoning war demands disturbing his slumber. That was one of the reasons Nimitz spent nearly every weekend and some weeknights of the war at the Walker's La'ie oasis. Sleep at Muliwai beat the distractions at Makalapa any day of the week!

The next morning, after awakening refreshed, Nimitz, Doc, and the Walkers had an early swim and a nice breakfast before the Admiral left. Nimitz initialed *Graybook* reports of massive strikes against the Marshalls and good news from natives of New Guinea that "The enemy's morale is severely shaken...the force is disintegrating into small detachments, and...all were critically short of food." [206]

At 4:30 p.m. that afternoon, the Walkers met Nimitz at his new headquarters, which was designed along nautical lines with exterior stairways and rooms opening from peripheral balconies, like decks, instead of from interior hallways. [207]

In this respect, his offices echoed Muliwai, as well as his

family's Steamboat Hotel in Fredericksburg, Texas, which his grandfather built to resemble a ship.

After touring the headquarters building, Nimitz took the Walkers to the CinCPac boathouse, to board his barge for the ride scrubbed after the L.S.T. tragedy.

Una described it as "a fine ride...all around Pearl Harbor!" Afterwards, they dined at his quarters, followed by the 1944 comedy, *Pin Up Girl,* with Betty Grable and Martha Rae, all while huddled in coats with rain pouring down in the open-air theater!

Though damp, they enjoyed a happy evening.

Michael A. Lilly

Chapter 12

Nimitz's Fall at Muliwai

ON JUNE 1ST, Nimitz played a foursome of tennis at the Walkers' court. The sun was blistering hot, with slight trade winds wafting through Surinam Cherry bushes lining the fence and cooling the players. A jade vine encircled the tennis pavilion from which dozens of talon-shaped blue blossoms hung in large clumps.

Una alluded to "great discussions" in her diary, but sadly did not enlighten us. They dined at Robert Purvis's home on the slopes of Diamond Head, followed by poker. Purvis was Vice President of Bishop National Bank, predecessor of today's First Hawaiian Bank. Two days later, on Saturday June 3rd, Nimitz and Lamar picked the Walkers up for walking, swimming and supper at Kailua.

The Normandy invasion (*Operation Overlord*) was launched on June 6th, followed shortly thereafter by the *Marianas*. Potter describes these two events as "The most titanic military efforts put forth by any nation at any one time in history." [208] The succeeding days were nerve-racking for Nimitz and his staff, as they awaited outcomes.

Three days after D-Day—Friday, June 9th—was significant for Nimitz. At 3:30 p.m., Sandy, Una and Hanko drove to the

University of Hawai'i in Manoa Valley to attend its 32nd Annual Commencement Ceremony, held at its outdoor theater. Wearing a black cap and gown, Nimitz was awarded an honorary Doctorate Degree in Science by University President Gregg M. Sinclair, while two professors placed the doctoral hood over his head and around his neck, where it draped down his back.

Una described the ceremony as "very impressive." The three, now extremely-close friends, celebrated his award that evening over dinner in Makalapa.

The next morning, Una says that Nimitz's driver "Beach picked us up [and] we met Adm at his office [and] Doc [and] Hal [and] went to Muli," with no inkling of danger facing the Admiral that day. Ginger and the Gremlins drove out separately.

From Muliwai, Nimitz, Doc and Una crossed the two-lane Kamehameha Highway for a repeat trek in the verdant foothills and mountains beyond. Directly across the highway, they followed an unpaved jeep road on top of a levee built to hold back Wailele stream, which was normally dry but in wet seasons could overrun its banks. Flanking the stream and to the base of distant hills were green fields of sugarcane grown by Kahuku Sugar Plantation. When fully grown, as it may have been that day, the cane towered high over one's head, blocking trade winds and intensifying the heat and humidity.

After a half mile, any one of several trails they might have taken ascended into the mountains. The soil of those trails was friable red clay grit on hardpan. When dry, as it was that day, the soil is rock hard, but it is covered with talcum-like powder as slippery as ice.

The trail dropped off one side or the other, depending on which switchback one was on, into scrubby forests of Strawberry Guava, Ironwood, Java Plum, Octopus (*Scheffelera arboricola*), banyans, and shrubs.

As they climbed farther into the hills, the sides became steeper and the drop-offs increasingly precipitous. At higher elevations, deep green valleys—dense jungle amphitheaters—cut deeply into the mountains below the trekkers. Through the foliage, their bird's-eye view brought grand vistas of turquoise ocean, sunken reefs and sand beaches against which waves slammed in frothy white foam. To the north was La'ie Point and flat Moku'auia Island known locally as Goat Island, a nesting ground for birds, such as the (now-protected) Wedge-Tailed Shearwater. To the south was Mokapu Hill with its giant sea turtle silhouette. The vaulted mountains, shimmering in the warmth, swept up above them like a gigantic wall with undulating clefts from which white waterfalls coursed during rainstorms. The day was bright and hot, with the sun high in a sky devoid of clouds. Sweat dripped from their brows and down their backs, staining shirts. The trio was in tropical heaven, enjoying some of the most spectacular scenery in the world and without a care. Even the war did not intrude on their reverie, which was free of any premonition of what was about to transpire.

I have hiked those hills for over sixty years and have seen people fall, and have fallen myself, so I know of what I write. At some point during their trek, Nimitz's foot hit a protruding Ironwood tree root or slipped on the gritty red earth, or both. Losing his balance, he "fell" (Una's word), tumbling some twenty feet or so down the sheer side of the trail into the forest and slamming into a tree or rock with such force that he hurt his back and broke [a] rib. Una screamed, mortified that a friend, much less the most important military leader in the Pacific, was hurt while she was host—worse yet, perhaps, in her presence.

As fate would have it, Nimitz's fleet surgeon, Doc Anderson, was with them. The fleet surgeon worked his way down the precipitous bank to help the Admiral, while Una watched in distress. Dazed from his fall, Nimitz's face was pressed into the red earth. With few handholds and no ropes, it was difficult for even an uninjured person to climb back up. Slipping on the crumbly soil with every step, Doc and his patient uncertainly worked their way upwards, clutching tuffs of grass and shrubbery, eventually reaching the trail where both of them collapsed from exertion. Doc nursed the Admiral as best he could.

With Nimitz in pain from his injuries, his chest stabbing sharply at every breath, the threesome slowly retraced the two or three miles or so back to Muliwai. There, Doc bandaged his chest and prescribed aspirin for pain. Fortunately, Nimitz's injuries were not life threatening, only very tender.

Despite Nimitz's injuries, they enjoyed dinner, danced and played poker. With more difficulty than usual, Nimitz trudged up the short grass path to the cottage on the bluff where he tentatively settled in for the night. It was one of the few nights at Muliwai that Nimitz had trouble sleeping. Every cough or turn brought sharp pains.

On Sunday morning, everyone walked the beach and had an early breakfast before leaving. Back at his headquarters by 10:00 a.m., Nimitz listened to the symphony broadcast. Reviewing the *Graybook*, he penned his red initials on Saturday's summary under the report that read, "For the fourth consecutive day B-24s from the 13th AF bombed Truk; for the first time in recent attacks, enemy interception was not encountered." [209]

On Tuesday, June 13th, the Walkers dined with Nimitz, Doc, and Soc at Makalapa. Una's diary notes that Nimitz was still feeling very miserable from his sore back and broken rib for which she felt personal responsibility. Nimitz intensely disliked being incapacitated, which Potter said made him impatient and irritable.[210]

Una would have consoled but not doted on the unhappy admiral that evening; that was not her nature. Instead, she tried her best to cheer up the normally upbeat Commander in Chief. She would have said, as she advised her children and grandchildren when facing adversity, "It may not seem like it now while you are in such pain, but a wise man once said, 'This too shall pass.' And so this shall, Chester."

With a broken rib, Nimitz was cautious about every movement, even getting in and out of a chair. In bed, he could not sit straight up, but had to roll to his side, drop his feet to the floor and carefully ease himself upright. Every breath and even a laugh grated rib against cartilage, bringing stabbing pain. Contrary to his nature, Nimitz restrained from laughing too hard that evening and for many successive evenings.

On Thursday, June 14th, the Navy took its most daring gamble yet with Operation Forager against the Marianas Islands with successful landings on red, green, blue, and yellow beaches on western Saipan. The Battle for Saipan would last a month.[211] The first B-29 "Superfortress" bombings of Kyushu were launched from bases in China.

That evening, the Walkers hosted a dinner at Nu'uanu for Nimitz and Rear Admiral John Jerome Gaffney, Commanding Officer of the Naval Supply Depot in Pearl Harbor. Guests included Rear Adm. Thomas Earle Hipp, 14th Naval District Supply Officer, then fifty and his Special Assistant, Lt. Cdr. Joseph "Joe" M. Lyle, thirty-one, Hanko and Ginger. Lyle frequently attended Walker gatherings; as the junior officer invited, he must have been a congenial and pleasant man. (He retired in 1967 as a vice admiral.)

Nothing was mentioned about Nimitz's injuries, but from painful personal experience, especially at his age, most likely it took at least six weeks of pain before the broken rib healed.

That day, Admiral Hart had completed his investigation into Pearl Harbor. Hart issued no findings, but preserved the recorded testimonies of forty witnesses. (It is a treasure trove of information and available online verbatim.)[212]

Territorial Governor Stainback consolidated two departments—Food Control and Materials and Supplies Control—under a single executive. Hence, with Sandy already heavily embroiled in managing American Factors, Food Control, and Leprosy Hospitals and Settlements, on June 17th he received an expected letter appointing him Director of Materials and Supplies Control.

MacArthur received a message from the Joint Chiefs of Staff proposing to bypass the Philippines in favor of attacking Formosa. MacArthur was incensed and responded on June 18 with a long and passionate appeal to the War Department, copying Nimitz. "It is my most earnest conviction," argued MacArthur, "that the proposal to bypass the Philippines and launch an attack across the Pacific directly against Formosa is unsound...The hazards of failure would be unjustifiable when a conservative and certain line of action is open. The occupation of Luzon is essential in order to establish air forces and bases prior to the move on Formosa." [213]

McArthur continued that America's "great national obligation" was to reoccupy the "territory where our unsupported forces were destroyed by the enemy." He stated further that our Philippine allies were "undergoing the greatest privation and suffering because we have not been able to support or succor them."

Finally, if the JCS persisted in its proposal, MacArthur requested an audience in Washington to "present fully my views." [214] In fact, he had his meeting with the President the following month in Honolulu.

The next day, Saturday, Una and Sandy joined Nimitz in target practice at his shooting gallery. Nimitz strained while shooting from his knitting rib. Sandy had grown up shooting firearms and had several antique guns. Nimitz had his boatswain's mates construct a tall hardwood gun case emblazoned in gold with Nimitz's name and four stars in which to store Sandy's guns.

After target practice they had a light lunch—"ate minis," wrote Una—and then they dressed at Makalapa for a dinner hosted by Pacific submarine commander Vice Adm. Lockwood for [his wife] Betty's birthday.

The next day, Nimitz and Lamar gave the Walkers a tour of Kaneohe Naval Air Station and Pearl Harbor. That evening, they danced and dined at Rear Admiral Gaffney's. Una described the evening as a "delightful party, best yet!"

Before retiring, Nimitz read reports full of good news from the Western Pacific. (When sleep is elusive, my father and I often let our minds call up Muliwai to relax and drift off. Since others have said the same thing, it is likely that when the war fed Nimitz's sleeplessness, as perhaps it did that evening, he too conjured up memories of Muliwai to hasten the Sandman.)

June 19th and 20th were the days of the first Battle of the Philippine Sea, popularly known as, "The Great Marianas Turkey Shoot," so-named because the Allied forces lost only about a hundred twenty-three aircraft to Japan's more than six hundred. Because the American forces under Spruance included battleships sunk at Pearl Harbor and raised from its depths (*West Virginia*, *California*, *Maryland*, and *Tennessee*) the Japanese losses marked the butcher's bill "Paid."

Nimitz, who was normally composed even with positive war news, was particularly jubilant because, in addition to planes and two oilers, three Japanese aircraft carriers were sent to *Davy Jones' Locker*.[215]

With remaining Japanese forces receding, Spruance elected not to pursue, a decision criticized by Nimitz in his summary, suggesting that had Spruance pursued the Japanese, "a decisive fleet air action could have been fought, the Japanese fleet destroyed, and the end of the war hastened."[216]

History was kinder to Spruance. Had he pursued the Japanese, there had been every possibility of a reverse disaster.

The last days of June, the Walkers and Nimitz were together daily. They dined and danced at Makalapa, and spent the weekend at Muliwai playing "horseshoes [and] swimming, dancing and [having a] cheery time." Dinner was likely Hara's charbroiled Kauai steaks.

Nimitz's broken rib was on the mend, but it was still painful. On Sunday they rose early to walk the beach and left after breakfast. That evening they attended a tea party followed by dinner at Makalapa. Two days later, the Stanley Kennedys hosted dinner including, Una's diary noted, "5 admirals—Great Scott!!"

The next day, the Walkers hosted dinner at Nu'uanu for Nimitz and Doc. Una's diary, however, noted "Blast!" Earlier that day, she had a flat tire and blowout. With replacement rubber tires hard to come by during the war, her blowout was troublesome. Adding to the flat tire, after so many endless festivities, Una awoke the following morning sick in bed with [a] bad cold. Even when she was seriously ill, Una never acknowledged it and only rarely gave in to it, so her remaining in bed that morning meant she was very ill, indeed.

Every day through the end of June, Nimitz's knitting rib continued to bother him as he initialed *Graybook* summaries of operations on Tinian and Saipan written with clinical and dispassionate objectivity. By June 29th, "Total enemy dead, buried by our troops reported as 4949." *

---

* Nearly fifteen hundred Americans were killed in action. Before Saipan was neutralized in early July, 24,000 enemy would die—a staggering seventy-seven percent of its force—against 3,426 Americans, or .05 percent of our forces. Twenty-three Zeros were captured on the ground in good condition. *Graybook*, 2002-03.

CHAPTER 13

Nimitz, MacArthur and Roosevelt: Philippines or Formosa?

ON THE FIRST day of July, Nimitz and Lamar drove Sandy, Una and Ginger to meet daughter Ann who arrived by ship from the West Coast at 12.30 p.m. When Lamar met Ann exiting the gangway, he was immediately smitten by her raven-haired beauty. From Aloha Tower, they drove directly to Makalapa for lunch.

Driving to Pearl Harbor for lunch never failed to bring to Sandy's mind an earlier humorous experience, which he later related to Nimitz with a gleam in his eyes:

> Invited to lunch with Nimitz in Pearl Harbor, the Walkers' car was stopped at the gate by a uniformed guard who asked, "Do you have a pass?"
> "No," Sandy replied, "I'm here to lunch with Admiral Nimitz."
> "I'm sorry, Sir, but without a pass you cannot come through the gate."
> "What should I do?" asked Sandy.
> "Turn around and go out the gate on the other

side."

Sandy dutifully turned his black Cadillac with its personalized number 1000 on the license plate around the guardhouse to exit the other side only to be stopped by another uniformed guard who asked, "Do you have a pass?"

"No," replied Sandy, "I am here to lunch with Admiral Nimitz."

"I'm sorry, Sir, but without a pass you can't go out the gate."

"What a fine kettle of fish," Sandy facetiously muttered aloud. "I can't go in the gate, and I can't go out the gate!"

(He never let on how he ultimately extricated himself.)

That evening, Nimitz, Lamar and Doc had dinner in Nu'uanu to celebrate Ann's return. Against protocol, Nimitz may have passed on the wonderful news emanating from Tinian and Saipan. Lamar doted on Ann that evening.

On Thursday July 6th, after two days of positive war news including a dozen Japanese ships sunk, Nimitz and Lamar dined with the Walkers, including Ann, after which they strolled in the garden in moonlight. The air was warm, and the moon was full, bathing the garden in a hoary light, casting shadows and lighting faces in a yellow glow and banishing from the minds of Nimitz and the Walkers all thoughts of even the good news from war in the Western Pacific.

Crossing the porte-cochère to a large grassy area between the house and Nu'uanu Avenue shaded by canopied Monkey Pod trees, Una explained that "Each of our gardens has a name. This front garden we call the *Wedding Circle*. The semi-circle rows of *Cattleya* orchids, *spathiphyllum* with their anthurium-like white flowers, tree ferns, Travelers Palms, begonias, and Ti plants make an attractive background for a wedding.

Michael A. Lilly

Una in Rainbow Garden

To the *mauka* (mountain) side of the house they entered the Rainbow Garden. "Rainbows arching over the valley inspired me to plant orchids in the hues of the rainbow. Beginning with violet, my orchids follow the spectrum through yellow hybrids and *dendrobium undulatums* which remind me of a swarm of butterflies and end with reds."

They strolled—*holoholo*, Una said in Hawaiian—under a Chicle Tree, the original source of chewing gum, and past a greenhouse to the entrance of a hedge rendered invisible by overlapping rows. Inside was her Red Garden of flowers in pastel shades of crimson.

A grass path lined with citrus led to the Pink Garden where dozens of pink *Vanda* orchids, shell ginger, and hibiscus were surrounded by rare old trees. In the center was a "Buddha Tree" (*ficus religiosa*) reportedly from a scion of the tree under which Buddha meditated.

The air carried scents of gardenia, jasmine and plumeria and pungent tamarind, as they continued along *alanui* (meandering paths) which took them around and sometimes behind gardens. "All of my gardens," said Una, "curve and bend. There are no straight lines in nature, so my gardens copy Mother Nature."

They ended up at the Japanese Garden and its koi pond reflecting moonlight like diamonds. The pond was crisscrossed by half-moon bridges, lanterns, and pagodas. Beyond was the teahouse.

One evening, Una recounted to Nimitz the history of their estate. "In the old days Hawai'i had a feudal system. The lands were held by *Ali'i* or royalty. In the Great *Mahele* or land division of 1848 they gave one-third of the lands to chiefs and chiefesses. Our property went to King Kamehameha's granddaughter, Chiefess Kekau'onohi. Many of our trees are over one hundred years old. So, I like to think she planted some of them. We call our home *Mamalu* for 'shady lawns'. Because the orange *ilima* flower grows here, we also call it *Pa Ilima*."

After Nimitz returned home late that evening, he turned in with an aura of the Walkers' beautiful gardens by the light of a full moon still swirling around his mind—a peaceful and relaxing sensation not unlike his weekends at Muliwai.

Two days later *Graybook* recorded, "All organized enemy resistance on Saipan ceased." All that remained were mopping-up operations—capturing or killing snipers and stray soldiers. A captured sailor had personally witnessed the suicide of Vice Admiral [Chuichi] Nagumo who had commanded the air attacks against Pearl Harbor and Midway.[217] By Nagumo's death, Nimitz partially avenged the "Day of Infamy."

With positive war news in mind, Nimitz's entourage drove to Kailua. Una joined them, recording that she had a swim and long walk at Kailua with Boss. That was the first time Una referred to Nimitz as "Boss" (with a capital "B") in her diary, a term later used by Lamar in his letters from Guam. It was an affectionate term given military commanders of high rank by their subordinates. Gen. Dwight D. Eisenhower, Supreme Commander Allied Expeditionary Force, was similarly referred to as "Boss" by his close subordinates. After the swim and walk, Nimitz enjoyed dinner, dancing and poker with the Walkers at their Nu'uanu home.

On July 10th, Nimitz appeared again on the cover of *Life* magazine. Page 82 bore the headline, "He Commands History's Greatest Fleet and a Watery Theater of 65,000,000 Square Miles." During his lunch period, the article reported that Nimitz would return to his quarters, remove his clothes and take "an hour sun bath in a convenient nook."

"Nothing is so restful and healing," he wrote Catherine, "as a good sunbath—and I attribute whatever good health I now enjoy— in large measure, to the midday sun bath I usually take in place of lunch."[218]

Sometimes Sherman joined him. "These informal groups," continued the article, "quite often turn out to be the meeting that determines the strategic trend of the Pacific war. In the course of one sun bath, Nimitz and Sherman laid the groundwork for the invasion of the Marianas which, following General MacArthur's mop-up of New Guinea, put the timetable of activities in the Pacific far ahead of schedule."

But Nimitz lamented to Catherine that the constant stream of visitors, especially VIPs, while pleasant, "forces me to eat lunch which I neither need nor want, and costs me my sunbath."[219]

On July 13th, the day after Brig. Gen. Theodore "Ted" Roosevelt, Jr., died in Normandy from a heart attack, Admiral King arrived in Honolulu for meetings with the Pacific commanders. Una dispatched Hanko with flowers to Makalapa for a lunch Nimitz was hosting for King. Later, the Walkers attended a USO show at the Nimitz Bowl featuring Bob Hope along with singer Frances Langford and comic Jerry Colonna. The red-tressed Langford, who sang like a 1944 siren, brought down the house, crooning her signature, *I'm in the Mood for Love*.[220]

Hope, a famous movie star and later television comedian, was one of the most prolific and certainly most well-known entertainers of troops in history. His entourage had flown to Hawai'i the month before on a four-engine C-54 (Army-configured DC-4) Skymaster, and had continued performing shows on islands and byways throughout the South Pacific, before returning to the United States in September. (Hope gave twenty-eight performances before a hundred eighty thousand servicemen, logged some thirty thousand miles, and had at least one non-fatal crash landing.)

After the Walkers returned home from the USO show, Boss phoned to say he was leaving for points west the next morning and would see them on his return. The next day, King and Nimitz departed for Kwajalein Atoll, Eniwetok and Saipan. They discussed future war strategies with Spruance who advocated taking Iwo Jima, followed by Okinawa. During the trip, numerous Japanese ships were sunk and landings on Guam took place on all beaches according to schedule,[221] although Nimitz's future forward headquarters was not secure for another month.

While on Sampan, General "Howling Mad" Smith nixed demands by King and Nimitz to visit the top of fifteen hundred-foot Mount Tapochau, because of straggling Japanese soldiers everywhere. Smith later said no one ever accused King or Nimitz of lack of guts or equilibrium.[222]

The party returned to Honolulu on July 20 in time for breakfast.[223] Despite the return trip taking about seventeen hours in the air, King, Nimitz, Doc, Soc and Lamar were guests at the

Walker's for dinner that evening. Nimitz brought photos of his trip, including several with King, Nimitz and Spruance on the *Indianapolis* and Saipan. After dinner, they climbed the stairs to Sandy's sitting room, where they played poker with Una cheering from the sidelines. Nimitz must have been so exhausted by the time he retired to his Makalapa quarters that he actually slept well.

Nimitz, King & Spruance aboard Indianapolis[224]

The following day, after two and a half years of blackout restrictions ended in Hawai'i, General Emmons dropped the title Military Governor, having served its purpose.[225]

That Saturday, Una (in her khaki Red Cross uniform) and Nimitz attended a very impressive ceremony, during which Admiral King gave awards to the destroyer USS *Buchanan* (DD 484) for operations in the Western Pacific. (On September 2, 1945, *Buchanan* would ferry Nimitz, MacArthur and Halsey to the *Missouri* surrender ceremonies.)

That afternoon, the Walkers, Hal Castles, Doc, Ann and Hanko drove to Muliwai. Nimitz and Lamar arrived later. Hal Lamar was so taken with Ann that he later wrote to Una from the Western Pacific that he was celebrating the anniversary of that weekend.

Hanko often took Nimitz for a ride on his 11-foot boat *Windy*, powered by a five horsepower Bendix Aviation outboard motor. One such voyage nearly wound up in a disaster, as Hanko recalled in his *Memoirs*:

> He also enjoyed going out with me in my little boat, *Windy*. On one Sunday morning, although the ocean was quite rough, he asked me to take him out to sea for a ride. Suddenly, sounds were heard as artillery shells flew over our heads and struck in the ocean beyond the reef. The Army field artillery units mounted in the hills behind us were engaging in target practice. He turned irritably to Lt. Cmdr. Lamar and said, "Hal, call the Army and have them stop this damn shooting. I'm going for a boat ride." In no more than five minutes the shooting stopped, and we took *Windy* out to sea.
>
> The water was indeed rough. I was terrified, first of all for exposing the commander in chief to possible danger, and secondly, for the inevitable humiliation of getting swamped and having to swim ashore. Nimitz, I reminded myself, was a strong swimmer. Nevertheless, I

could see the newspaper headlines: "Admiral Nimitz nearly drowns in boating accident with Henry Walker." I don't ever recall having a life preserver in Windy.

The Admiral and I chugged out into the open ocean four or five hundred yards off shore and outside the protection of the reef. The seas were steep and breaking at the top. At that point even Nimitz began to think better of our voyage. "Henry," he said, "I think we had better go back." I hastily obeyed and as little Windy nosed onto the beach, a breaker crashed into the stern, swamping us. By that time, of course, it was simply a matter for laughter.[226]

In the 19th century, La'ie and nearby Kahuku and its sugar mill were remote outposts of O'ahu, reached primarily by boat. Sugar from the mill was loaded onto steamers anchored near the pier fronting Muliwai. In January 1898, the packet *Ka'ala*, after offloading freight and taking on several thousand bags of sugar, weighed anchor for Honolulu.

Soon, its captain and crew returned in lifeboats with a harrowing tale. Just as it had cleared the reef, the *Ka'ala* was hit by fierce swells, lost steerage and was thrown onto the reef, where it was pounded into rubble near the place where a schooner had foundered a week before.[227] All that remained of the *Ka'ala* was its large boiler, which became embedded permanently in the coral reef about a few hundred yards offshore from Muliwai, where its top can still be seen today at low tide.

The boiler attracted a host of tropical fish and coral, and its apertures made perfect apartments for spiny [Hawaiian clawless langosta] lobsters.[228] Nimitz loved to eat lobsters and often asked Hanko to get some for his meal. Dutifully, Hanko snorkeled to the boiler where many lobster feelers poked out from its apertures. With a gloved hand, one or two were stuffed into a net hanging from his belt and returned ashore, where they were plunged into boiling water for Nimitz's meal.

The next morning, Sunday, everyone left after a walk on the beach and breakfast, although the Walkers were back at Makalapa that evening for dinner with Nimitz and Mercer to meet Captain Marion Eppley, who endeared Una as a nice man. At age sixty-one, Eppley was already a noted physical chemist who was recalled to active duty at the start of the war as a captain. He arrived that month to oversee servicemen voting in the Pacific and later as Nimitz's chief of censorship. Eppley had a high opinion of his leader, Nimitz, writing the Walkers after the war that the Fleet Admiral was "The greatest and best" of old friends who won others "by his fine simplicity and unconscious dignity mixed with easy manners." The feeling was mutual. As Nimitz wrote his wife, "The more I see of him [Eppley] the better I like him...because of his great value to me & the Navy." [229]

Just before noon that day, Tony Lilly's ship, USS *Bush* (DD 529), was conducting shore bombardment exercises off the Hawaiian "Target" island of Kaho'olawe when one of its five-inch anti-aircraft rounds hit an antenna and exploded, killing five and wounding thirteen, including George Beartrap Triede, who had introduced Tony to Ginger. Normal peacetime regulations, which required gun "stop settings" to prevent rounds from hitting parts of a ship, were relaxed in times of war. Navy Bureau of Ordnance instructions authorized "a slight acceptable hazard during wartime."

During the investigation, Tony testified that the antenna was apparently installed after plotting the stop settings on the five-inch gun. No one was faulted for the accident. That afternoon, *Bush* pulled into Pearl Harbor and moored at dock M-1. For the next week, whenever he could escape the investigation and his duties as Executive Officer, Tony was in Nu'uanu wooing Ginger and playing with the Gremlins. "And this is when my romance with Ginger blossomed," recalled Tony. "And she was a blossom," he added with a wide grin.

On July 24th, the Navy landed on the Marianas island of Tinian, which was not secure until August 1st. That same date, the Navy convened a Court of Inquiry into the attack on Pearl Harbor.

Its proceedings, which took the testimonies of thirty-nine witnesses, were conducted into October.*

Meanwhile, MacArthur continued pushing to invade the Philippines in fulfillment of his promise—"I shall return"—while Nimitz favored the JCS proposal to bypass the Philippines for a drive on Formosa and China. President Roosevelt decided to consider the opposing views in a joint conference in Pearl Harbor. Nimitz first heard of the President's plan, when a secret service officer arrived to locate a hotel for the President. Nimitz was asked to invite MacArthur, who, when invited, replied tersely, "We have nothing to talk about." [230]

To Admiral King's invitation, MacArthur was too busy. However, MacArthur could not refuse the next one, which came in the form of an order from Gen. George Marshall, Chief of Staff of the Army.

On July 26th, after a quiet and uneventful night for the troops on Tinian, the Boss came to call on the Walkers in Nu'uanu. It speaks volumes about the importance of their relationship that Nimitz called on his friends, just before the start of a stressful two-day conference.

That afternoon the three giants posed for photographs aboard the heavy cruiser USS *Baltimore* (CA 68). Only the President was smiling in between two somber military leaders.

---

* All told, there were seven investigations of the attack by the Navy and Army. No formal proceedings were ever initiated under which Kimmel and Short could confront witnesses and present their defense. Not content with seven investigations, Congress initiated its own from November 1945 to May 1946, resulting in thirty-nine volumes of record. Hardly anyone emerged unscathed by the majority opinion of that investigation.

MacArthur, Roosevelt & Nimitz aboard USS Baltimore, 4:15 p.m., July 26, 1944[231]

Considering the state of the President's health, the next day, July 27th, entailed a grueling, seven-hour tour of Oahu with MacArthur and Nimitz. They departed Waikiki mid-morning in open-air touring cars, stopping at four military installations. After driving up the Waianae Coast, they crossed Kolekole Pass into Schofield Barracks for a reception, lunch, and inspection of the 7th Infantry Division. Returning to Waikiki at 5:00 p.m., they had dinner, followed by substantive discussions on the next strategies for the Pacific War.

MacArthur advocated his return as promised. "Leyte and then Luzon," he urged.[232] Even as MacArthur was making his pitch, the JCS sent him and Nimitz a *Top Secret* message that the occupation of the Philippines was not to be accomplished before occupation of Formosa. The former made political sense, the latter military sense.[233]

Using a long bamboo pointer against a huge map of the Pacific, Nimitz urged bypassing the Philippines. MacArthur successfully convinced the President of the moral responsibility America had to that country. MacArthur would return as promised.

Roosevelt suddenly announced that he would have lunch the next day at Nimitz's quarters, which set off a frenzy of last-minute preparations. The Secret Service quickly employed a huge crew of Seabees, who virtually rebuilt the residence, making it accessible by wheelchair, repainting it, and adding a driveway to the back, which required the removal of two palm trees.[234]

Nimitz half-seriously warned, "If you injure my palm trees, you're all going to be fired." [235]

Lamar called Una for help with decorations. Una and Ginger frantically gathered a carload of orchids, birds of paradise, heliconia and gingers from their garden, with which they adorned Nimitz's quarters in time for the Roosevelt lunch.*

So many flag officers attended the one-hour lunch that Lamar counted, depending on the source, a hundred thirty-six or more stars on their collars and probably as many flowers from the Walkers' garden.[236]

Roosevelt departed at 7:30 p.m. Nimitz immediately dispatched Beach to bring the Walkers, Ann and Ginger to Makalapa for dinner. Nimitz was dog-tired from the stressful conference and, having lost the battle between the Philippines and Formosa, he needed to relax with friends. He thanked Ginger and Una profusely for the beautiful flowers still gracing his home.

---

* Although Nimitz gave the Walkers several photos of Roosevelt's trip, nothing in the diary indicates they met with the President, who was a Harvard classmate of Sandy's. Sandy, being reserved and gentlemanly, recalled Roosevelt as boisterous, self-centered and opinionated. "No sooner a professor would finish a lesson," Sandy told me, "than Roosevelt would ask a question, as if he hadn't heard a single thing the professor said."

(Lamar, who had placed his nametag next to Ann's, was falling hopelessly in love.)

Dinner Nametag Hand-Painted by Nimitz's Staff for Sandy Walker

Michael A. Lilly

Chapter 14

Hanko Joins the Navy

GRAYBOOK RECORDED ON August 1st that mopping-up operations continued on Saipan in the Marianas, with an average of fifty enemy soldiers killed each day.²³⁷ On Saturday, August 5th, Sandy and Hara, with a car full of provisions, left for Muliwai at noon. The Boss picked up Una and Maile and "drove to Muliwai separately."

Hanko launched his boat *Windy* with Nimitz and Una as passengers for a fishing voyage. Running through breaking surf was always precarious, with passengers getting soaked. Once underway, they bounced through waves and over the shallow waters, narrowly avoiding coral heads.

Once they were into a deep blue sea, choppy waves gave way to swells, as they trailed a fishing line along the outer edge of the reef. The little boat often wandered into a maelstrom of porpoises playfully racing back and forth, arching their backs and disappearing into the deeps, only to suddenly reappear and sprint away. From shore, the trio cast a curious silhouette—a soon-to-be-commissioned most junior ensign in the Navy at the tiller, an admiral who commanded the largest armada in history tending a fishing line, and Una, regal under one of her ubiquitous floral parasols.

After cocktails and dinner, they danced by moonlite—indeed, a radiant, full moon rose above the horizon at about 8:00 p.m. All night, the bright tropical moon lit up Muliwai, casting shadows from every tree and shrub and illuminating the white caps on the ocean with iridescence. Una recorded afterwards, as she often did, that it was a happy day.

As Nimitz walked up the grass path to the cottage, the brilliant moon was already high in the night sky, bathing him with a brilliant opalescence. All was right in the world as Nimitz's chronic insomnia was exiled in favor of thoughts of a serene tropical garden and the roar of the surf below.

Maile recalls that one such Muliwai weekend a terrible tragedy befell the Walker family. At home in Nu'uanu or at Muliwai, they were never without their cherished Scottish Terriers, Dirke and Boykin. However, they awoke one Sunday morning at Muliwai to find Boykin missing, to Una's great anguish. The dogs never strayed, so he must have been stolen. Nimitz came to the rescue, enlisting several sailors to conduct periodic searches for the missing pet.

After several weeks, the mystery was solved when the sailors found Boykin locked up in a family's backyard in nearby Hau'ula. With the scarcity of fresh meat during the war, Boykin was being fattened up with sweet potatoes to be eaten. Some people considered dog meat a delicacy. With the terrier's reprieve, Una's heartbreak turned to relief for which she thanked Nimitz profusely. Summing up, Maile remembered both the furor and the relief so many years ago.

On Monday, August 7th, Nimitz was off for Guam, which was generally secure, although the enemy had been driven into the extreme northeastern part of the islands.[238]

Control of the Marianas provided the Allies with a springboard from which attacks were launched against Tokyo, just fifteen hundred miles to the north.

Michael A. Lilly

Admiral Nimitz with Major Gremlin and Minor Gremlin, Kailua Beach, 1944

Nimitz was back in Pearl Harbor that Saturday. Ginger and her daughters, who were soon to leave for the East Coast, moved in with the Walkers. At 2:30 p.m., Nimitz picked everyone up to walk Kailua beach with a large party.

Nimitz and the Gremlins posed for a photograph on Kailua Beach with Mokapu Hill (part of today's Marine Corps Base Hawai`i) in the background. In the picture, one can see Nimitz's "stub of a ring finger from an accident in 1916, as he built the first American diesel engine. The stub was saved when the machine jammed against his Annapolis ring." [239] When sitting in the back seat of his flag car, Sheila said, "Nimitz would amuse me with magic by pretending to pull off his missing finger."

She squealed every time he magically did this. His grandson Chet Lay said Nimitz played the same trick on his grandchildren when they were growing up.

Nimitz was one of the first persons in the world with a car radiotelephone—the first mobile phone—installed in his flag car to maintain contact with his headquarters. The device was cumbersome and consumed a lot of battery power. Young Maile (Major Gremlin) often rode with Nimitz to or from La'ie or Makalapa and enjoyed toying with the heavy black *Bakelite* handset and cord long enough to reach into the backseat.

On one trip, Hal Lamar, who had by now become a surrogate uncle to the Gremlins, began teasing Maile, as he often did. Absentmindedly reacting, little Maile sharply swung the hard handset by its cord, smacking Lamar in the face. The force broke his front tooth. Maile was mortified and still is today. Poor Lamar's next stop was the CinCPacFlt dental clinic to have his fractured tooth capped.

Michael A. Lilly

Hal Lamar with Sheila (Minor Gremlin) & Maile (Major Gremlin), Muliwai

Hal Lamar with Sheila (Minor Gremlin) & Maile (Major Gremlin), Muliwai

On August 10th, after three weeks of bitter fighting, the Marianas campaign and the Battle of Guam were officially over, but at an enormous cost. Over five thousand American lives were lost, while nearly sixty thousand Japanese were destroyed.[240]

On Guam, dozens of indigenous Chamorro children were found bound, bayoneted, and beheaded in the forest. *Graybook* listed over eleven thousand enemy buried on Guam, but cautioned the figures would doubtless change considerably as mopping up operations have just gotten underway.[241] (One lone Japanese soldier continued to hide in a cave for the next twenty-seven years, refusing to believe the Japanese Empire had lost the war.)

Hanko had been trying to join the Navy for nearly two years, but was repeatedly rejected for extreme nearsightedness, a malady suffered by all three Walker children. Finally, "Through the intervention of Nimitz…, despite my poor eyesight, I was finally granted a Navy commission."[242]

Hanko felt that he was fully qualified, except for his eyes, but the "Good Admiral overcame that handicap...," and he "was sworn in as a Navy ensign." Before departing for Navy schools in the East, Nimitz had a serious talk with Hanko, explaining, "If you do well, I will arrange a position for you on a combat ship."

That month, Hanko left Hawai'i for Navy schooling to the tears of his parents, Ann, Ginger, and the Gremlins, as they watched him depart. Una lamented in her diary, "Somebody went away! My darling boy!"

Before Hanko left, Nimitz handed him a photograph on which he inscribed in his hand, "To Ensign Henry A. Walker, Jr., USNR—With kindest regards and best wishes & success in your new appointment. C.W. Nimitz, Admiral, USN."

While he was in the Navy Communications School at Harvard, the Commander demanded to see Hanko, asking why a letter was addressed to him from the Commander in Chief, Pacific Fleet.

"Walker, do you know who this is from?"

"Oh, yes, Sir," my uncle sheepishly replied. "It must be from Admiral Nimitz."

"Why the hell would he be writing to you? Do you know Admiral Nimitz?"

"Yes, Sir," Hanko replied, "He's a good friend of my parents." [243] The commanding officer "looked at me with horror and was unable to respond."

Meanwhile, on Sunday, August 13th, Nimitz, the Walkers, Ginger, the Gremlins, Ann, Doc and Lamar boarded the Admiral's barge for another lazy tour around Pearl Harbor, circling Ford Island and passing the rusting remnants of the Battleships *Utah* and *Arizona*. Cruising the calm waters of Pearl Harbor that night under a waning crescent moon was very peaceful. Returning, they dined at Makalapa with Nimitz. (Lamar, no doubt, had the stewards place his nametag next to Ann's.)

Nimitz's Barge and Crew, 1944[244]

Two days later, Una served Chinese dinner at their residence for a large group, which included Nimitz, Doc, Lamar; a prominent Straub Hospital obstetrician and gynecologist—Dr. Guy Champion Milnor—and his wife, Nell; and Ginger and Ann. Lamar again spent as much time as possible that evening with Ann, who was leaving the next day with Ginger for the East Coast.

On August 18th, Ann, Ginger and the Gremlins left Hawai'i. Una bemoaned, "All our girls sailed away on the 'Permanenti'—So Sad!"

On the pier at Aloha Tower, seeing them off, were Una, Sandy, Lt. Cdr. Joe Lyle, Rear Admiral Gaffney, Ginger's ex-husband, Richard Rice, and Hal Lamar—all lonely hearts, said Una's diary. Ann was off to Vassar College. Ginger was on her way to marry Alfred Wright, Jr., a handsome *Sports Illustrated* senior editor, whom she met while he had duty in Honolulu as a naval officer.* (Fortunately, she wound up marrying Tony Lilly instead [See the Epilogue].) That was the last reference to Ginger and the Gremlins in Una's 1944 diary.

The next day, a Saturday, Sandy and Hara drove to Muliwai in the morning. Then, Boss and Lamar drove Una out separately. Upon entering the grounds, Una yelled with delight when they flushed a Plover, which had just returned from summer nesting in Alaska. The bird, likely the same one who had left the previous April, was thin from its twenty-five hundred mile flight.

That afternoon, they played croquet, walked, enjoyed good weather, swam and had a fine dinner. Hara often served his signature dessert, blackberry steamed pudding, which Ginger said was so delicious it "was only beaten by Nimitz's crepe suzettes!"

I asked Nimitz's daughter Kate and grandsons Chet and Dick Lay what the recipe for the crepe suzettes might have been. Among their old family cookbooks in Cape Cod, was one published in 1941, *The Best Men Are Cooks*, with a recipe for crepes with flaming Suzette Sauce. The sauce included 1 pony brandy and 1 jigger Curacao.[245] (A "pony" is a small glass also called a "small beer," whose name derived from early horse races, when patrons needed a fast drink.) Chet wrote that "would certainly have appealed to our grandfather!" (Including mine.)

August nights in Hawai'i are often hot and muggy, especially Makalapa in those days, before air conditioning. I lived at Makalapa and even stayed at Nimitz's quarters in the 1950s, when Adm. Felix Stump was in command and had a son my age. Even circulating fans were of marginal help against sultry nights, exasperating Nimitz's insomnia. Not so at La'ie. Falling against Sandy's pillow in the cottage that evening, the Admiral was thankful for the cool marine air blowing through the cottage, hastening sleep. Instead of repeatedly tossing and turning as at Makalapa, he usually slept through the night.

---

* Wright would later marry the actress, Joan Fontaine, who was as beautiful as Ginger.

Nimitz at Ease

The next morning, they walked the beach before having breakfast, after which Nimitz and his entourage left in time to catch the 10:00 a.m. symphony broadcast from San Francisco. The Walkers had a quiet day, but were back for another nice dinner [with Nimitz at] Makalapa.

On Thursday, August 24th, the Walkers attended a dinner at Nimitz's quarters in honor of British Governor of Fiji, Major General Sir Philip Mitchell, fifty-four, and his aide, Major Harrop. Sherman was not present, having left that day for Washington. After dinner, they watched a movie at the outdoor theater. Two days later, the Walkers hosted a dinner at Nu'uanu for the same guests and several Walker friends, including the Dillinghams and von Holts. Dinner was followed by singing girls and dancing and poker in the upstairs smoke-filled room. The next day, Nimitz and Soc picked the Walkers up at 4:30 p.m. and drove them to the destroyer base for Planter's Punch and to attend the opening of the new Pearl Harbor Officer's Club, opposite Alpha piers, after which they dined at Nimitz's quarters.

Nimitz, Una (to his left), Ginger (two to Nimitz's right) and Red Cross Volunteers, 1943

Still chairing the Red Cross Surgical Dressing Corps, Una noted on August 29th that she had a busy morning with many dressings finished. She was also lonesome for Hanko who was still at Navy Communications School at Harvard and her two daughters who were travelling to the east coast.

The next day, Nimitz initialed a report that the submarine USS *Bowfin* (SS 287) (now a Pacific Historic Site and museum next to the Arizona Memorial) sunk two destroyers, two cargo ships and a trawler.[246]

Chapter 15

Nimitz finds Relief from War Demands

EARLIER IN THE war, Nimitz's flag car and driver had an amusing if awkward encounter. One of his young marine drivers, Robert Allen, drove the Admiral's black Buick, with a cover hiding the four stars on its license place, to pick up a package at a drugstore in Chinatown. Unable to find an open stall, he double-parked while he ran into the store. What Allen did not know was that one of the largest happy houses in the city was above the drugstore.

Most such brothels operated from the second floor of Chinatown buildings, so the phrase, "Let's climb the stairs," became a common euphemism for visiting them.[247]

Allen returned to the car and found several Military Police (MPs) examining the Buick with evident curiosity about Nimitz's flag car parked next to an ignominious flight of stairs. Allen convinced the MPs he was alone and on a proper mission for the Commander in Chief. Instead of confessing the incident at headquarters, Allen said nothing, hoping it would simply go away. *Wishful thinking*. Nimitz had countless sources of information. A few days later, Allen was summoned by Admiral Nimitz, who "said to me in his quiet voice, with a twinkle in his eye, 'Allen, we're going to have to be careful where we park our car, aren't we?'" [248]

Nimitz's last involvement with Chinatown Happy Houses occurred in September 1944. With the pressures of war winding down in the Hawaiian Islands, the brothels, which had operated legally by license since 1942, were officially shut down that month.[249] Responding to a letter from the "Do-good" Honolulu Council of Social Agencies, asking for his position on the subject, Nimitz ambiguously agreed with its suppression, where it adversely affects the efficiency, health and welfare of naval personnel, although war made the issue an extremely difficult one where large numbers of men...are concentrated.[250]

Governor Stainback wrote Nimitz that he had directed the Police Commission under George Sumner to enforce strictly the laws against prostitution, because he believed, incorrectly, that segregation and control of open prostitution does not minimize the spread of venereal disease, being the only excuse for its toleration in this community. (Contrary to Stainback's assertion, brothels helped control VD, with Hawai'i having the lowest incidence among service members nationwide.) [251]

Stainback asked for Nimitz's assurances of full enforcement of the laws against ladies of the night, which will redound to the benefit of all of the services as well as the civilian community.[252]

Nimitz, the consummate gentleman, assured the Governor of his cooperation in...efforts to enforce the Federal and Territorial laws against prostitution.[253] Meanwhile, a newspaper editorial applauded the "fall of the fallen" as "an affront to public decency" and a "relief to the civilian population." [254]

Effective the first of September, Nimitz announced that the World War I-era battleship USS *Oklahoma* (BB 37) (which had capsized and sunk at Pearl Harbor, but which had been salvaged and later saw action against the Imperial Japanese Navy in the Pacific), was decommissioned.

By that month, Nimitz commanded more men and machines of war than all the fabled conquerors of antiquity combined, and his staff operated at an intensity level, best described as controlled frenzy—peaking with the mount-out of each new campaign.[255]

Every day Nimitz made decisions that decided the fate of men under his command. Thousands of his soldiers, sailors and airmen were dying on remote, previously-unknown and difficult-to-pronounce islands of the Western Pacific from orders he issued. The Japanese, who stubbornly refused to surrender, launched suicide attacks and had to be rooted out of crevices and caves in savage hand-to-hand, bloody combat. By the end of September, one marine division on Peleliu alone suffered more than five thousand battle casualties (killed and wounded). Nearly every day, *Graybook* listed Japanese ships torpedoed and sunk, sometimes with the unintended loss of thousands of Allied POWs crammed in their holds, as happened on September 11th with the sinking of the transport, *Kachidoki Maru*.

Nimitz handled these pressure-cooker demands of command by pitching horseshoes, firing his target pistol,[256] and spending time with friends, such as the Walkers, with whom he could let his hair down and leave war burdens behind.

The following entries in Una's diary should be considered in light of the overwhelming war demands on Nimitz that month. The Walkers and Nimitz were together seventeen days in September, a necessary fellowship for coping with his heavy responsibilities of command that month.

On Saturday, September 2nd, after the Walkers planted seven coco-husks with *dendrobiums*, Nimitz picked them up. In a caravan of two or three cars, the Walkers, Nimitz, Commodore Paul Hammond, Doc, Lamar, and Sueki and Matsuko Goto, went to Muliwai, where they pitched horseshoes, swam, danced, played cribbage and ate dinner.

At 8:21 p.m., while still playing cribbage, a soft radiance glowed on the clear eastern horizon, before a blood-red, full moon burst forth, like a ship exploding from torpedoes. That was the night of a super full moon which, because it was at its closest approach to earth, appeared unusually brighter and larger. (Only those who have witnessed it know how exquisitely beautiful such a moon is at La'ie.) All night, the moonlight was so intense that every tree and structure cast shadows. One could read a book from its silvery beams. Transparent puffs of clouds drifted across the moon's face, as it slowly rose and arced across the night sky. The white caps of breaking waves glittered like phosphorescence in the moon's glow. One could almost hear one of the symphonies Nimitz was fond of listening to or the haunting poetry of Omar Khayyam in an old volume on the side table next to where Nimitz slept.

> *Ah, Moon of my Delight who know'st no wane,*
> *The Moon of Heav'n is rising once again:*
> *How oft hereafter rising shall she look*
> *Through this same Garden after me—in vain!* [257]

With all the exigent pressures of war, when the Nimitz and the Walkers retired that evening at Muliwai, they had no inkling that, precisely one year later, the war would end with the Japanese signing the formal Instrument of Surrender.

The next morning, as the sun replaced the moon and burst from the eastern horizon just after 6:00 a.m., Muliwai and its guests awoke. On many such early mornings at Muliwai, a pulsating motor roared in the distance and rose in intensity, until just overhead when it briefly hovered soundlessly, before starting up again and disappearing toward the mountains. When Nimitz first encountered the sound, he curiously stepped out from Sandy's room to find a Sopwith Camel-like, yellow single-engine biplane, making measured sweeps of the sugar cane fields across the road, where it released clouds of pesticides. The plane made its wide turns directly over the Muliwai buildings, often waking guests from their slumbers.

The guests donned floral bathing suits and threaded the barbed-wire barriers to an unspoiled beach for an early walk and swim. Afterward, with appetites whetted, they ate breakfast, before Nimitz and his staff departed. At Makalapa, Nimitz initialed reports of numerous Japanese and planes destroyed off the Bonin Islands and elsewhere in the Western Pacific. Sandy and Una remained for another day, enjoying another glorious full moon over Muliwai. On Monday, they were home by 3:00 p.m., but received a last-minute call from Nimitz; and off they dashed to Makalapa for dinner.

On Thursday, September 7th, in another spontaneous event, Nimitz, Doc and Hal came to call at the Walkers' Nu'uanu home. They played horseshoes and stayed for dinner. The next day, they played golf. With Una and Lamar watching from the gallery, Sandy and [Dr.] Milnor were two up against Nimitz and Doc. That evening, they all had a pleasant and happy dinner at Doctor Milnor's. On Saturday, they drove to Kailua for walking and swimming at Prostate Rest, followed by dinner in Nu'uanu.

On Wednesday, September 13th, before a crowd of twenty thousand fans, including the Walkers, Nimitz tossed out the first ball in the second game of the Army-Navy World Series baseball game at Hickam base's, Furlong Field. The newspaper published a photograph of a bareheaded Nimitz, with his arm twisted high behind his head, winding up for the toss.

That afternoon, Boss called for them at Nu'uanu and he played another game of horseshoes with Sandy and Hanko. Nimitz's skill earned him an inscription on Sandy's brass plaque, as its third and last Double Ringer. After horseshoes, Una told her diary, "We went to Dinner at Louise" Dillingham's, in honor of Admiral Roger Keyes of the Royal Navy, who was on a goodwill tour of the Pacific. His wife, Lady Keyes, accompanied him. Lord Keyes had had a long and distinguished naval career with the Royal Navy and was considered one of the great military heroes of Britain. At the time of his trip, Lord Keyes was in failing health and died fifteen months later in England at the age of seventy-three.[*] Una described it as a lovely eve.

---

[*] Keyes' daughter maintained that his death was brought on by pneumonia caused by flying at too high an elevation in unpressurized airplanes during the goodwill tour.

The next day, Una was involved in a horrid accident, colliding with a motorcycle that veered suddenly in front of her, just a block from her home on Nu'uanu Avenue. Her bumper caught the cycle, whose two servicemen riders were slightly injured and rushed to the hospital. Una was mortified and recorded a summary in case there were any questions. The accident unnerved her.

Still trembling from the traumatic incident, Una hosted a lunch in honor of Lady Keyes with several friends, including two of Sandy's sisters and Matty Kennedy. Nimitz and Ghormley posed for a photograph of Lady and 1st Baron Keyes at the *Arizona* wreckage. That evening, the Walkers attended a dinner hosted by Nimitz at Makalapa in honor of Lord Keyes.

Admirals Nimitz & Ghormley with Royal Navy Fleet Admiral Roger Keyes & Wife, Arizona[258]

When Nimitz became Commander in Chief, Pacific Fleet, in 1941, he replaced his two stars of a rear admiral with the four stars of a full admiral. Such war-time promotions were only temporary, while holding the office, after which the officer reverted to his permanent rank. On September 15th, however, President Roosevelt made Nimitz's promotion permanent, signing his commission as a full admiral.

Two other critical events occurred that day. The Joint Chiefs of Staff directed MacArthur to start landings on Leyte on October 20th. And Marine and Army forces finally landed on the island of Peleliu, deploying troops and flame throwers, supported by tanks, artillery, and naval and air bombardment…against strongly prepared defenses…along the entire front.[259]

Peleliu was not declared secure for over two months. At the last minute, Halsey recommended canceling the attack, but Nimitz overruled the suggestion. Historians, Samuel Eliot Morison and Nathan Miller, opined that the Battle of Peleliu was Nimitz's worst mistake of the war. Allied casualties were over twelve hundred killed and five thousand wounded or missing. Of the approximately eleven thousand Japanese defenders, only about two hundred survived.

The resulting carnage at Peleliu shocked Nimitz, as it did the amphibious force. While tactical errors were committed by senior Navy and Marine officers, who should have known better, the greatest shortfall of the campaign proved to be poor combat intelligence. Perhaps not surprisingly, Peleliu was the only major Western Pacific island Nimitz chose not to visit.

Against the tragedy at Peleliu, perhaps the newspaper editorial the next day in Honolulu gave Nimitz some small comfort:

> Admiral Nimitz, to whom the great share of credit is given for cracking Japan's back, is gifted with the judgment of a scientific fighter who knows where, when and how hard to hit. Above all, he has the rare ability to pick the best man for each job.[260]

Michael A. Lilly

Una clipped the editorial and filed it with her other papers about Nimitz. Later that morning, Sandy drove Hara to Muliwai with weekend supplies. Una followed with Nimitz, Lamar, and Nimitz's Chief of Censorship, Capt. Marion Eppley. Even with the Battle of Peleliu raging, and no doubt troubling Nimitz's mind, his mind found relief enjoying a "Happy day!" at archery, horse-shoes, paddle-tennis, walk, [and] swim. That evening after dinner, they danced and had a dice game. Sandy and Una congratulated Nimitz on the positive editorial.

With the sun dipping behind the Ko'olau Mountains, the tufted clouds turned from brilliant white to rose, and from rose to gold. Slowly, the tints dulled, until the radiance faded eventually to a dull gray. The once-green mountains became shadowed. In the tropics, darkness quickly followed, along with the pleasant mating call of cane toads. Trudging up the well-warn path in the dark to the cottage, Nimitz changed into pajamas, crawled into the ample bed and was soon fast asleep, despite deeply-troubling thoughts of Peleliu and his next campaign. Nimitz's unique "down time" with the Walkers was essential to freeing himself physically and emotionally from the extreme pressures of command and remaining an able and effective leader.

The next morning, Nimitz joined the Walkers and their terriers for an early walk on the beach. Threading their way again through nine rows of barbed wire, they stepped onto washed sand and headed to the right toward Pounders Beach. The pier pilings on the left were eerie specters in the early morning light. Pale flocks of small gray and white *Hunakai*—Hawaiian Sanderlings—raced ahead, up and down the beach, just outside the reach of the waves, probing the sand with their beaks for food. To the right was the large pond behind a high sand bar where Black-crowned Night Herons were often startled into flight. Crabs of all sizes scurried in circular motions before them, disappearing into holes or burrowing themselves backwards into the sand.

Ahead of them, high on the bank, was a round object with bits of green seaweed trailing toward the ocean. "Eureka!" shouted Una with delight. Before them was a large green Japanese glass ball, lightly etched from the actions of sand, sun and salt and full of air bubbles. It had floated thousands of miles, before landing on the beach at Muliwai. (In a letter from Guam on February 19, 1945, Nimitz wrote, "I wish I could join in those early morning expeditions" on the beach finding glass balls. He regretted that "no glass balls are to be found" on Guam.)

Returning from the Muliwai beach with the treasured glass ball, they ate breakfast before the gang went home. At his headquarters, Nimitz stowed his treasured glass ball, before initialing a report that the 1st Marine Division at Peleliu was operating "against strong enemy opposition" while "all resistance had been overcome on the southern part of the island." [261]

That evening, the Walkers had dinner at Makalapa with Nimitz, no doubt recalling their luck that morning on the beach.

That same day, Rear Adm. Sherman left Pearl Harbor to visit Hollandia, the Dutch half of New Guinea. Hollandia was under the headquarters of MacArthur, a teetotaler, who forbade liquor for his troops, an unpopular decree. Tony Lilly recalled that the Navy got "around MacArthur's prohibition rules" by constructing "anchored rafts that served as officer and enlisted clubs, where booze was available for officers and beer for men. We had the same kind of arrangement in the Admiralty Islands, except there we had a small islet in the ring around the lagoon."

MacArthur's thirsty troops flooded into those makeshift clubs.

On Tuesday, September 18th, Nimitz broadcast a speech live to the American Legion Convention in Chicago through the *Mutual Broadcasting System*. He summarized the war to date and warned against the struggles ahead to victory. "When we have won the war," he said, "we must not fail in striving for a lasting peace."

To the members of the American Legion, he said they had "shown…the courage and resolution to face war with all its horrors and to win through—despite the blood, sweat and tears—despite the mud, filth, flies and stench of rotting dead."

In conclusion, he asked, "in the peace to follow," would they have the "courage and resolution to face your fellow citizens and insist on adequate national preparedness to maintain this peace?" Nimitz gave Una a copy of his speech.

Nimitz also sent a letter to Ginger and the Gremlins in New York. At the bottom, he penned a note to "Give the 'Gremlins' my best with some for yourself. We miss you here."

September 18 1944

Dear Ginger, Maile and Sheila:

 Thank you very much for your nice letter of September 13 which reached me yesterday - Sunday - in time to show to your family when Una and Sandy had dinner with me at 37 Makalapa.

 I am so glad to know that you reached your destination safely, and that Maile and Sheila are going to such a nice school in Greenwich, Connecticut.

 Am I correct in assuming that when Maile says in her letter, "I am waiting for Friday," that she means that she is waiting to start school, or waiting to go to a party?

 I expect before the winter is over you will have all the snow and more too than you like, and that you will wish to get your bare feet into the sands at Kailua or at Mulinai.

 I am glad to hear that you like New York, although I can't imagine anyone liking to live in a large city like that.

 We miss you out here, and hope that you will not be gone too long.

 Hal joins me in

  Aloha nui loa,

   C W Nimitz

Mrs. V. Rice,
Care: American Factors,
341 Madison Avenue,
New York, N. Y.

Dear Ginger: Give the "Gremlins" my best with some for yourself. We miss you here.

Nimitz Letter to Ginger Lilly & Daughters Maile (Major Gremlin) and Sheila (Minor Gremlin) September 18, 1944

The next day, September 19th, Una turned fifty-seven years young.

Even in her later years, Una had a youthful spirit. When she was ninety-five, I asked what it was like, having reached that advanced age. "Michael," she replied serenely, "Inside I feel the same as I did when I was nineteen. I'm a nineteen-year-old girl trapped in a ninety-year-old body."

That evening, the woman who felt inside as if she was still only nineteen enjoyed a birthday, hosting her own dinner party at Nu'uanu for Boss, Lamar, Lt. Cdr. Joe Lyle, Rear Admiral Gaffney, and other friends. Lyle was still beaming from Nimitz's Letter of Commendation for his material contributions to the Pacific Fleet and Advanced Bases. Nimitz brought Una a birthday present of Salmon, writing, "Here is one of your birthday presents which I am sending you to-day so that you can get it ready. Many happy returns of the day. Aloha nui loa, C.W. Nimitz."

After dinner, they moved upstairs for a game of poker, cheered on by the birthday girl.

Over the next five days the Walkers and Nimitz were constant companions. On Saturday, September 23rd, Nimitz's Chief of Staff and Walker poker partner, Soc McMorris, was promoted to the temporary war rank of a three-star vice admiral. "Hal [and] Boss called for us [and] we went walking [and] swimming at Kailua" Beach, followed by dinner in Nu'uanu. One of the Walkers' guests that evening was Lt. Gen. Simon Bolivar Buckner, Jr., who was in Hawai'i preparing for the *Battle of Okinawa*. The fifty-eight-year-old Buckner was the son of a Confederate major general who fought against Gen. Ulysses S. Grant's forces during the Civil War, and later became Governor of Kentucky. White-haired with blue eyes and a passion for exercise like Nimitz, Buckner, a veteran of World War I, was a soldier's soldier. Sandy and Una would have instantly taken to that brawny, outgoing general and deeply mourned his loss nine months later by a Japanese sniper. After dinner, Sandy, Nimitz and Buckner repaired upstairs for poker, overseen by Una cheerleading through the haze of smoke in the background.

On Sunday, September 24th, Nimitz released a *Communiqué* that Halsey's "Third Fleet have forced the enemy to withdraw his naval forces from their former anchorages in the Philippines, and to seek new refuges,...have disrupted their inter-island communications, and have broken his air force." He gave Una a copy of the communiqué. Left unsaid were the mounting daily casualties at Peleliu listed in *Graybook* over Nimitz's initials.

That afternoon, Sandy and Nimitz played horse-shoes while Lamar and Una visited [Aiea Naval] hospital, chatting with service members wounded in the war, followed by dinner at Nimitz's quarters. Two days later, they had dinner at the Cy Damon's. The Damons, who owned the Kailua beach house from which Nimitz took his frequent walks, resided less than a mile up Nu'uanu Valley from the Walkers, along the 15th hole of Oahu Country Club. The next day, "Sandy [and] I drove to Maka to call on Nimitz before he departed for S.F. in his Coronado Flying Boat."

For the next six days, Nimitz was in San Francisco for his regular meeting with King. He brought with him several senior officers, including Rear Adm. Forrest Sherman and Lt. Gens. Buckner and Millard F. Harmon, Jr. (Harmon commanded the army air forces in the Pacific until December, when Nimitz would assign him command of the Strategic Air Command, Pacific. He and his plane would disappear without a trace on February 25, 1945, after departing Kwajalein for Hawai'i.)

Spruance, who was in California at the time, joined them at Nimitz's request. They debated whether the next major target would be Formosa or Okinawa. Generals Buckner and Harmon convinced King that Formosa was too heavily fortified and would needlessly cost tens of thousands of casualties. King agreed to recommend to the Joint Chiefs, who later concurred, that Nimitz should attack Okinawa and Iwo Jima, instead of Formosa. The Admirals also resolved to support MacArthur's return to the Philippines. In discussing Iwo Jima, King approved the plan to land there, but intuitively called it a "sinkhole." [262]

While Nimitz was gone, Una broke her toe. The next day, she told her diary, "Sore toe[,] so rested all day!" (As I previously mentioned, this indicated an extreme condition for her, as it was against her nature not to be out and about.)

By the end of the month, against the losses on Peleliu, *Graybook* listed 69 Japanese ships sunk with the loss of only one U.S. ship, the World War I-era high speed transport USS *Noa* (APD 24), from a collision.[263] All sailors on the *Noa* survived.

On October 3rd, Nimitz phoned the Walkers to say that he and Lamar had landed in Pearl Harbor. Opening *Graybook*, Nimitz penned his initials in red, below a report that the destroyer escort USS *Shelton* (DE 407) had been torpedoed and sunk in the southern Pacific. *Shelton* was the first major U.S. warship sunk since December 26, 1943, when the USS *Brownson* (DD 518) was bombed during the landings at Cape Gloucester, New Britain.

By contrast, during the same period, *Graybook* lists numerous major Japanese vessels sunk, including one carrier, two cruisers, 24 destroyers, 117 cargo ships, 34 oilers, nine freighters, 20 transport ships, three submarines, and one-armed merchant ship.

The next day, Nimitz received formal orders from the Joint Chiefs of Staff to seize Iwo Jima and Okinawa. Nimitz assigned Spruance to the Iwo Jima operation. In 1945, Iwo Jima would grind through five cruel weeks, and Okinawa, twice that. Buckner would command the marine amphibious forces at Okinawa. The following day, Nimitz and Lamar called on the Walkers and stayed for dinner. Poker capped the evening upstairs—another nice evening, Una noted.

That weekend, Sandy and Hara drove to Muliwai in the morning, and Nimitz, Doc and Lamar picked up Una and drove over that afternoon. They had a "busy time" at archery, horseshoes, swimming, dinner and dancing. After dinner at La'ie, Una brought out her ukulele and sang "Muliwai," the plaintive, Hawaiian song about a beautiful home that was her beach place.

`Aia i ka Muliwai	(There at Muliwai)
Ku`u home nani	(My beautiful home)
Ka `i`ini pau `ole	(Is the endless yearning)
A ka pu`uwai	(of my heart)

(As we grew up, Una's rendition of "Muliwai" became the family favorite.)

After a restful sleep, the gang walked the beach early in the morning. There, in the early sunlight was the green reflection of another Japanese glass ball. Nimitz, carrying his new treasure, along with his entourage, left at 9:00 a.m., in time for Nimitz to tune into the symphony broadcast from San Francisco.

He also congratulated Halsey that his carrier operations in the Philippines were "Beyond praise and will be remembered as long as we have a Navy."

That afternoon, the Walkers drove into town before heading to Makalapa for dinner with Nimitz, the Milnors, Pearl Harbor Medical Director, Capt. W.W. Nesbit, "& several more."

Night Pass for the Walkers, October 8, 1944

Chapter 16

Leyte and a Record Cache of Japanese Glass Balls

MONDAY OCTOBER 9TH, Nimitz had some fun at the expense of journalists. Everyone knew that Admiral Halsey's Third Fleet had been attacking the Japanese around Okinawa and, in fact, had that day destroyed almost a hundred planes and sunk numerous submarines, merchants, transports and ships.[264] Nimitz read a *Communiqué* of a great allied naval victory over a Japanese fleet at the tip of the Korean peninsula. Intrigued, the journalists faithfully took down every word. Reveling in a classic Nimitz joke, he revealed at the end that the rout actually happened in 1592, when Chinese and Korean forces had attacked the Japanese.

The Associated Press broadcast the *Communiqué* just as it was delivered. And in San Francisco the dispatch was put on AP transcontinental wires as rapidly as it was received.

The message was rebroadcast all over the mainland and as far as England, before anyone realized the mistake. One newspaper stopped the presses, while it prepared a new front-page story about the triumph. "Correspondents for other wire services were awakened at all hours during the night by Mainland messages about,

Michael A. Lilly

'Where were you during the big naval battle?'" [265]

An editorial concluded, "Can anyone with confidence predict that Admiral Halsey may not perform an act just as audacious?" [266]

The afternoon of Tuesday, October 10th, while U.S. naval air forces strafed Luzon and Formosa, Nimitz joined the Walkers at a Chinese Tea party, held at the Honolulu Academy of Arts, along with some four hundred guests, to celebrate the thirty-third anniversary of the Chinese Republic. The event is known as the *Double Ten*, for the Republic was founded on the tenth day of the tenth month of 1911. A photograph of Nimitz, resplendent in his "choker" Dress White uniform with submarine gold "Dolphins" device and ribbons appeared in the *Star Bulletin*. Afterwards, Nimitz took the Walkers to Makalapa to dine. "Nice dinner and eve," Una noted.

In the prelude to the Battle for Leyte, the Walkers and Nimitz were together eight out of the nine days in mid-October for a nearly endless, and exhausting, sequence of dinners, parties, walks, and functions. On Saturday, the 14th, Nimitz, Doc and Lamar took the Walkers for a swim and walk at Kailua. They returned to Nu'uanu for dinner, followed by a game of poker, along with several friends in the smoke-filled upstairs room.

The following morning, Una gathered orchids and ginger from their garden and decorated Nimitz's Makalapa quarters for a luncheon he was hosting for British Major General Sir Philip Mitchell and his wife. Afterwards, they attended the opening of *Fuller House*, the new USO club for service members at Pearl City. Nimitz spoke of the importance of the United Service Organization to sustaining positive morale among the troops:

> ...[T]his work is an important contribution to winning the war. If anything, the importance of these facilities is destined to increase as the military population of these islands expands, and as the duration of the individual's absence from his home lengthens.
>
> Homesickness in varying degrees seems to be an

> *occupational disease of the military. It usually appears in mild form, but it can become acute, and when it does it can impair health and efficiency. In one sense these clubs are as essential as hospitals. In them are available the tonics of companionship, relaxation, active sports and congenial surroundings. They keep our fighting men in good psychological health.*

Nimitz's words—"the tonics of companionship, relaxation, active sports and congenial surroundings"—came from his heart and echoed the value of his own recreational time at target practicing, tossing horseshoes, walking Kailua Beach, spending weekends at Muliwai, and dining with the Walkers. Nimitz enjoyed his own private USO with the Walkers.

The next day, Sandy, Una, Nimitz, and Lamar drove to the Naval Ammunition Depot at Lualualei on the western Waianae Coast of O'ahu to call on its Inspector of Ordnance in Charge, Capt. J. S. Dowell. Mirroring a tour by President Roosevelt the previous July 27th, they drove through the Depot and its many humped magazines and storage facilities, before climbing over Kolekole Pass in the Waianae Range and down into Schofield Barracks. Contrary to popular belief, the Japanese *did not* fly through the pass during the attack on Pearl Harbor.

Once in Schofield, the party passed rows of tanks and motorized vehicles, hangers and planes parked at Wheeler Field, winding up at Lieutenant General Buckner's quarters for dinner. After returning home late that night, Una summed up the day as a "lovely outing."

On the 17th, Nimitz "called for us [and] we went to Eva and George Sumner's home for dinner." On the 19th, while Nimitz drove the Walkers to dinner and dancing at the von Holt's, the Naval Court of Inquiry into the attack on Pearl Harbor issued findings exonerating Admiral Kimmel. Chief of Naval Operations Adm. Harold Stark, however, was faulted for failing to adequately advise Kimmel about vital information before the attack:

> ...[T]he Court is of the opinion that Admiral Harold R. Stark, U.S.N., Chief of Naval Operations and responsible for the operations of the Fleet, failed to display the sound judgment expected of him in that he did not transmit to Admiral Kimmel, Commander in Chief, Pacific fleet, during the very critical period 26 November to 7 December, important information which he had regarding the Japanese situation and, especially, in that, on the morning of 7 December 1941, he did not transmit immediately the fact that a message had been received which appeared to indicate that a break in diplomatic relations was imminent, and that an attack in the Hawaiian area might be expected soon.[*]

The findings provided no immediate solace to Kimmel, as they would remain sealed until after the war, in part based on a letter from Nimitz to King dated November 3, 1944, stating that the release would adversely affect current military operations.

In keeping the record secret, Secretary of the Navy Forrestal said he was guided by the following question: "What will best serve the continued successful prosecution of the war?"

Those exigencies required it to remain under seal. Neither Kimmel nor the public knew of his exculpation until August 29, 1945, after the war had ended.

Carrying out the directives of the Joint Chiefs of Staff to the day, the next night, October 20th, MacArthur waded ashore on the island of Leyte, where he broadcast to the Philippines his now-famous message of return, since his departure from Corregidor Island two years and six months before:

---

[*] Adm. William H. Standley, a member of the Roberts Commission of Inquiry, flatly concluded that Kimmel and Short "were martyred," and had they been "brought to trial, both would have been cleared." "More About Pearl Harbor," (*U.S. News and World Report*, April 16, 1954).

Nimitz at Ease

I have returned. By the grace of Almighty God our forces stand again on Philippine soil—soil consecrated in the blood of our two peoples. We have come dedicated and committed to the task of destroying every vestige of enemy control over your daily lives, and of restoring upon a foundation of indestructible strength, the liberties of your people.

While MacArthur was wading and broadcasting, Nimitz drove the Walkers to the Stanley Kennedy's for dinner and poker. The next morning, Una, Chimey Walker, and Betty von Holt donned Red Cross uniforms and drove to the submarine base at Lockwood's invitation to board a submarine returning from patrol that day. Una described the tour as very interesting. They lunched at Lockwood's quarters.

Early that morning, Sandy and Hara drove to Muliwai. Una was back in Nu'uanu in time for Beach to pick her up at 2:00 p.m. for a drive to Makalapa from which she, Nimitz, Lamar and Doc went to Muliwai via Haleiwa. Before departing Pearl Harbor, Nimitz announced that regular U.S. currency could henceforth be used interchangeably with the Hawaiian Series overprints throughout the Pacific.

At Muliwai, they broke all records in horseshoes, danced, and enjoyed dinner by the sound of ocean waves breaking against the shore. Early Sunday morning, they walked through the barbed wire to the beach. Half-way to Pounder's Beach, they found another green Japanese glass ball. "Eureka!" shouted Una. Then another glass ball! And still another. Finally, a cluster of them. All told, they found eight green Japanese glass balls. A large find of various sizes and shapes, but not a record.

One time, Ginger heard that planes from the Naval Air Station in Kaneohe[*] were going to pound nearby thirteen-acre Moku'auia

---

[*] The then-Naval Air Station Kaneohe, attacked during Pearl Harbor, was later turned over to the Marines and is now Marine Corps

Island (Goat Island to the locals) as target practice at 9:00 a.m. About a quarter mile offshore, the island was reached at low tide by walking across the reef.* Ginger, being sometimes overly adventuresome, struck out for the island at dawn. From its beaches, she gathered a record thirteen glass balls and hastened back to Muliwai, not long before bombs began exploding on the island.

After an early breakfast, Beach arrived to return Nimitz to Pearl Harbor, where he initialed a report of "three definite [Japanese] battleships and two possible carriers headed south in Mindoro Strait." [267]

That evening, the Walkers drove to Makalapa for dinner with Nimitz, bringing orchids to decorate the quarters. Among the guests were several friends of the Walkers, including Alice and Philip Spalding and Florence and Lawrence McCully Judd.

The fifty-five-year-old Spalding was President of C. Brewer & Company, the smallest of the Big Five companies in Hawai'i. Judd, a fifty-seven year old missionary descendant, served as Governor of Hawai'i from 1929 to 1934 and again after the war. Judd had originally appointed Sandy as Chairman of the Board of Leper Hospitals in 1932.

After dinner, they repaired to the outdoor theater to watch the 1943 drama, *Lost Angel,* starring Margaret O'Brien.

Dinner Nametag Hand Painted by Nimitz's Staff for Una

Base Hawai'i.

* Today, visitors can still walk out to the Island at low tide, but its interior is preserved as a bird sanctuary, providing nesting grounds for the threatened Wedge-tailed Shearwater and other birds.

Nimitz at Ease

On October 23rd, Halsey informed Nimitz that his Third Fleet was moving toward what turned out to be a Japanese diversionary force to the north. It was a trap intended to lure the sometimes-impulsive Halsey away. It worked.

With Halsey gone, between October 23 and 26, 1944, the Allied forces fought the Battle of Leyte Gulf, also known as the Second Battle of the Philippine Sea.

It was the largest naval battle of World War II and, perhaps, in all history.

In Japan's first deployment of large naval forces in combat since Guadalcanal two years before, two massive Japanese armadas, comprising nine battleships and three carriers, converged on Leyte in a pincer movement—Vice Admiral Shoji Nishimura's forces through Surigao Strait in the south, and Vice Admiral Takeo Kurita's forces through San Bernardino Strait to the north. The Allied forces at Leyte faced utter annihilation.

October 25th was already a famous date in military history—the day the Seljuk Turks defeated German crusaders (1147); the Battle of Agincourt, when the outnumbered King Henry V vanquished the French (1415); the Second battle of Cape Finisterre when the British fleet defeated the French (1747); the Battle Balaclava (1854), made famous by Tennyson's 1854 poem, "Charge of the Light Brigade"; and now, Leyte. For the first time since the Battle of Tsushima Straits, and the last time in history, allied naval forces at Surigao Crossed the 'T'—this time the Japanese T—which, like knocking a baseball out of the park with the bases loaded, utterly obliterated Nishimura's armada.

Nishimura died when his flagship sank. Some historians credit Jutland during World War I as the last great battleship-to-battleship battle. Not so. It was, in fact, Surigao where battleships fought battleships for the last time in world history.

Meanwhile, Kurita's fleet of five battleships, including two of the world's largest, emerged to the north from San Bernardino Strait. Kurita was unaware that Halsey, aboard the battleship USS *New Jersey* (BB 62), had fallen for a Japanese feint and had disappeared far to the north, leaving an open backdoor for Kurita's massive armada to crush Vice Adm. T.C. Kinkaid's inferior Task Force 77 off Leyte Gulf.

Nimitz worried about the location of Halsey's Third Fleet and whether he had left a force guarding San Bernardino Strait. On October 25th at 12:44 a.m. HWT, Nimitz sent Halsey the famous message, "Where is Task Force 34? The world wonders."

Unknown to Nimitz, his staff added the "world wonders" phrase as security padding, but Halsey took it as a personal slight. As all men of his day, Halsey had studied Tennyson's poem memorializing the six hundred, who had unwisely ridden into the *valley of death,* while all the world wonder'd. Not realizing the wording was padding, and incensed at being compared to those foolish and suicidal cavalry on the anniversary of their charge, Halsey threw his hat to the carrier deck and turned his task force around.

Two hours later, Kinkaid pleaded with Halsey that with "Enemy fast battleships and heavy cruisers" attacking his force, his situation has "become very serious" and "Your assistance badly needed."

Halsey arrived the next day, too late to be of any significant help. The firepower of Halsey's Third Fleet, exceeding that of the entire Japanese navy, was only employed during the battle to sink two wounded ships.

Nimitz was "perturbed" when he learned that Halsey had "left the gate open for the wolves to jump the sheep." * Halsey dispatched Nimitz a bitter letter and a message, archived in *Graybook,* defending his strategy. He wrote that to "Statically guard San Bernardino Straits until enemy surface and carrier air attacks

---

* *"And I Was There": Pearl Harbor and Midway—Breaking the Secrets,* 491. A month later on December 17, 1944, Halsey steamed his battle force through the heart of Typhoon Cobra and lost three destroyers and almost 800 lives. Nimitz recommended that Halsey be relieved, but was turned down. Interview with Hal Lamar, 95.

could be coordinated would have been childish" and lamented having had to break off "my golden opportunity and head south to support Kinkaid[,] although I was convinced that his force was adequate to deal with an enemy force that was badly weakened by our attacks." [268]

With his subordinate admirals managing Leyte operations, there was little Nimitz could do in Pearl Harbor except stress over developments. He needed healthy distractions. *Life* magazine discussed Nimitz's stresses of command and noted that the British naval commander of the Battle of Jutland during World War I was once considered "the only man in history who was in a position to lose a war in an afternoon. This may have been true at the time but Nimitz has more than once been in a position to lose an even bigger war in an even shorter period of time." [269] Leyte was nearly one of those losses.

So, while Halsey was steaming south toward Leyte, and the battle was still in doubt, at 4:00 p.m. on October 25th, Nimitz, Doc, Una's nephew, Chester Sims, and Sandy played golf at the stunning O'ahu Country Club, only about a mile up Nu'uanu Valley from the Walker Estate. Una told her diary that it was "great fun, but tense with war." (Una's use of the words, "Tense with war," was one of only a couple of allusions to the war with Japan in her diary.) While Nimitz was playing golf, his staff delivered messages on the progress of Leyte—not the best circumstance under which to concentrate on one's golf stroke. But the time spent on the course was essential to his peace of mind.

Everyone was anxious about Leyte that evening, even as they dined at Lt. Gen. Benjamin Holmes, Jr.'s residence. Since 1943, Holmes had been the chief of staff of the Army's Hawai'i Department. War talk was still generally verboten, but Leyte, no doubt, was discussed. Back at Makalapa, Nimitz added his initials in red at the end of a long and intense *Graybook* summary of the events in Leyte.

The First Duke of Wellington might have been describing Leyte instead of Waterloo, when he said the British victory over

Napoleon "Was the nearest run thing you ever saw in your life." Leyte could easily have been an allied debacle, rivaling the Japanese defeat of the Russian Imperial fleet in the Tsushima Straits in 1905. Instead, it was a key victory, "One of the most decisive battles of naval history." [270]

"All war," the ancient war strategist Sun Tzu taught, "is based on deception." Fortunately for the Leyte forces, Kurita was deceived—although not because U.S. forces intended it. He thought the forces before him were Halsey's formidable Third Fleet, and he acted accordingly.

In fact, he was attacked by inferior destroyers, submarines and planes from small escort carriers. Kurita could easily have crushed Kinkaid's Task Force 77. But he lost nerve and turned tail. Kinkaid wired Nimitz a Top Secret message, reporting his "deepest regret" at "the loss of 2 CVE's 2 DD's and 1 DE," but they were among the ships which "with superb determination and skill fought and defeated a strong enemy surface force supported by repeated attacks by shore based enemy aircraft." [271] Kurita's superior force was defeated by confusion, timidity, a great deal of luck and American heroism.[*]

October 27, 1944, was "Navy Day," celebrated every year in honor of the birth of President Theodore Roosevelt, called the "father" of the modern U.S. Navy. That morning, Nimitz sent Sandy's nephew Jack Walker and his daughter Jill, a note written in longhand with a box of "Navy Day cookies which I baked myself— (??) for you and your father and mother. Aloha nui loa, C.W. Nimitz."

I asked Chet Lay what he thought his grandfather meant by the two question marks. "My take is this is a joke," Chet replied. "I

---

[*] Coincidentally, the Lay and Lilly families were represented during the Leyte battle. Chet and Dick Lay's father, Cdr. James T. Lay, Jr., was with "Taffy 3," a small task force of escort carriers and destroyers. My father, Tony Lilly, was about a hundred thirty miles to the south in Surigao Strait aboard the *Bush*.

don't think CinCPac was baking any cookies two days after the Battle for Leyte Gulf."

At 3:30 p.m. that afternoon, Sandy and Una attended a change of command. Nimitz was the keynote speaker, wearing his choker white dress uniform. Una described Nimitz's speech to her diary as "Very, very interesting" and "so impressive." In those days, wearing white uniforms in Pearl Harbor held a special peril. The sugarcane fields of O'ahu Sugar and other plantations were torched before harvest to rid the plants of leaves. The billowing fires carried enormous quantities of black charred leaves aloft, which often rained down on official gatherings, settling on white Navy uniforms. "Hawaiian Snow," as Sandy called the black filaments, were blown off white hats and shirts, and never rubbed, which would grind them into clothing in ugly black streaks.

After the ceremony, Una notes that Nimitz drove the Walkers to his house at Makalapa where they had dinner and a musical evening, returning home late. The next day, Nimitz and the Walkers were back walking and swimming at Kailua beach, followed by dinner and poker at Nu'uanu.

On Sunday, October 29th, Nimitz released a five-page *Communiqué No. 168* that, in the Second Battle of the Philippine Sea, the "Japanese Fleet has been decisively defeated and routed."

When Nimitz landed in Pearl Harbor Christmas morning in 1941, his fleet was on the bottom of Pearl Harbor. Out of the Japanese-caused-graveyard rose marine specters, which avenged with unrelenting ferocity the attack that awoke a sleeping giant.

Of those specters, Nimitz proudly listed the "Following battleships seriously damaged at Pearl Harbor [which] took part in these actions: *West Virginia, Maryland, Tennessee, California,* and *Pennsylvania.* The new carriers *Lexington, Wasp* and *Hornet* also participated." *

---

* Of the remaining Pearl Harbor battleships, *Oklahoma* was sold for scrap, *Nevada* was resurrected and fought off Normandy, and the *Arizona* and the target ship *Utah* remained on the bottom of the harbor, both

The *Communiqué* summed up, "Much of the credit for the destruction inflicted on the Japanese Fleet goes to the naval airmen who gallantly and relentlessly pressed their attacks home with telling effect."

Left unsaid was the fact that Halsey's Task Force 77 had been AWOL. A New York Times editorial extolled that "No finer ... description of a complicated action has come out of this war than Admiral Nimitz'[s] *Communiqué 168*... it throbs with the stimulating pace of direct statement; it leaves room for the imagination to picture the exciting events."

In fact, Nimitz's trusty deputy, Rear Admiral Sherman, actually wrote the *Communiqué*.[272] Nimitz wrote to Sherman that he "would be guilty if I did not make due acknowledgement to you who wrote it."

Nimitz gave the Walkers a copy of the *Communiqué*, which they preserved.

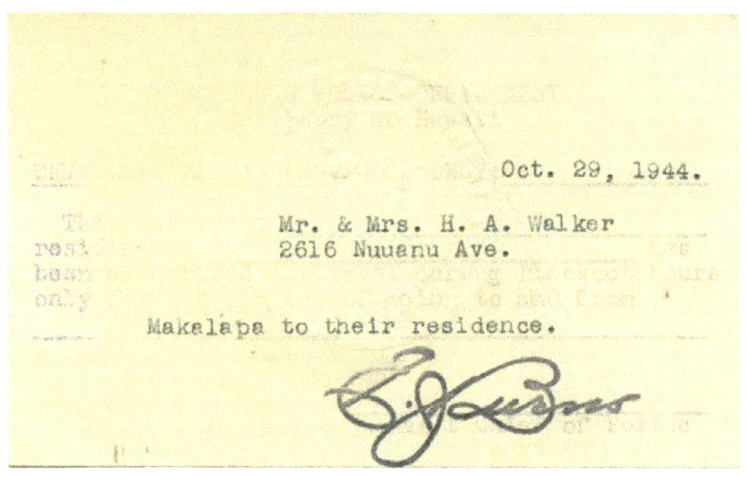

Night Pass for the Walkers, October 29, 1944

That afternoon, the Walkers drove to Makalapa to arrange orchids from their garden for Nimitz's dinner in honor of Adm. Royal Eason Ingersoll. Ingersoll, who was then sixty-one, had served as Commander in Chief, U.S. Atlantic Fleet, but was being reassigned as Commander, Western Sea Frontier as of November 15th. In 1942, the World War II *Fletcher*-class destroyer USS *Ingersoll* (DD 652) was commissioned in his honor, as well as his grandson, who was killed in the Battle of Midway. (Four years after his death in 1976, the *Spruance*-class destroyer USS *Ingersoll* (DD 990) was commissioned in his honor.)

In his new command headquartered in San Francisco, Ingersoll would be responsible for the sea defense of the Pacific coast of the United States and Mexico during World War II.

Mummy Nametag Hand Painted by Nimitz's staff for Una Walker, Halloween, 1944.

At dinner that evening with Nimitz, Admiral Ingersoll and the Sumners, Una was surprised by what she found at her place setting. In honor of Halloween two days later, Nimitz's staff had hand-painted a special name tag for the chair of the Red Cross Surgical Dressing Corps of Honolulu—a mummy, wrapped in surgical bandages. After poker and classical music, the Walkers were home before midnight.

About five hours later in the early morning hours, while everyone was fast asleep, a rare *Blue* Moon—the second full Moon that month—rose above the Ko'olau Mountains, bathing all of O'ahu in a soft light.

With the Japanese Empire on the defensive, the enemy launched a terrible new weapon—service members willing to commit suicide *(Kamikazes)* for the Emperor. The *Graybook* began recording such suicide attacks. On the last day of October, *Kamikazes* piloted by *tokkotai* (special attack units) hit the carriers, USS *Franklin* (CV 13) and USS *Belleau Wood* (CVL 24), while they were operating near Leyte. War photographs show both ships with billows of smoke rising from flames. The fires were brought under control, but at an enormous cost—ninety-two sailors killed on *Belleau Woods* and eight hundred seven aboard *Franklin*.

On November 1st, the Japanese launched Mitsubishi "Betty" Bombers, Zeroes or "Zekes," and *Kamikazes* against U.S. Navy ships in the Leyte Gulf and the Surigao Straits. While patrolling the lower Leyte Gulf to protect MacArthur's beachhead, the *Fletcher*-class destroyer USS *Abner Read* (DD 424) was sunk and four destroyers damaged by *Kamikazes*. All but twenty-two of *Abner Read's* crew were recovered. That same day, another *Fletcher*-class destroyer, USS *Bush* (DD 529), was on patrol duty in the Surigao Straits. Lieutenant Tony Lilly, U.S. Naval Academy class of 1941, was the ship's Executive Officer, whose general quarter station was on the bridge. The deck log that day, from 2:42 a.m., when the ship went to general quarters, until 8:37 p.m., when the ship was relieved of patrol duty, chronicled continuous combat operations for hours, and the downing of two of ten attacking Japanese planes. The following summary was published in *The Sacred Warriors: Japan's Suicide Legions*:

> *The destroyer Bush, on antisubmarine patrol in South Surigao Strait, fought a running battle with numerous planes all morning, beginning at 9:40 a.m., when she*

opened up on a Betty that came in on the ship's starboard beam, dropped a torpedo, and swept off. Bush maneuvered to avoid the torpedo and hit the plane with her forty-millimeter guns. Four minutes later another Betty rushed the destroyer, and Bush, zigzagging furiously, dodged another torpedo and brought the plane down close to her side. A third, fourth, fifth, and sixth Betty pounced on the destroyer, as though she were the only ship on the high seas, the tail gunner of one plane strafing with his machine gun.

After the Bettys came the Zekes. Bush hit one and it swung low, dropping a bomb that missed before plunging afire into the sea fifty yards astern.[273]

At 10:47 a.m., one Betty swooped down on the *Bush*, strafing her with gunfire, wounding Tony Lilly in the back. After being patched up, Lilly was soon back on the bridge, where the action continued with frequent encounters with Japanese warplanes.

"I have a vivid memory," Tony recalled, "of one Betty coming low on the starboard hand flying through all our gun fire, dropping his torpedo, actually seeing the pilot's face when his plane was hit, and he went careening into the water as his torpedo passed astern."

During the war, broadcasts by a woman the Allies dubbed "Tokyo Rose" were made from Japan. In fact, several women served as *Tokyo Rose*, whose transmissions were intended to deteriorate morale among U.S. service members. Most often, the opposite resulted, as she became a form of entertainment. Marine Corps Commandant Gen. Vandegrift said she competed with American radio comedians by "inciting the longest and loudest laughs." [274]

Sometimes, however, she was fairly accurate in her reports of American units. Indeed, that was the case during her November 2, 1944, broadcast overheard by *Bush*, as described in its after-action report. Rose said that Japanese "Aircraft attacked a lone American destroyer which had automatic five-inch guns" in the Surigao area."

Michael A. Lilly

Bush concluded, "This command is sure Tokyo Rose referred to the U.S.S. *Bush* and is especially proud that we should have been singled out for a portion of Tokyo Rose's excellent program. Tokyo Rose identified the attacking planes of that day as the Kamikaze Corps, who had sworn to take a ship with every plane."

This author is glad that the worst damage Japan inflicted on *Bush* that day was only two wounded personnel, including Lieutenant Lilly, who survived the war.[*]

---

[*] Lilly was soon reassigned, and fortunate for him and this author he was. Five months later, on April 6, 1945, off Okinawa, three *Kamikazes* crashed into *Bush*, sinking her. Some eighty-seven of her crew were lost.

Chapter 17

Ambassador Grew on Japanese Tenacity

ON FRIDAY, NOVEMBER 3rd, the Walkers and Rear Adm. William Rhea Furlong,* Commandant of the Pearl Harbor Navy Yard, attended the Wahine Baseball game. After the game, they dined with Nimitz at his quarters.

The next morning, Sandy, Hara and American Factors Vice President, William Monahan, drove to Muliwai with provisions. Nimitz and Lamar picked up Una at Nu'uanu and drove separately to the country. At Muliwai, they enjoyed archery, horseshoes, a walk and a swim. After dinner, they danced and played poker.

The next morning, everyone enjoyed the normal early walk on the beach, washed immaculate from the nighttime tide and breakfast, before an early departure for Makalapa. The Walkers had lunch at Muliwai before leaving for town, where they gathered flowers from their garden to decorate Nimitz's quarters that evening for dinner. The Walkers returned home late. Before

---

* On the day of the Pearl Harbor attack, Furlong was aboard the minelayer *Oglala* (CM 4) and, thus, the Navy's senior officer present afloat (SOPA) that day.

retiring, Nimitz initialed a report that "Land operations on Leyte continue to progress favorably."²⁷⁵

Early the next morning at 12:40 a.m., November 6th, Nimitz's headquarters received a message from Task Force 57, enclosing a transcription of a Japanese psychological warfare pamphlet dropped on Allied forces at Peleliu. The pamphlet, with fractured English and revisionist history, no doubt brought smiles to Nimitz's lips, especially its misspelling of his name—"Nimmit":

> Poor reckless Yankee-Doodle. Do you know about the naval battle wone by the American 58th Fleet at the sea near Taiwan (Tomosa) and Philippine. Japanese powerful air firce had sank their 19 aeroplene carriers, 4 battleships, 10 several cruisers and destroyers along with sending 1,261 ship aeroplanes into the sea. From this result we think that you can imagine what shall happen next around Palau upon you. The fraud Rousevelt, hanging the president election under his nose and from his policy ambition, worked not only poor Nimmit but also Maccasir [MacArthur] like a robot. Like this, what is pity. Must be sacrifice you pay. Thanks for your advice notes of surrender. But we haven't any reason to surrender to those who are fated to be totally destroyed in a few days later. Add to you, against the manner of your attack paying no heed to humanity, your god shall make Japanese force to add retaliative attack upon you. Saying again, against the attack paying no heed to humanity contrary to the mutual military spirits, you shall get a very stern attack. We mean cruel attack. Japan Military.²⁷⁶

Until Friday that week, the Walkers were with Nimitz only on Wednesday for dinner. That evening, Nimitz handed the Walkers a small, wrapped package containing a slender twenty-four page book entitled, *Your Son and Six Fighting Admirals,* by a Seaman,

Donald Wilhelm, which Nimitz inscribed with the date "7 Nov 1944." [277] The book was illustrated with photographs and short summaries of the six full Navy admirals in 1944, including Nimitz and Spruance, who signed their respective prints with salutations to "Una and Sandy Walker."

About Nimitz, it wrote, "Seems an eminently simple man with the simplest tastes. He likes simple food, simple sea stories, symphonic recordings, pitching horseshoes, swimming, tennis. With what thought we can only guess, he likes each morning, toward noon, to step from his office, pistol in hand and, on an improvised range, fire twenty rounds at a target, inspect it, then, feeling better, go back to work."

That accurately described the Nimitz the Walkers knew so well.

Photo of Nimitz in Your Son and Six Fighting Admirals inscribed by Nimitz to the Walkers

Michael A. Lilly

The U.S. Marine Corps celebrated its hundred sixty-ninth anniversary on Friday, November 10, 1944. Reviewing the Corps' victorious record in the Pacific war, Nimitz broadcast that, "You may be certain that your hundred seventieth anniversary in 1945 will find the Marines even closer to Japan."

While Nimitz broadcast his message, Una was on horseback. A lifelong lover of horseback riding, in the 1930s Paul Fagan* gave Una a Magnificent Texas quarter horse who was a pacer. The legs on both sides of that big young bay gelding moved forward and back in unison, providing a most comfortable ride.[278]

"Tex" was maintained below Diamond Head at Kapiolani Park stables, owned and operated by Walter Dillingham, principally for polo ponies.

Wearing jodhpurs, stiff-brimmed ranger hat, scarf, long-sleeved floral shirt and high boots, she often rode Tex, as she probably did that Friday, east across the face of Diamond Head over to Kahala, where she galloped along the three miles of beach to the present-day Waialae Country Club and back.

She returned in time that afternoon, when Nimitz drove her and Sandy to dinner at "Dagmar" Cooke's. (Dagmar was a founder of the Honolulu Academy of Arts.)

---

* Paul Fagan was an entrepreneur with a home on the slopes of Diamond Head, who purchased Hana Ranch on Maui in 1944. In 1946, he and Sandy built Hana Ranch Hotel. Fagan owned the San Francisco Seals baseball team, which he brought to Hana, Maui, to train in 1946. (Sandy was Fagan's executor.) (*Henry Alexander Walker, Jr.*, "Watumull Foundation Oral History Project," 1987, 8.)

Photo of Una Riding her Quarter Horse "Tex," Kailua Beach, 1940s

The next day, the anniversary of the end of World War I (Armistice Day), Iwo Jima was bombarded by the U.S. Navy. Marines landed the following February 19, 1945. The Battle of Iwo Jima, made immemorial by the image of five marines raising the flag atop

Mount Suribachi, lasted over a month, with nearly all the Japanese defenders perishing.

Meanwhile, Una recorded that the sixty-four year old former Ambassador to Japan, Joseph Grew, arrived in Honolulu. At 1:45 p.m., Sandy and Una arrived at Nimitz's quarters in Makalapa. Nimitz, Ambassador Grew, the Walkers, Lamar, and Doc left for [the] Crow Bar, where they went riding and swimming. That evening, they all had dinner at Rear Admiral Furlong's. Afterward, they attended another Wahine Baseball game—another altogether happy day for Una.

The next day, Sunday, Lamar and a group of Sailors arrived at Nu'uanu to trim trees in the Walkers' garden and stayed for luncheon. That evening, the Walkers had dinner at Nimitz's quarters. The guest of honor was Ambassador Grew, a handsome man with piercing eyes, chiseled face and an aristocratic carriage. Other guests included Vice Adm. Towers, Soc, the Walkers' good friends the A. L. Castles and several others. Castle had headed the Hawai'i Red Cross since the Great War, was its Chairman on December 7th, and had been the President of Honolulu Rapid Transit until 1940. He lived next door to the Walkers.

After dinner, the mustachioed Ambassador Grew gave a talk, no doubt a gripping discussion of Japan and the war. With his head cocked slightly to the right, Grew spoke assertively with clipped words and a clear firm voice. Two years before, Nimitz and the Walkers had read a *Honolulu Advertiser* article on the publication of his book, *Report from Tokyo*, which grimly described the Japanese soldier as "An able and ruthless fighter whose greatest ambition is to die on the battlefield." [279]

Grew had impeccable credentials on the subject, having been Ambassador to Japan when war broke out, and was interned and repatriated nine months later. On January 27, 1941, Ambassador Grew telegraphed Secretary of State Cordell Hull that he heard from a source that, in the event of hostilities, the Japanese planned to launch a surprise attack against Pearl Harbor.[280] (Unfortunately, with the mentality of an ostrich, naval intelligence in Washington gave no credence to his report.)

In 1944, Grew published an autobiography, *Ten Years in Japan*, filled with personal insights into Japan, during a very turbulent time when Japanese Prime Ministers and Military leaders were repeatedly assassinated, and Japan had invaded Manchuria, not to mention the attack on Pearl Harbor. In an essay published in 1942, he warned that, having lived in Japan for ten years, he knew the Japanese intimately—they held Americans with a "cold, withering contempt," and "will not crack morally or psychologically or economically, even when eventual defeat stares them in the face. ...Only by utter physical destruction or utter exhaustion of their men and materials can they be defeated." [281]

Grew also argued that the Japanese would not surrender, unless the Emperor was retained. What prescient words, for that is exactly what it took by August 1945 to force the Japanese Empire to capitulate—near annihilation, but a willingness to keep the Emperor. And what an education the Walkers and Nimitz had listening to Ambassador Grew. Oh, to have been the proverbial fly on Nimitz's wall that evening!

On Monday, November 13th, Una drove to Kapiolani Park stables and rode Tex, her quarter horse, across the face of Diamond Head, along Kahala Beach and back. That afternoon, Nimitz and Ambassador Grew picked up the Walkers and drove to Louise and Walter Dillingham's elegant Diamond Head home, La Pietra, for dinner.

The next day, Nimitz and Ambassador Grew picked them up for another dinner, this time at the "Anderson's" to celebrate their 25th wedding anniversary. While Una, who, like Nimitz and Sandy, rarely uttered a negative word, she summed up the evening as "not [a] very good time"!

Whatever caused Una to pen those words was not explained, but it must have been significant for her to record it. Una never publicly complained about anything and disliked hearing complaints from others. (Once, she stopped herself from asking a hypochondriac how she was, telling me later she did not want to hear the person's endless list of ailments.)

On Thursday, Ambassador Grew departed Honolulu. In another spontaneous event, probably because Nimitz was then relieved of a lot of protocol and formalities with Ambassador Grew's departure, he suddenly called the Walkers at 6:15 p.m. and asked them to dine with him. They cancelled their plans and drove to Makalapa, where they toured his headquarters and had a happy eve. With such last-minute invitations from Nimitz, Sandy, no doubt, continued to obtain his night passes on short notice through his friend, Honolulu Police Commission Chairman George Sumner.

The next day, November 17th, the Navy Department issued *Communiqué No. 554,* which was published verbatim in the December issue of *All Hands.* "Overwhelming Victory" reported that, based on still incomplete reports, the Japanese lost two battleships, four carriers and eight cruisers in "a series of naval engagements...which may turn out to be among the decisive battles of modern times."

The magazine later quoted Nimitz's review of 1944 as "A year of continuous progress and gratifying success" and that the Navy would continue to exploit any opportunities "to bring the enemy to decisive defeat at the earliest possible time." [282]

The following Saturday, the Walkers drove to Muliwai with their cook, Hara, maid, Hassie, and the terriers. Nimitz came out separately by way of Haleiwa. They practiced archery, pitched horseshoes, walked on the beach and swam. That evening, as the sun set behind the Ko'olau Mountains, they enjoyed cocktails and dinner, followed by dancing and a game of dice. It was, noted Una, the "happiest time ever."

The next morning, as always, they headed down through the rows of barbed wire for an early walk on the smooth beach, followed by breakfast. Nimitz and his entourage left about 10.45. Before retiring, Nimitz initialed a long summary of war activities in the West, including a list of casualties to date at Leyte: "Allied—1,072 killed, 4,277 wounded, and 22 missing; Japanese—18,778 killed, 95 captured." [283]

Two days later, November 21st, Una recorded that Nimitz and his staff left for the Coast for the regular war strategy meetings with Admiral King in San Francisco. King informed Nimitz that the Royal Navy Pacific Fleet would soon be commanded by Admiral Bruce Austin Fraser, 1st Baron Fraser of North Cape.[284] Fraser would be under Nimitz's operational control, but based in Sydney, Australia. King warned Nimitz that the British wanted to pool resources, but he wanted it understood that the British had to supply their own resources—although local Area Commanders could provide supporting elements when needed.

Una recorded that Nimitz returned to Hawai'i on the evening of Monday, November 27th. Nimitz initialed reports that *Kamikazes* had slammed into the carriers USS *Intrepid* (CV 11), USS *Cabot* (CVL 28), USS *Essex* (CV 9) and USS *Hancock* (CV 19), killing seventy-three crewmembers and wounding another hundred seventeen. The next day *Kamikazes* were back in the air, diving on ships of opportunity. Some forty-seven Allied ships would be sunk by Japanese suicide bombers in the war.

Halsey never understood a psyche so anathema to western culture. "The psychology behind it was too alien to ours; Americans, who fight to live, find it hard to realize that another people will fight to die." [285]

The next day, Nimitz delivered wonderful apples to the Walkers. That evening, they drove to Makalapa for dinner with Nimitz and General Richardson.

On the last day of November, Sandy and Una dined at "37 Makalapa" with Nimitz, Doc, Lamar, and the Walkers' friends, the Sumners and Dr. Milnors. They had enjoyed a "2nd Cheery Thanks[giving] dinner," followed by poker. On their way home, a full Moon cast so much light that Sandy could drive without his little sliver of headlights.

Despite the endless work and partying consuming his time, Nimitz wrote Catherine, "I have finally caught up with my papers sufficiently to take more exercise—which I need badly to keep me feeling fit." He also "cut out lunches until my weight gets back to

180—which is a good weight for me." He asked that she not "worry about [his] dieting because Dr. A. keeps a close check on my condition. So much of my work must be done at my desk & this is very confining." [286]

Meanwhile, Roosevelt nominated Ambassador Grew to serve as Under Secretary of State, a position he assumed the following month.

Chapter 18

A Pentagon of Stars

ON SATURDAY, DECEMBER 2nd, Sandy and Hara left early from Nu'uanu to Muliwai. With all his stress, socializing and travel, it was Nimitz's turn to become ill, perhaps from a recurring bout of malaria he contracted during a visit to Guadalcanal in 1943. Una recorded that Nimitz was suffering from a sore throat. Despite his sore throat, Nimitz invited Una for lunch at Makalapa with Lamar and Captain Eppley, before driving together in a tropical storm to Muliwai for the afternoon and evening. Nimitz wrote Catherine that the "Weather was not good and there was much wind and rain which did not help me, [with the]…cold and sore throat I had picked up from several running around my H.Q." 287

His illness did not prevent him from walking the beach that afternoon and finding "4 glass balls—two of which I gave [Marion] Eppley." For dinner, he wrote to Catherine, "We had charcoal cooked island steaks…and then a long sleep."

Exacerbating his cold, as Nimitz walked up the path to the cottage that evening against the chilly rainstorm driving in from the ocean, he became thoroughly soaked. Even an umbrella would have provided little protection against the gale.

Nimitz's condition worsened in the night. Una's diary recorded that he "wakened with [a] bad cold," and, out of character, "didn't swim or walk" the beach. While he skipped the beach walk, Sandy "...netted three more glass balls for Eppley who was very pleased to have them." The stream broke through the sandbar from all the rain, spewing brown mud well out to sea and blocking the way to the end of the beach.

Nimitz was back in Makalapa in time for the opening of the new Towers Pool, named for Admiral Towers because, as Nimitz wrote Catherine, "He was the driving force behind the idea. The pool was a much-needed exercise and recreational facility for the five hundred plus young officers in this immediate area." Nimitz gave the Walkers a photo of himself smiling, despite his cold, next to a grim-looking Admiral Towers with a cigarette dangling from his mouth.

Photo of Nimitz and Towers at Opening of Towers Pool, Makalapa, December 3, 1944[288]

That evening, the Walkers celebrated Matty and Stanley Kennedy's twenty-fifth wedding anniversary with a dinner-dance. Nimitz was invited, but wrote his wife that his cold "was a help, in a way, because" it allowed him to decline the invitation and avoid "many callers at my office today, thus letting me make much progress on my work."

He enjoyed a quiet evening "with only McMorris and Anderson" while enjoying "Brahms # 2 & 3." [289]

On Monday and Tuesday, Nimitz was still sick and, against character, remained in bed. To Catherine, he wrote that his "cold has advanced to the wet nose & laryngitis stage—but I am well cared for & so far have no fever." (However, he dutifully penned his initials on war summaries in *Graybook*.)

Una called Nimitz to say she was stopping by with gifts from her garden to cheer him up. She arrived at 37 Makalapa Tuesday afternoon with a cache of flowers and fruit, as Nimitz noted in a letter to Catherine. Una was not one to dote on ailments and would have drawn from her eternal pool of optimism and good will to humor her friend.

In the Western Pacific, the submarine USS *Gunnel* (SS 253), operating in the home waters of Japan, sunk a Japanese passenger-cargo ship, the *Hiyoshi Maru*. The commanding officer of the submarine was a young Lt. Cdr. John S. McCain, Jr., son of a vice admiral and father of a future Vietnam War POW and U.S. Senator, John McCain, III. The young commanding officer would later be promoted to a four-star admiral and, from 1968 to 1972, succeed Nimitz not only as Commander in Chief, Pacific Command, but also as a close friend of the Walkers and a frequent weekend guest at Muliwai.*

---

* This author chatted with Admiral McCain at Muliwai many times. A man's man, McCain was ruggedly handsome and outspoken and puffed on cigars while drinking on the Muliwai lanai. A subject never mentioned was his son's incarceration as a POW. It must have always been difficult commanding the Pacific forces bombing the North Vietnamese, who held

Michael A. Lilly

That Thursday was the third anniversary of the attack on Pearl Harbor and Sandy and Una's wedding anniversary. Sandy and Una attended an early morning Catholic Mass at Pearl Harbor ("At least 5000 service men" attended, Nimitz wrote Catherine) and War Bond rally at the Navy Yard, where Nimitz gave a speech reporting that every Japanese aircraft carrier that participated in the attack on Pearl Harbor was sent to Davy Jones' Locker—the "Happiest day" of Nimitz's life:

> *This date, the 7th of December, and this site, the Pearl Harbor Navy Yard are a fitting time and place for me to tell you that all six of the Japanese aircraft carriers that opened this war by attacking us here three years ago now lie on the bottom of the sea.*
>
> *Of these six, we got four—the KAGA, the AKAGI the SORYU and the HIRYU—in the decisive battle of Midway on the 4th and 5th of June, 1942.*
>
> *That was four down and two to go. ... We got a good bite into the SHOKAKU in the Battle of the Coral Sea in May 1942. We got another bite in the battle of Santa Cruz in October 1942. Then, for 20 long months, we patiently waited. Finally in the First Battle of the Philippines Sea on the 19th and 20th of June this year—she was sent to the bottom.*
>
> *That left ZUIKAKU, the pride of the Japanese Navy. ... It took nearly three years to bring her to book. ... Finally, on the 25th of October, just six weeks ago, our Third Fleet caught the ZUIKAKU northeast of Luzon. The sea is just three miles deep where she lies on the bottom.* [*][290]

---

his son captive. McCain made no secret of his distaste for Vietnam War protesters, once publicly giving them a one-finger salute in Waikiki.

[*] Nimitz's speech can be watched at:
https://www.youtube.com/watch?v=6n4nEA-x4sU

Nimitz "speaks so charmingly," Una's diary recorded.

Catherine gave a similar speech at Pacific Grove, California. "My speech," Nimitz admitted to his wife, "is not as good as yours by a long shot." [291]

Afterward, the Walkers and Nimitz attended a luncheon with [Rear] Adm. [John Dale] Pride who was involved in making the still-secret atom bomb. That evening, the Walkers celebrated their wedding anniversary at a dinner hosted by Nimitz in Makalapa.

Nimitz lamented that he had been besieged for days on end by congressional delegations, military leaders and dignitaries and that "if they are as weary as I am they will sleep hard tonight." [292] On December 10th, he wrote Catherine that "I have finally enjoyed a reduction in numbers of visitors," giving him a "three (3) day respite" before the next deluge. Until the end of the month, "I will be visited to death." He sarcastically concluded, "The Japs are not the worst of my troubles." [293]

That evening, the Walkers dined at Makalapa with Nimitz and several Waves, including Lt. Winifred R. Quick and Lt. Cdr. Eleanor G. Rigby (no relation to the Beatles' song). Waves was the acronym for Women Accepted for Volunteer Emergency Services program enacted in 1942 for women to serve in the U.S. Navy during the war. In 1944, Congress allowed Waves to serve overseas in non-combatant roles. Rigby and Quick were the first two women ordered to Hawai'i. Quick, supervised arrangements to accommodate forty-five hundred Waves expected in the following months, including a Quonset hut-city with Chapel, mess hall, open-air movie, several recreational halls, tennis courts, ship's service store and access to swimming pools. [294]

Rigby eventually commanded three hundred fifty officers and over three thousand enlisted Waves in Hawai'i. Nimitz earlier wrote Catherine that he was inviting the Walkers to meet Rigby and Quick along with other "Honolulu people to maintain a friendly interest" in them. [295]

Over dinner that evening, they discussed preparations for the upcoming influx of Waves in Hawai'i, beginning early January.

Nimitz played Brahms 3rd Symphony for his dinner guests, which Una described as very nice!

"The Walkers," Nimitz wrote to Catherine, "thoroughly enjoyed" meeting the Wave officers.[296] But Nimitz also needed the Walkers that evening as a buffer because, as a rule, he did not care for women in the war zone or even in uniform and would have prohibited Waves from Hawai'i altogether, except that Congress had mandated it.[297]

On Thursday, December 14th, the *Honolulu Advertiser* reported, "Admiral Nimitz tonight announced that he would soon establish headquarters in the forward area in order to be nearer the actual fighting zones in the war against Japan."

In fact, he was preparing to move to the island of Guam, a location that was to remain secret; but Nimitz lamented to Catherine that "The news leaked out about my advance H.Q. in Guam."[298] Nimitz was referring to the page 1 article of the previous evening's *Honolulu StarBulletin* headlined, "Nimitz Moving To Guam." The news was leaked by an Australian radio dispatch from Guam.

The announcement was sad news to the Walkers, but not a word of it appears in Una's diary. Rather, she proudly recorded that the Most Reverend James Sweeney, Honolulu's Catholic Bishop, presented Nimitz with an honorary Doctor of Laws (*Legum Doctoratum*) from Fordham University in New York City. The actual date of the degree was the anniversary of Pearl Harbor and the Walker's wedding anniversary, December 7th.

Afterwards, Nimitz, Doc and Lamar celebrated his Doctorate over dinner at the Walkers' home. The conversation may have included the planned move to a secret forward headquarters. On a cheerier note, they would soon learn that, earlier that day, Congress had approved a new rank of Fleet Admiral of the United States Navy with five stars—the highest grade attainable in the Navy—which would be officially awarded to Nimitz by President Roosevelt on December 19th.

On Saturday, December 16th, Nimitz and Lamar stopped by

the Walkers' Nu'uanu home on their way to meet the arrival of the newly-assigned Commander in Chief British Pacific Fleet, Bruce Fraser, who was fifty-six at the time. In late November Nimitz had sent Fraser a "Most Secret" message that he would be "Delighted to have you as my guest at Pearl Harbor," which he had accepted. Fraser arrived with a party of twelve, including two Wrens—the Women's Royal Naval Service. Nine months later, Fraser would sign the Japanese Instrument of Surrender on behalf of the United Kingdom.

Ignoring storm warnings, on December 18th, Halsey directed his Task Force 38, comprising thirteen carriers, eight battleships, fifteen cruisers and fifty destroyers, into what became the massive *Typhoon Cobra,* about three hundred miles east of Luzon in the Philippine Sea. Three destroyers capsized and sank. Other ships were heavily damaged. Dozens of airplanes were destroyed. Almost eight hundred servicemen lost their lives. A court of inquiry held Halsey responsible, although his errors of judgment oddly did not amount to professional negligence. Alluding to Halsey, Nimitz later wrote a confidential memorandum that some commanding officers remained on station too long. That event delayed and nearly cost Halsey his fifth star.

December 19th "was quite the longest day" Nimitz had had "in many months," he wrote Catherine at 11:00 p.m., because he had been promoted to Fleet Admiral.[299] (At first it was uncertain whether Nimitz would continue to wear only four stars or would add a fifth star. Sometime between December 19 and the next day approval for a fifth star was given and Lamar commissioned sailors to fashion the pentagon insignia from those of lesser flag ranks.) Nimitz received many congratulations, including one that day in a dispatch from the British Chiefs of Staff.

That evening, the Walkers and Nimitz celebrated his promotion over dinner. A "very nice party," Una noted.

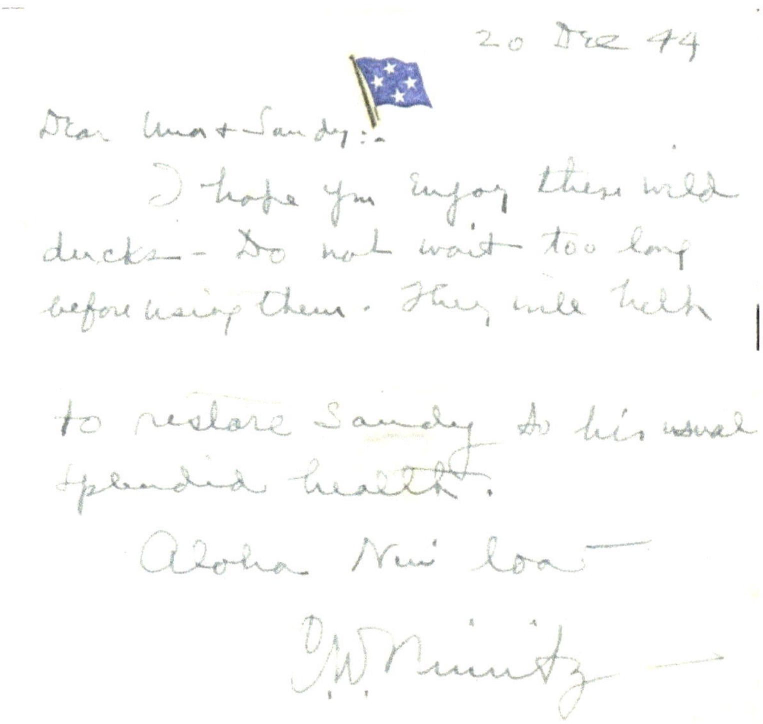

Michael A. Lilly

[Handwritten note:]

20 Dec 44

Dear Una & Sandy:—

I hope you enjoy these wild ducks — Do not wait too long before using them. They will help to restore Sandy to his usual splendid health.

Aloha Nui loa —

C.W. Nimitz —

Nimitz Note to the Walkers, December 20, 1944

The next day, Nimitz, Lamar and Doc called to say they had opened their Christmas stockings early, including the Walkers' regular gift of homemade Mango Chutney, but sadly that they were bidding, adieu. Nimitz and Lamar were flying to the Western Pacific for a tour. Meanwhile, Sandy had come down with a cold and was not feeling well. In response, Nimitz sent him a present of "Wild ducks" with a note, hoping they would "restore Sandy to his usual splendid health. Aloha nui loa, C.W. Nimitz."

On Thursday, December 21st, Nimitz, Sherman and Lamar left for the west to meet with MacArthur in Leyte to confer about the invasion of Luzon. MacArthur, who was also promoted to a five-star General but had not received the insignia of that rank, was

Nimitz at Ease

instantly irked,[300] when he spotted Nimitz's pentagon of stars. He ordered his staff to fashion a set for him by morning. They did.

Nimitz was in his seaplane returning to Pearl Harbor, landing on December 30th at 10:30 a.m. Had he been with the Walkers the night before, he would have joined them in watching an ethereal Penumbral Lunar Eclipse, as the moon passed through the Earth's shadow.

Despite his exhaustion after flying more than five thousand miles, Nimitz immediately drove to Muliwai, where he had his "First exercise for days—walked—swam & looked for Jap fisherman balls but found none." [301]

With the final chapters of the war in the Pacific before him, after dining, dancing, and playing poker at the Walkers, Nimitz trudged up the familiar path to the cottage on the bluff over the ocean and turned in early to peaceful ocean sounds below. The afternoon swim had helped stretch out the knots from his long journey.

Next to the bed in which Nimitz lay were a large five-band shortwave radio with oversized dials and a familiar row of books—a collection of Shakespeare's plays, the recently published, *Legends of Old Hawaii*, a 1904 edition of the *Rubáiyát of Omar Khayyám*, Don Blanding's poems in *Vagabond's House*, William White's 1942 best seller, *They Were Expendable* (the gripping story of MacArthur's evacuation from Corregidor), and Agnes Newton Keith's delightful, *Land Below the Wind* (recounting her life as a wife of a British government official in remote Borneo in the 1930s).

How many times had Nimitz tried picking up one of those books to read over the previous three years, only to succumb to the Sandman? Muliwai brought him needed rest that eluded him at the Makalapa helm.

Michael A. Lilly

Sunrise from Nimitz's cottage

The last morning of 1944, Nimitz and the Walkers awoke to a brilliant Muliwai sunrise at 7:10 a.m. The sun transformed the grays of night to tinges of gold followed by brilliant rays setting the entire horizon ablaze. The air was still and cool, Una's favorite La'ie weather—"winter Kona"—which she told Nimitz was delicious. All night the temperature had dipped to the low sixties, perfect sleeping weather. With not the slightest breeze or cloud in the heavens, the green Ko'olau Mountains drew a pencil-line against azure skies. Takeo was busy picking up leaves, smiling and nodding to Nimitz, as he emerged wearing only his floral bathing suit. "Top O' the morning, Chester," greeted the ever-cheerful Sandy.

The gang zigzagged through the barbed-wire strands and passed the obsolete guard post for an early walk and swim. Afterward, Nimitz showered and dressed in the cottage and ate breakfast," cooked by Hara in the main house before departing for Pearl Harbor and his cherished 10:00 a.m. symphony broadcast refreshed and relaxed.[302]

Sandy and Una returned to Nu'uanu for lunch, but according

to plan were back with Nimitz again at Makalapa by 6:00 p.m.

For Christmas 1944, Nimitz inscribed this whimsical painting of Santa Clause over the Statue of Liberty by John R. Ellerbusch to the Gremlins, writing: "To Maile and Sheila – Since you left Honolulu, I have let my beard grow – and will continue to do so until you come back. This is a picture of me at ten pm today and I expect to see you tomorrow at 7 am. CW Nimitz – Admiral USN." *

They walked half a block from Nimitz's quarters to tour the new

---

* This painting led the author as a young child to believe Nimitz was Santa Claus.

Towers Pool for the first time, had dinner and opened Christmas presents. Nimitz gave the Walkers a painting of Santa Clause over the Statue of Liberty to be passed on to the Gremlins. Ambassador Grew had left Una a picture of "Japan." Una gave Nimitz a handsome colored print of a Hawaiian on a Surf Board.

Sandy gave Nimitz a glass pitcher for mixing martinis, on which he had a pentagon of five stars etched.[303] The Walkers' maid and butler, Matsuko and Sueki Goto, gave him two sleeping coats, one silk and one cotton, which he later had embroidered with five stars. With gifts in hand, the Walkers, tired from a long weekend and a late night, drove home.

Thus ended Una's 1944 diary. The first page of Una's missing diary for 1945, no doubt, began with the words, "Still at War!"

Chapter 19

1945: Path to Victory

THE YEAR 1944 ended with the war still raging in the Western Pacific, as well as in Europe. Though there were glimmers of hope for an end, many military strategists thought Japan could not be defeated without invading its homeland, which would be a bloody contest. The Office of War Information predicted that it would take "An absolute minimum of one and a half to two years after the defeat of Germany to defeat Japan"—perhaps, not until 1947.[304]

At the start of 1945, the consensus was that Japan's "Defeat will not be easy or speedy." [305] Nimitz said hopefully, "It will definitely end before 1946 ends." [306]

No one had an inkling that Germany would surrender in only four months, followed by Japan on September 2, 1945, on the 0-1deck of the *Missouri*.

By January 1945, most of the Allied Pacific island-hopping campaigns were successfully completed. After two and a half years of brutal Japanese occupation and the victories of the Battles of the Philippine Sea, the Philippine Islands were nearly secure. Thousands of abused and emaciated POWs were liberated from camps all over the Western Pacific. Iwo Jima and Okinawa were the last major enemy bastions remaining, before the Allies could mount an invasion of the Japanese homeland. Based on losses suffered in securing Okinawa, estimates of Allied casualties from such an invasion were up to a million. Because "Okinawa had been so bloody," Nimitz wanted to avoid it. He feared that "We'd have to kill even women and children, for they would try to defend to the last man, woman and child!" [307]

On January 6th, to Nimitz's chagrin, over two hundred Wave officers and enlisted, wearing summer uniforms of gray and white seersucker and newly-authorized garrison caps, filed down the gangplank of a transport in Pearl Harbor. Greeting them was Lieutenant Commander Rigby, 14th Naval District Director of Waves, whom the Walkers had met over dinner at Nimitz's quarters the previous month.

That evening, Nimitz, Lamar, Doc Anderson, the Milnors ate fish chowder at the Walkers, followed by poker. "I was tremendously lucky," wrote Nimitz, "in this 1½ hours of poker. With 10¢ chips—(2 chips limit) I won $21.00—winning both high and low—in two large pots." [308]

As was often the case at Makalapa, Nimitz read dispatches at his headquarters before retiring at 11:00 p.m.

January saw MacArthur's force of about a hundred thousand soldiers discharge from eight hundred troop ships onto Luzon. Supported by air and naval forces, they pressed toward Manila, although Nimitz complained to Catherine that he always got his "first information about MacA's operations ashore from the newspapers." [309]

Surface and air forces continued to batter Iwo Jima from which the *Graybook* reported, "Enemy air opposition was feeble." [310] Nimitz announced that the Third Fleet's carrier planes were bombing Formosa and Okinawa. U.S. submarines sunk their first aircraft carrier and scores of other ships. And B-29 Superfortresses from the Marianas and China hammered Japanese bases in Singapore and Japan.

Suicide planes continued to harass U.S. ships. The carrier USS

Nimitz at Ease

Ommaney Bay (CVE 79), operating in the Sulu Sea, was so badly damaged by a *Kamikaze* that she had to be sunk by torpedoes from one of our destroyers on January 4th.[311] Navy Ens. Clarence "Spike" Borley was flying from the USS *Essex* (CV 9) near Formosa, when he shot down four Japanese fighters before his Hellcat was mortally hit. While floating in the water wearing his "Mae West" life preserver, two Japanese in a sampan tried to capture him. Spike pulled out his .38-caliber service revolver and dispatched them. The hero was rescued five days later. (Seventy years later he was awarded the Congressional Medal of Honor!)

In movie theaters, audiences watched the color documentary, *Fighting Lady,* narrated by popular actor, Lt. Robert Taylor, U.S. Naval Reserve. The film used actual war footage to chronicle the story of an aircraft carrier (later revealed as the USS *Yorktown* [CV 10]) from her initial cruise through her action at Kwajalein, Truk and the Marianas.

At the end of the movie, Taylor says, "Battles we have fought on the sea and in the sky were only the beginning. Still hungry for battle[,] we'll steam our carrier, serene, powerful, unafraid. She and her planes will come home again someday, God grant. But not until the bitter, glorious end. For she is, and we salute her, the *Fighting Lady*."

The Walkers, Nimitz, and Lamar watched the movie together after dinner in the Makalapa outdoor theater and agreed with Soc McMorris, who called it "The finest motion picture concerning the war yet made." [312] Nimitz praised the movie in his January 1, 1945, letter to his wife Catherine, writing, "It should be a 'must' for all good Americans."

Sailors surveyed worldwide, however, preferred movies in the following order: Musicals with girls (Judy Garland in *Meet me in St. Louis*); comedies with girls (Abbott & Costello in *Here Come the Co-Eds*); dramas with girls (Frederick March in *Tomorrow the World*); and mysteries with girls (the *Thin Man* series with William Powell and Myrna Loy). What they did not care for were war films and old newsreels.[313]

Michael A. Lilly

In Honolulu, twenty-two hundred service members filled Furlong Stadium for the Poi Bowl football game. The Navy All Stars won the championship of the Pacific Ocean Areas when they routed the Army Air Force, 14 to 0. The Walkers and Nimitz were likely in attendance.

With his departure for Guam set for January 26th, Nimitz's remaining days on O'ahu were whirlwinds of parties, swimming, hikes, poker and packing.

On January 10th, the Walkers gave Lamar a surprise birthday party, with presents from lovely young Honolulu girls.[314] Two days later Nimitz was at Muliwai for his first swim and much-needed exercise in ten days. For dinner, "We had fish chowder [and] outdoor cooked steaks."

Nimitz's contribution was an apple pie baked by Ramirez. After a good night's sleep, he had a swim and walk, in which he picked up four more Jap fisherman balls and now had six to add to Catherine's collection.[315] He was back at headquarters in time for the classical music broadcast.

On January 19th, Nimitz donned his new Guam khaki uniform—garrison "fore-n-aft" cap, khaki shirt but not tie, khaki shorts and khaki belt, long hose (Boy Scout—cotton) and rough, tan hiking shoes, which he wore on a two-hour hike to Aiea Hospital and back.[316]

While Nimitz was on his long walk, Hanko experienced one of those serendipitous moments of life. While Hanko was in naval Communications School at Harvard, Nimitz told him that his "Grades were good enough that [he] could be assured of getting any billet [he] should request," and directed [him] to apply for the Pacific Officer's Pool at Pearl Harbor and said he would then personally handle [Hanko's] further assignment.[317] Hanko had done well, made the application and was dutifully assigned and ordered to depart to Hawai'i via the West Coast.

Awaiting ship transportation to Pearl Harbor from San Francisco, a wait that was expected to last six weeks or more, Hanko was walking up Powell Street, when he ran into none other than McMorris, Nimitz's Chief of Staff.

"Henry Walker! What are you doing here?"

Hanko replied, "Awaiting transportation to Pearl Harbor, Sir."

McMorris ordered him to "Be in this hotel at nine o'clock tonight and I'll take you out in one of Nimitz's flag planes, the Blue Goose,* a Douglass C-54 Skymaster."

Hanko, who had been in town for only twelve hours and who was looking forward to several weeks of idle pleasure in San Francisco, muttered "But, Sir…"

"No buts," replied McMorris sternly.[318]

Departing from Alameda Naval Air Station, the trip took thirteen hours, before landing on the waters of Keehi Lagoon in Honolulu.[319] Nimitz and the Walkers, alerted to his return, were on the dock to greet him.

That evening, everyone gathered at Muliwai for a reunion. Nimitz arrived in time to have a good swim and supper—and an hour of poker, the entire winnings of which ($8.75) were donated to eight-day-old Mary Higuchi—the newly arrived daughter of the Caretaker (Mr. and Mrs. Takeo Higuchi).[320]

Over dinner, Nimitz told Hanko, "How fortunate I was to have encountered Adm. McMorris just after my arrival in San Francisco, so that no time had to be wasted waiting to get my ship." Hanko continued, "I detected a twinkle in his eye, as he spoke."[321]

While Hanko had privately hoped for liberty in San Francisco, Nimitz described his quick return as "much to Henry's delight."[322]

That was Nimitz's last weekend at Muliwai before leaving for Guam.

On January 24, 1945, the Walkers hosted a farewell dinner for Nimitz, Lamar, and Doc Anderson and an hour or so of poker afterwards.[323] Hanko, wrote Nimitz, "was to be included in the farewell, but his orders to a ship required him to start moving this

---

* Nimitz had several flag planes—the "Pink Lady"; the "Gray Goose"; and the "Blue Goose"—all named for the color of their upholstery.

morning. I have never seen a young officer so radiantly happy."

The commanding officer of the Battleship *Missouri*, Capt. William M. Callaghan, had expressly asked for Hanko's assignment.

Before departing for Guam, Nimitz gave the Walkers another photograph of himself and inscribed, "To Una and Sandy, With great aloha, C.W. Nimitz, Fleet Admiral, USN."

"Great Aloha" from Nimitz to the Walkers

He also issued a War Bond certificate to Maile (Major Gremlin) for her investment "in this country's fight for human liberty and a contributor in a world struggle to make life free and forever peaceful for all men."

A colorful chain of Disney cartoon characters, including Snow White's seven dwarfs and Mickey Mouse encircled the certificate.

War Bond for Maile (Major Gremlin) by Nimitz

He thanked Una "and all the members of the Surgical Dressing Group" for their "loyal support of the Naval Service" for "three and one-half years." He was deeply appreciative that in "The last six months more than three million dressings have been provided"—a "Notable achievement."

The wheels of Nimitz's primary flag plane, the Pink Lady, left the ground at 8:30 p.m. on January 26th, and, after a perfect flight, landed at Wake Island the next morning at 6:30 a.m. With a range of four thousand miles at a cruise speed of 190 miles per hour, he could have made it nonstop to Guam, but chose to land for breakfast with the atoll commander and fill up on fuel.[324]

Graybook recorded that "CinCPac and CinCPOA arrived Guam 27 January 1945."[325] Nimitz took *Graybook* with him, which henceforth noted each daily entry as "Guam Date." All war operations, except for activities east of Hawai'i, would be conducted from Guam.

Nimitz wrote the Walkers that he had "Arrived at our destination at noon." Departing from his plane, he spotted a familiar face, awaiting transit to the *Missouri* as its newest crewmember:

> *Who do you suppose I saw standing at the edge of the airfield as I jeeped away from my plane yesterday? Yes, it was none other than Hanko, who had to rub his eyes and look twice before he was willing to recognize me in the jeep. We had inquired about him at an Island stop on our way, intending to pick him up in case he had lost his priority by reason of somebody's dog. Henry looked to be in the best of spirits, and was to leave early this morning for his final destination, where no doubt he is now on board his ship.*

"We shall never forget," Nimitz wrote, alluding in part to weekends at Muliwai, "the wonderful hospitality and the many kindnesses of Una and Sandy to me and my mess, and we look forward to the time when we can again renew those pleasant associations."

He also thanked them also for "your martini mixer and your lovely ash trays which added greatly to the smart appearance of our house."

Ens. Henry A. "Hanko" Walker Jr. aboard USS Missouri (BB 63)

Nimitz's new quarters were a "Beautiful white clapboard cottage with four bedrooms and four baths, opening onto a square court with grass and flowers in the middle. We had a large living room-dining room and a long, screened porch right on the edge of a cliff overlooking the harbor.³²⁶ The view—both from the H.Q. administrative bldgs—and from the Quarters—is superb. We are almost eight hundred fifty feet above sea level and the air is cool and pleasant." ³²⁷

The gardens were, however, non-existent. Nearly "all of the coconut trees" and forests on Guam had been destroyed "during the heavy pre-invasion bombardment. Admiral Nimitz was very anxious to have the island reforested...." ³²⁸

Accordingly, Nimitz asked the Walkers to send him "any spare seeds of flowering trees, monkey pod trees, lichee nut seeds etc. that you may have."

The Walkers soon gathered trees, flowers, gingers, orchids—both seeds and seedlings—and loaded them aboard the regular flag plane from Pearl.

Before the advent of bottled soda water, special bottles were charged with CO_2 "Sparklet" cartridges, creating seltzer or soda water. (Children watching the Howdy Doody TV show in the 1950s laughed as *Clarabell the Clown* squirted fellow actors from seltzer water bottles.) Among the items the Walkers gave Nimitz when he left for his western headquarters were soda water bottles and a supply of cartridges. On January 30th, Lamar wrote that they "Had guests for dinner every night so far and the thing that pleases everyone the most is the 'soda water'. The bottle makes [seltzer] beautifully and the water has all the pep the Admiral wants. Thanks again for your assistance in this direction."

He lamented, however, that they could not make Nimitz's favorite "old fashion since we have neither oranges nor cherries." The Walkers soon accommodated him.

On February 2nd, Nimitz flew by seaplane to Ulithi Atoll, where he boarded Spruance's flagship, the heavy cruiser USS *Indianapolis* (CA 35), on which he "broke his flag."* Ulithi had been a Japanese radio and weather station before liberation in 1944. Tony Lilly's ship stopped at its lagoon, which he described as "a vast anchorage." Nimitz returned to Guam two days later.

On February 6th, Nimitz wrote that he had received a report of someone who had been aboard the Battleship USS *Missouri* (BB 63) and described Hanko as "extremely happy and cheerful."

Nimitz's new quarters at his still-undisclosed location were very comfortably established. Outside, Nimitz built a horseshoe court, which he was going to try that afternoon—"if I can find an opponent." Enclosed in the envelope were pictures of his new

---

* Seven months later, the *Indianapolis* would deliver critical parts of the first atomic bomb to Tinian Island.

quarters and grounds. His salutation reminisced their wonderful times together, including Muliwai:

> We shall not soon forget...the many lovely times we spent with you both in Nu'uanu and at Muliwai, and those good times will always be the high spots of our Hawaiian experiences. This does not mean that we are never coming back to Hawai'i. On the contrary, you will see us many times.

In a letter dated the same day, Lamar revealed who Nimitz's first horseshoe opponent was that day.

"This afternoon we didn't take the usual two-hour hike and instead I was the Admiral's partner at horseshoes in the first game played on his new court. Of course, he beat me badly and produced a number of ringers just to make me feel badly." Lamar closed, "We miss the Walkers, Muliwai and Nuuanu very much."

He included photos of Nimitz's Guam quarters. On the back of one photo, Lamar drew in pen the horseshoe court and its orientation to the quarters and the sea.

Nimitz also recreated his shooting range at Guam, enlisting anyone and everyone to join him at target practice, including his intelligence chief, Edwin T. Layton, with whom he practiced daily with Colt .45s, until they departed for the surrender ceremonies.[329] Since he had no marine orderly, Layton doubled as security for the Fleet Admiral.

"There we practiced with Colt .45s every day until we left for Japan," where Layton followed Nimitz ashore carrying a heavy pistol in a shoulder holster.[330]

Michael A. Lilly

To the Surgical Dressing Group of the Honolulu Chapter, American Red Cross with best wishes and great appreciation of your outstanding contribution to the war effort in the Pacific Ocean Areas.
—**CW Nimitz, Fleet Admiral, USN**

On February 9th, Nimitz dispatched to the Walkers "a photograph of myself in blue," addressed to the Surgical Dressing Group of the Hawai'i Red Cross. Nimitz and his staff had flown to be with Spruance for two days. Doc saw young Henry several times, reporting, "He is extremely happy and cheerful, and has begun to acquire some suntan to counteract that 'life under a board look.'"

Nimitz had no worries about Hanko "Because he is not only in good hands, but is extremely pleased to be with [Captain William M.] Callaghan. I have every confidence that Henry will soon be pulling his weight in the boat."

Una (Center, back) & Her Surgical Dressing Corps, Walker Estate, March 1945

Chapter 20

"Guam Bombed!"

THE UNITED PRESS finally reported on February 14th that Nimitz had "today lifted the secrecy covering the location," and disclosed his new headquarters were in Guam to be "nearer the scene of air and naval action now raging in the enemy's front yard."

Lamar dispatched a letter that day. "All of us will be thinking about Sandy on the 19th and will drink a special 'old fashion' toast in his honor." Meanwhile, the flag plane landed from Pearl with "two boxes of fancy cocktail napkins and matches and one box of paper coasters." He thanked the Walkers for "these welcome and necessary presents."

Aboard the *Missouri* in the South Pacific, Hanko served as a communications officer. Because of the Walkers' close relationship with Admiral Spruance, Hanko, among the most junior ensigns in the entire U.S. Navy, was invited to accompany the Captain of *Missouri* for dinner aboard Spruance's flagship, the *Indianapolis*. Before departing *Missouri*, Hanko rushed to decode recent radio messages, one of which was in "Airplane Mode," a complex process.

"As best I could make out, the code message I was deciphering indicated that Guam had been bombed." Hanko was shocked, realizing Nimitz had just returned from Ulithi to Guam when it was bombed, but had no time to tell anyone. Later, sitting at Spruance's elegant flag mess dining table, around which Filipino stewards in white jackets circulated with platters of food, he needed to unburden himself of the dire message. Leaning over to a Captain next to him, he reported, "Sir, before leaving *Missouri* I deciphered a message that Guam had been bombed."

"Guam bombed?" the perplexed Captain replied. "That's really bad news!"

The Captain turned to Admiral Spruance. "Sir, did you know that Ensign Walker decoded a message that Guam has been bombed?"

"Guam bombed?" an anxious Spruance replied. "No, I know nothing about it."

Spruance summoned his fleet communications officer, a Captain Stone. "Stone," Spruance commanded, "Break radio silence and find out what the damage may be to Guam. Walker here says a message was received on his ship that Guam was bombed."

"Guam bombed?" replied a shocked Captain Stone. "First I heard of it. I'll find out immediately, Sir."

Returning a few minutes later with a puzzled expression on his face, Stone said, "Admiral, Guam most definitely has not been bombed. Oh, there was a Japanese intruder that flew nearby last night, but they quickly scared him off and certainly no damage was done."

After a stony silence, a relieved four-star Admiral Spruance turned to the junior ensign of the Navy's Pacific Fleet and, before a table surrounded by senior officers, remonstrated, "Henry, I think your communication skills need polishing." [331]

"In the boldest challenge of the Pacific war," went the *Stars and Stripes* issue of February 17, 1945, "An estimated 1,500" warplanes from Spruance's Fifth Fleet struck Tokyo. Nimitz had "sent the most powerful fleet in the Navy's history to within 300 miles of Japan." Nimitz described it in a wire to the entire Pacific command as "A crushing blow which will long be remembered."

Nimitz wrote the Walkers, "Congratulations to both of you on having a veteran son in your family. Hanko participated in the heavy air strikes on Tokyo—16 & 17 Feb (your 15 and 16 Feb) and is now a veteran." Nimitz envied "him the active participation in these interesting operations which are continuing with little pause from now on." And Hanko "will have much to talk about when you next see him—and much to be proud of after the war."

Meanwhile, Nimitz somewhat lamented being "back here in the safe rear area [where] life runs along smoothly, and we have settled into a routine of work—food—exercise—sleep (and) their repeat. Our horseshoe court is in commission and is used frequently."

Nimitz and company "...usually assemble for old fashioned at 6:30 p.m. on our lanai—with its wonderful view over the western Pacific—and your cocktail napkins and coasters (and) matches are in daily use. However—we do not need these material things to remind us of the Walkers and their wonderful hospitality."

Nimitz and Staff on Guam Quarter's Lanai: Soc McMorris (2nd from left), Nimitz, Lamar, Forrest Sherman, Brig. Gen. H.C. Mandell, and Doc Anderson[332]

That day, a lone U.S. minesweeper, surveying the coast of Iwo Jima, withdrew when fired on by artillery ashore. Tokyo's radio reported, "The enemy attempted landings," which their "defense garrison promptly repulsed." While that false information was published, the actual Allied invasion was launched. *Graybook* recorded that Iwo Jima was free of "underwater obstacles" and the beach "suitable for all types of landing craft." [333] Minesweepers found no mines.

"No bigger than a comma on the map," began *All Hands* magazine, "Iwo Jima flamed into a giant exclamation mark in the headlines," when the "U.S. Marines were landed by the Navy on the volcanic dot on 18 February and planted the American flag within waving distance of the Jap homeland." [334]

Graybook recorded that the landings "were carried out as scheduled following intense naval gunfire and air bombardment." While the landings went well, the forces immediately met the first of what became repeated fierce counterattacks by artillery, tanks, and suicidal squads. Iwo would not be secure for over a month of bitter fighting. America would lose 6,800 to Japan's 18,800. Una's surgical dressing corps cancelled everything "to fill a rush order for 5,000 face masks for marines who were being choked to death by the volcanic dust of Iwo Jima." [335]

The next day, Nimitz wrote in long hand, "Congratulations and many happy returns to Sandy on his [sixtieth] birthday, which comes today (our date) and tomorrow (your date)."

Lamar added, "We drank our toast to Sandy and all the mess wished him well."

In honor of Nimitz's 60th birthday, the Walkers loaded the next flag plane from Pearl Harbor with birthday gifts. Lamar wrote he had difficulty keeping Nimitz from opening the presents. On February 24th, with ground forces on Iwo Jima reporting a relatively quiet night, Nimitz thanked the Walkers for their presents—"the lovely Kalakaua covered bowl, the wooden sandwich tray and bowls, the glass balls, the handsome swim outfit, and the bath mitt." He said he was "overwhelmed by your generosity."

Lamar wrote that his Filipino steward, Ramirez, baked a "Monumental creation [cake] highlighted by a globe of the world in sugar which will be illuminated by flashlight from the inside." A five-star flag flew from its apex. Hal hoped "We can give the boss a cheery day, but it won't be like a party with the Walkers." (Pictures of the cake and steward were included in the letter to the Walkers.)

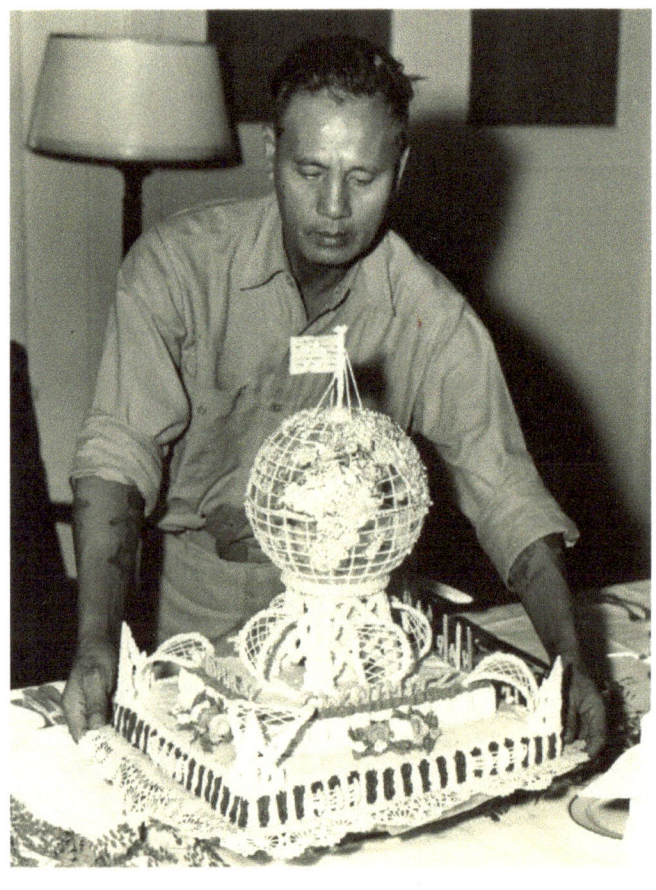

Nimitz's Steward, Ramirez, with the Cake he spent a Week Preparing for Nimitz's 60th birthday, Guam

Nimitz at Ease

Nimitz noted the reports of the *Missouri* from which "You can readily surmise what a wonderful experience young Henry had, dashing around the ocean just south of Tokyo." Nimitz then described a recent photograph of himself pointing with a swagger cane Sandy had given him that appeared on page 1 of the February 20, 1945 issue of the *Honolulu StarBulletin*:

> You have no doubt seen in the newspaper a photograph of me pointing to Tokyo on the chart with a short pointer. I am sorry the newspaper photograph did not give you the details of that pointer, because it was your [Sandy's] swagger cane.

The next day, he penned another letter, thanking the Walkers for "the four handsome trees, the litchi, fig, pomelo, and naval orange" for which he was "most agreeably surprised." The Walkers continued loading seedlings, presents and provisions on the flag plane from Hawai'i to Guam, which Nimitz continued to plant everywhere around the devastated Guam.

The birthday letters between Nimitz and the Walkers were exchanged during intense fighting on Iwo Jima, summarized in gritty detail in *Graybook*. Japanese defenses were "Expertly planned and fanatically defended," with four-foot-thick concrete pillboxes and blockhouses providing "mutually supporting" and murderous crossfire. Enemy infiltrations during the nights were repulsed.

By the 26th, against "stubborn resistance," it was reported that American "Troops occupy the most important terrain," commanding the "high ground" from which they can "observe the entire northern part of the island." When American troops confiscated a 300,000 gallon-per-day desalination plant on March 4th, captured Japanese soldiers reported having only rainwater in barrels to drink. The commander of the Japanese defense force had previously ordered that any water not "removed to the rear" be poisoned "with hydrocyanic acid." Marine divisions reported high morale with "reserves adequate to complete the mission of capturing Iwo Jima." By the 14th, *Graybook* recorded that the "backbone of the enemy appears to have been broken." [336]

Meanwhile, Tony Lilly wired Ginger from Guam *not* to marry Alfred Wright, but to wait for him. Somehow, from half way around the world, they arranged to meet below the clock in the Biltmore Hotel in New York, a common rendezvous spot. But Ginger had a long wait. Tony traveled by plane from Guam to Kwajalein to Pearl Harbor to San Francisco, where he boarded a train. He stopped in Kentucky to see his father. On the train again to Chicago, a snowstorm delayed him for six hours. Ginger paced back and forth in New York below the clock waiting for him, getting more and more exasperated by the hour. They nearly missed one another forever, but, in one of those rare moments of chance, came face to face below the clock.

"By the time I got there, Ginger was quite put out with me, first for going to Kentucky and second because I was late." Tony added with a wry smile, "But, all's well that ends well."

Two weeks later, on March 18th, they were married in Lee, Massachusetts, with Ginger's sister Ann, the Gremlins and nanny, Tamiye, in attendance.

On March 1st, Nimitz, Sherman and Lamar had departed Guam for Pearl Harbor with ultimate destination Washington D.C., to meet with Fleet Admiral King and President Roosevelt about the war in the Pacific. While in D.C., Nimitz and his wife Catherine attended the marriage of their daughter Catherine Vance ("Kate") to Cdr. James Lay.

During the weekend of March 3rd, Lamar made his way from Washington to New York City, where Ginger reported that he and Ann went to the Hawaiian Room of the Lexington Hotel. The Hawaiian Room and its South Sea motif had become one of the most popular restaurants in America, since it opened in 1937.[337] Ginger gave Ann a pair of black suede flat evening shoes...to wear for the occasion. Ann "had been *terribly* excited the day before, and was all a-twitter afterwards, too. Hedy [Lamar] is a bit 'seriousish' about her! Ann had a lovely time." (As did the lovesick Lamar, who hated for their reunion to come to an end.)

With the war winding down in Hawai'i, Sandy's workload at American Factors became more demanding. Thus, on March 6th, after more than three years at the helm, he wrote to E.E. Black, Director of Civilian Defense, that, with "Increased pressure of work in connection with my regular duties as President and Manager of American Factors," he was submitting his "resignation as Director of the Office of Food Control and of the Office of Materials and Supplies." Sandy Enjoyed working with them for the last three years, but regretted that, "It now becomes necessary for me to terminate my services."

On March 12th, Black accepted Sandy's resignation "With regret," noting his "very sincere thanks for all the time and effort you have been generous enough to give the Offices of Civilian Defense," and how "greatly I appreciate the good work you have done." Black told reporters that "[Walker] did an excellent job in obtaining food for the territory." [338]

Fleet Admiral Nimitz, pilot and General of the Army Hap Arnold, and Superfortress B-29 bomber, Guam 1945[339]

Michael A. Lilly

On Nimitz's return flight, he stopped in Honolulu and spent a weekend at Muliwai with the Walkers. Nimitz convinced Sandy to return with him on the Pink Lady to Guam, landing on March 15th. Sandy and Nimitz fished from a fifteen-ton, forty-five foot Chris Craft cabin cruiser the Commanding General of the Army Air Forces had given Nimitz, who christened it "Catherine—for my sweetheart." [340]

Ever since Nimitz shifted to Guam, he and his staff wore khaki uniform shorts. But Sandy arrived in a suit and tie, shedding only the jacket and tie for fishing.

Lamar sent "Pictures of our fishing trip." One showed Sandy and Nimitz with a famous dramatist and then-Director of Overseas War Information, the mustachioed and towering six-foot eight Robert E. Sherwood.* Sherwood's craggy face mirrored Humphrey Bogart's snarling expression as the hardened criminal in the *film noir*, *Petrified Forest*, which was adapted from one of Sherwood's Broadway hits. He had been one of Nimitz's first guests in Guam the month before, when he consumed a number of Hal's old fashioneds before dinner. The year before, Sherwood had provided Nimitz and Delos Emmons with a propaganda leaflet they strewed over Japan by the thousands, warning that under the "Greater East Asia" banner, their military leaders had "betrayed all Japanese from the lowest to the highest in the realm and they have thought only of making names for themselves and their own personal desires." [341]

Joining them in a fedora was Sandy's old friend Walter Dillingham.

---

* Among Sherwood's screen credits were Hitchcock's thriller, *Rebecca*, and *The Best Years of Our Lives*, for which he received an Academy Award.

Sandy, Hal Lamar and Nimitz, Guam[342]

Playwright Robert E. Sherwood, Nimitz, Sandy and Walter Dillingham, Guam[343]

Lamar did not mention Sandy's success at fishing, but Nimitz hauled in a five-pound barracuda.

In the evenings, Sandy, Sherwood and Dillingham played cribbage with Gen. Holland "Howling Mad" Smith, beating him badly. Nimitz wrote that they "had great difficulty in collecting many cribbage winnings" from "Smith and his partner," for the "General is indeed a tough egg, either as a cribbage opponent or as a battle opponent, as the Japs well know."

Meanwhile, Nimitz said, "Spruance, Mitscher, and your son, Henry are giving the Japs merry H in the Western Pacific now, and my thoughts are constantly with them, as I know yours are, also. What a lot Henry will have to tell you when you see him again!"

Nimitz took his guests swimming. Sandy would have entered the water, but not swum far. However, the admiral struck out at a furious pace. Lamar never forgot Sherwood "nearly drowning trying to keep up with the Admiral's swimming."

The Battle for Iwo Jima ended on March 16th. Nimitz was still entertaining Sandy when he announced one of his most famous messages: "Among the Americans who served on Iwo Island uncommon valor was a common virtue." [344]

With Sandy still on Guam, Nimitz was planning *Operation Iceberg*—the invasion and conquest of Okinawa. *Kamikazes* hit the carrier USS *Franklin* (CV 13), Japanese ships were sunk, "Mopping up operations continued on Iwo Jima," and Nagoya was "bombed with incendiaries." [345] Nimitz wired subordinate commanders that because the "Emperor of Japan is not at present a liability" but "may later become an asset, his palace at Tokyo will not be attacked until further orders."

On March 21st Nimitz wrote Una that he "had no sooner seen Sandy safely on the plane for the return trip to Oahu than I succumbed to the cold I had been resisting ever since I left Washington recently." On the subject of the war, he was unusually candid:

> Early this morning I released the news of our last strikes in Kyushu and in the Inland Sea where our planes destroyed several hundred Japanese planes and also damaged some eighteen Japanese combatant ships. You may be sure that Henry had a front-line seat—not on the delivery end, but on the receiving end of that party,

> *as he undoubtedly saw many of the attacks that came in on our own fleet from Japanese planes. Although I have not specific information on the subject, I am positive that Henry himself is safe and that his ship, the lovely MOE, escaped injury. What a lot of exciting news Henry will be able to give you when you next see him!*

He also thanked them "for the fresh eggs, fern roots, and other plants which you have been sending. As it has rained every day since Sandy's departure, all of our plants are thriving." He said that he would appreciate "some more maiden-hair fern roots and some ginger roots when you have some available."

In another letter, he wrote, "In later years when you two visit Guam and see all of the fruit and flowering trees and nice plants, you can take great satisfaction in your share in this program."

Chapter 21

Una: "The Number 1 Exponent of Hawaiian Hospitality"

TEN DAYS AFTER seeing Sandy and Walter Dillingham off on his flag plane, it was Easter Sunday Eve. Sandy and Una had loaded the flag plane with a cache of Easter presents for his staff, including a pile of aloha shirts, orchids, scarves, and ginger roots for Nimitz's garden. "The orchids are doing well in their coconut husks, and so far the 'Miss Joaquin' [*vanda*] orchid outside is thriving, as are also the fern roots and the ginger roots."

Nimitz thanked them for gifts of *dendrobium* orchids and coconuts. "I have just learned from Hal that you have sent some colored Easter eggs for us to search for tomorrow – How kind & generous of you & how like you!"

As the five-star Fleet Admiral and his high ranking staff searched for the Walkers' colored eggs the next morning, Easter Sunday, the brutal *Battle of Okinawa* began with the largest amphibious landing of the Pacific war. Vice Adm. Marc Mitscher, Commander Task Force 58, wired Nimitz that Okinawa was "honeycombed with caves," into which "tanks and armored cars" entered. "It will be probably be tough," he dryly concluded. Far down the chain of command below Nimitz, Hanko's *Missouri* had been bombarding the southeast coast of Okinawa with her formidable sixteen-inch guns. Its nine barrels could discharge a round every thirty seconds, hurtling two-ton projectiles some twenty-four miles. Up to twenty-seven rounds could be on their way, before the first one hit its target. Each shell was lethal within three hundred yards of impact. (Enemy troops surviving such bombardments suffered extreme psychological trauma.)

During Easter dinner, Nimitz and his staff were decked out in the floral aloha shirts the Walkers had sent. Lamar wrote that Soc "has just come in the office wearing your Easter shirt and looks very chic. He says that he was below normal until he put it on but is now 'fair, fat and forty again'." Sherman received a special blue aloha shirt. Five years later, when he was a four-star Chief of Naval Operations, Sherman mentioned shyly to Ginger how touched he still was by the blue aloha shirt Una had sent him.

"Sherman was so tickled about the gift," Ginger wrote her mother in 1950 from Washington D.C. "He batted his blue eyes and grinned and cast his eyes down and finally said, 'It was a blue aloha shirt which your mother said just matched my eyes!' He was so tickled and a little embarrassed to admit it!"

Meanwhile, the entire flag mess endorsed Una in a citation dated April 4th as "The No. 1 Exponent of Hawaiian Hospitality."

With classic wit, Nimitz's postscript described how Una's generosity had softened his hard-boiled staff:

> *CinCPac-CinCPOA says that although the eggs that sat round the table, dressed in the gaudy shirts were as hard boiled as the eggs in the pretty shells, they were softened by your gracious generosity!*

Nimitz at Ease

4 April 1945

Dear Una:

Easter dinner at Cincpac Flag Mess was an unusually pleasant occasion. Not only was the table setting punctuated with brightly colored eggs in the traditional colors, but the diners seated round the table vied with the eggs for color, for they all were wearing the gorgeous aloha shirts which you in your generous kindness had sent. We all join in endorsing you as the No. 1 Exponent of Hawaiian Hospitality.

C. W. NIMITZ   C. H. McMORRIS
F. P. SHERMAN   H. C. MANDELL
J. B. CARTER   JAMES PENFIELD
T. C. ANDERSON   H. A. LAMAR

P. S.

Cincpac-Cincpoa says that although the eggs that sat round the table, dressed in the gaudy shirts were as hard boiled as the eggs in the pretty shells, they were softened by your gracious generosity!

Mrs. H. A. Walker,
2616 Nuuanu Avenue,
Honolulu, Hawaii.

Staff Easter Letter to Una

Lamar was writing the Walkers from his desk in white shorts, given to him by Admiral Sir Bruce Fraser, and Muliwai slippers on his feet. Mentioning Muliwai "Makes me wish I could be there Saturday. Instead we shall be besieged by the party of fourteen labor executives."

Doc, Lamar noted, had been promoted to one-star Commodore and was "decked out in his new Walker shirt. "The Boss has recovered from his cold," so for "the last three days we have had grand walks through the Guam countryside. On Monday we gave Lt. General [Albert C.] Wedemeyer a heavy work-out by taking him up to the peak of [1000-foot] Mt. Tenjo."

Wedemeyer, who had replaced General Joseph Stilwell five months before in command of U.S. forces in China, was with them briefly on his way back to China. The two-hour trek up Tenjo Mountain became one of Nimitz's favorite outings on Guam. Closing, Lamar lamented that their flag jeep, the Grey Ghost, had a hole in its muffler and can be heard for many miles away."

Inhibiting Nimitz's daily hikes was the threat of "A considerable number of Japanese soldiers," hiding in the hills of Guam, who "are killed or captured in appreciable numbers each week. It is practically impossible to starve them out because there is so much accessible food in the island...available to them."

Captured Japanese were used to induce them to surrender with some success. But, he said that their presence "keeps us from taking walking trips to many desirable spots although only a few of our men have been shot at recently."

Nimitz comforted Catherine that she could "rest assured that we only walk in areas where lots of our men are working—for I have no desire to stumble on a Jap & get a grenade or bullet." [346]

Nimitz later revealed, "A group of submarine men strayed away from their recuperation camp...and despite many warnings, seven of them were ambushed by a party of about 20 Japs—who killed 5 and wounded the other two. I do all my walking," Nimitz added, "in the main roads, along which many trucks & autos are in constant sight." [347]

Anxious to halt the inexorable Allied island-hopping march north toward its homeland and to protect Okinawa from invasion, the Japanese dispatched their super battleship *Yamato* with a task force of nine escorts south. *Yamato* carried eighteen-inch guns—the largest caliber of naval artillery ever installed in any ship in history, making her a formidable naval power. But she did not get far. Spotted south of Kyushu on April 6th, carrier-based planes sunk the mighty battleship with numerous bombs and torpedoes.

Vice Adm. Mitscher tersely reported to Nimitz: "Total force attacked 1 Yamato BB, 1 Agano CL, 1 CL or large DD, 7 or 8 DD. Sank 1 BB, 1 Agano CL, 1 CL or DD, 3 DD." [348]

Yamato's only engagement against U.S. forces wasted her guns on small escort carriers, destroyers and destroyer escorts during the *Battle of Leyte Gulf* the previous October. In a parody of a popular song from the 1930s, a squadron that helped sink the battleship sang, "*Yamato* been a beautiful BB, but BB, you ought to see yourself now." [349]

With the dreadnaught's demise, Japan could no longer mount any serious naval defense. Turner, the admiral expected to lead the amphibious landings on the Japanese homeland, sent Nimitz a curious cable. "I may be crazy, but I think the Japs have quit this war at least for the time being." (Turner was a bit premature, for the Japanese still had quite a lot of fight left in them.)

On April 8th, Nimitz proudly wrote the Walkers that Hanko:

> In his good ship, the "MOE" has helped drive another nail into the coffin of Japan's Naval strength. Although he was not where he could see the [Japanese Battleship] "YAMATO" and the cruiser and destroyers with her sink when Mitscher's planes struck them yesterday, his ship was with the carriers and contributed her share toward this splendid result...Another generous slice has been whittled off the rapidly-shrinking Japanese Fleet, and they are now without any modern battleships.

Nimitz enjoyed [and envied] "The description of your visit to Muliwai; and thank you both very much for the lovely glass balls which now rest in the wooden bowl you gave me on my departure from Oahu."

In a postscript, Nimitz reported the good news that the Walker's friend, "Commodore [Doc] Anderson (Medical Corps), received his star night before last and was duly inducted into his higher rank. You may be sure both he and we are very happy in this well-deserved promotion."

Another flag plane arrived with Walker gifts of *Cup of Gold* vines (*solanda maxima*) and a rare commodity on Guam—another cache of eggs. Lamar thanked the Walker for the gifts, writing, "For breakfast this morning we had Major General [Harry] Schmidt who has been doing all the good fighting on Iwo [Jima]. He certainly did enjoy his poached eggs. The first he had eaten since he left here for the operation."

Schmidt commanded the Marine's Fifth Amphibious Division in the Battle of Iwo Jima. Robert Sherwood had visited Schmidt on Iwo the month before, telling *Life* magazine that after the war, "I hope and pray we will hold onto the islands we paid such a tremendous price to win." [350]

On April 12, 1945, the nation mourned the death of President Roosevelt. Nimitz wrote the Walkers on the loss of his friend who sent him to Pearl Harbor in December 1941:

> *I was very much shocked and grieved at the death of President Roosevelt, who was a great and true friend of the Navy. Whatever faults he might have had to others, he was a friend of the Navy and of the country, by reason of his wisdom in building up a big Navy. All of us will miss him.*

At the end of the month a carrier named for the late President, USS *Franklin D. Roosevelt* (CV 42), was christened by Pierrette Towers, the wife of Nimitz's deputy, Vice Adm. John Towers, at the New York Navy Yard.

Secretary Forrestal warned Lamar, "Expect a barrage of VIPs for the next few months."

Says Lamar, "Barrage was not the word for it! We had VIPs on every day of the week, two at a time, and sometimes their arrival and departures overlapped." [351]

Lamar was overwhelmed by so many visitors: "We hardly have time to change the sheets on the beds before the new people arrive."

In another letter, Lamar lamented having "Just completed a siege with 3 French correspondents—only one of [whom] could speak English," Capt. Stuart S. Murray (on his way to assume command of the *Missouri*), Commo. Bernard "Count" Austin (Nimitz's Asst. Chief of Staff), Commandant of the Marine Corps General Vandegrift, representatives of the AFL-CIO, and "a newspaper publisher from Oregon as house guests. There is never a lack of visitors on this island!"

Yet another letter complained that the "List of visitors for the next three days…only total 16 officers most of them of rather senior-rank—the kind you have to be particularly careful with. The poor steward and I have our troubles…" finding enough food and drink for the guests. "Tell Hara that I could use him to perfection out here in helping make luau out of strange weeds when vegetables are scarce."

Lamar got his "First concrete evidence of how many we had entertained in April this morning with my grocery bill – really, it was stupendous." Another round of visitors brought Maryland "Senator [Millard E.] Tydings and the Filipino President" in exile, Sergio S. Osmeña, Sr. When they finally had a "respite from visitors," Lamar was pleased "to see the Admiral feeling cheery and like himself again."

Commenting on the spate of Guam guests, always the optimist, Una responded, "The visitors seem endless but probably lend variety to table-conversations and break the monotony of daily life."

When on one occasion, they had "only ten guests for dinner," Lamar lamented that the guests "were reluctant to go home…[but]…they finally did."

Later, Lamar was deluged with guests, including the Walkers' close friends, Henry and Clare Boothe Luce. Lamar must not have known or recalled the close connection between the Luces and Walkers when he wrote, "You will remember that Luce is editor of *Fortune*[,] etc[.,] and Clare Boothe's husband—plus his stooge [*Time* magazine Managing Editor] Roy Alexander." And he certainly would not have endeared himself when he described Luce as "a distinct liability and sourpuss."[*]

Another guest of Nimitz's was Brooklyn Daily Eagle owner, Frank D. Schroth, whom Lamar described as a "gentleman and a scholar," whom they "enjoyed having aboard."

Nimitz surely wished the congenial Walkers were present to help entertain his endless chain of dignitaries, although he acknowledged to Catherine that he did not mind them, since they helped "'sell the Navy' to other VIPs." [352] If the evening went on too late, Nimitz would excuse himself to the war room.

Nimitz loaned his guests beachwear, such as to Admiral Furlong, whom they entertained for two days. "He looks most stylish in the owner's shorts and the handsome aloha shirt you gave him."

One guest he enjoyed but also lamented was Under Secretary of State Joseph Grew, to whom he loaned a "pair of fancy colored swim trunks." They were a gift from the Walkers which Grew "walked away with." The pragmatic Nimitz summed it up to Catherine as, "Thus is life." [353]

---

[*] This author admired Henry Luce, but he could be a bit of a stuffed shirt. In the summer of 1965 I was at Muliwai when Henry Luce and Howard P. Jones, the recently-retired U.S. Ambassador to Indonesia, were embroiled in a heated discussion about Indonesian President Sukarno. Luce insisted his information was correct. Jones personally knew Sukarno and insisted Luce was wrong. An exasperated Jones finally asked, "Henry, what is the source of your information about Indonesia?"

"*Time* magazine correspondents," replied Luce smugly.

Bringing the dispute to an abrupt halt, Jones replied with an air of absolute authority, "There are no *Time* correspondents in Indonesia, Henry. They were all expelled."

"Yesterday afternoon," wrote Lamar on April 16th, "as we came back to the quarters hot and tired from a walk, we were so happy to find all the lovely orchids and pretty pictures." He continued, the "Steward is busily engaged in putting them in the patio. These new orchids together with the ones already sent have made the CinCPac's quarters a real show place."

The Walkers had also included several small paintings. "Commodore Andy [Doc] picked the waterfall scene—said 'it would help give him that cool feeling on a hot day.' I have one of the flower scenes."

Lamar lamented that MacArthur's outfit, which included the General's Chief of Staff (and lackey) Lt. Gen. Richard Sutherland, had arrived on April 13th. Shockingly, Sutherland reported that MacArthur demanded all army units in the Pacific be placed under his command. The *Graybook* recorded that Sutherland explained that the current arrangements of shared responsibility "had been 'unsatisfactory' and that unity of command was an unworkable 'shibboleth'."

"No army troops," Sutherland audaciously told Admirals Nimitz, McMorris and Sherman, "would be allowed to serve under an Admiral."

Nimitz would have none of it. In a Top Secret message to King, Nimitz refused to cede to MacArthur control of any forces "essential to the defense and functioning of the Pacific Ocean Areas." *

---

* See *Graybook*, 3226, and *Nimitz*, 378-79. The issue of command and control of Navy and Army forces continued to fester into late May 1945, when Nimitz sent MacArthur a long message detailing their respective responsibilities. While Nimitz had "no desire to exercise any command or control over Army forces" after invasion of Japan, Army troops embarked on Navy ships would remain under "naval control," even through landings ashore "until appropriate Army commanders [ashore] are willing to assume their normal command responsibilities." *Graybook*, 3256.

To Nimitz's relief, King responded the next day, "I am in complete agreement with your views expressed." However, MacArthur never let the matter rest. On July 14th, in a Top Secret message to Nimitz and Marshall, MacArthur lamented that the April conference was "unfruitful," which "has become increasingly embarrassing for me to plan future operations with the Army resources of the Pacific when I am denied the authority to control" the forces needed for "the invasion of Japan." (*Graybook* reveals no response to MacArthur and, perhaps, events in August overshadowed the subject.)

On April 22nd, Nimitz, along with Vandegrift, Sherman, and Lamar, flew to Okinawa, just four days after the United States' beloved war correspondent, Ernie Pyle, was killed by a Japanese sniper on a small nearby island.

Lamar did not mention Pyle, but found the place "most interesting" with his "first contact with things really Japanese. I was impressed with the state of cultivation of the place, even down to patches of land no bigger than the top of my desk. The old Jap [sic] women seemed annoyed at the havoc wreaked in their gardens although they bowed deeply and frequently while we were nearby."

Two days later, they were back on Guam, weary from travel and saddened by the Walkers' report that Princess Abigail Wahiʻikaʻahuʻula Campbell Kawananakoa had died ten days before.

Chapter 22

Columbus: "An Early MacArthur?"

THROUGHOUT APRIL AND May, Nimitz initialed reports of scores of attacks by suicide planes, boats and sappers, which inflicted considerable damage. Numerous ships sank or were damaged. After shooting down three dive-bombers (Aichi D3A "Vals"), the USS *Sterrett* (DD 407) had been hit in her starboard hull by a third on April 9th. The *Arizona's* sister ship, USS *New York* (BB 34), was severely wounded on April 14th. The destroyer USS *Pringle* (DD 477) had been sunk on April 16th. A Canadian cargo ship anchored off Okinawa sank in ten minutes on April 27th. Nineteen suicide boats were reported destroyed on April 29th. On May 2nd, several suicide attacks scored hits on ships on radar picket stations.

May 4-5th brought *Kamikaze* hits on two cruisers, six destroyers, and several cargo ships, and they also sank an escort carrier. Another *Arizona* sister ship, USS *New Mexico* (BB 40), and the escort carrier USS *Bunker Hill* (CV 17) suffered extensive damage from *Kamikazes* on May 12th. (Tony Lilly had fortunately gone east and married the Walker's daughter Ginger. Had he remained as Executive Officer of the destroyer *Bush*, he would have been among the ship's eighty-seven killed or two hundred twenty-

sive survivors, when it sank off Okinawa by two *Kamikazes* on April 6th.) The battleship *Missouri* and Hanko met their destiny with a *Kamikaze* on April 11, 1945, when nineteen-year old Setsuo Ishino crashed his Zero into the starboard quarter of the battleship off Okinawa. Ishino's suicide plane was repeatedly hit with ship's antiaircraft guns. It kept flying toward the ship through a hailstorm of gunfire, glancing off the ocean, crashing into the starboard side and ending up on a gun mount, where it erupted into flames and scattered shrapnel.

"The whole ship shook," Hanko recalled. "It was quite a blow. Everyone felt it...The Captain decreed that we bury the pilot's remains at sea," Hanko continued. "And we did. The Captain read the Navy regs. He was wrapped up in his country's flag, which the sailmakers had made the night before. Over he went."[354] (The indentation in the hull is still evident today on the *Missouri*.)

Alluding to the attack, Nimitz cryptically wrote to Sandy and Una:

> *If your son, Henry, could drop in on you today I am sure that he could give you a vivid episode in his life—perhaps the most exciting one he will ever experience. I hasten to assure you that he is well and no doubt very happy in his work. I envy him in his front seat at some of the most daring events in the history of our war against Japan.*

Another day, a Japanese Betty tried to crash into *Missouri's* port side. Hanko clearly saw the two pilots through the cockpit window. "It kept coming and coming."

Hanko told me something about that *Kamikaze* that Tony Lilly also related, when his ship was attacked off Surigao Straits—one had the eerie feeling the pilot was aiming directly for you. "Finally, the airplane was hit [with anti-aircraft fire]. I thought surely it was going to crash into the port side of the *Missouri*, but it fell just a little short. People swore the splash hit the ship. Frightening. Scary."

Hanko pulled out a pack of cigarettes, shook one out and put it in his mouth. Flicking his Zippo lighter, he tried to hold its flame to the cigarette, but "My hands were shaking so [hard] I couldn't do it." [355]

Kamikazes had been a closely guarded secret, in part to keep from the Japanese how successful they were, and also for morale purposes. But they were about to be disclosed publicly. On April 12th, Nimitz cabled King, "Because suicide attacks are now the rule rather than the exception...I consider it necessary gradually to divulge the situation to the American people. My previous requests for secrecy are withdrawn." [356]

Although no response appears in *Graybook*, King apparently agreed, because the next day Nimitz withdrew "Censorship regulations regarding suicide attacks." He also issued a statement, summarized in the May 1945 issue of *All Hand's* Magazine, that "'Do-or-die' suicide pilots have been attacking units of the Pacific Fleet for several months without seriously interfering with our operations." It continued that these "fanatical methods" by an "enemy trapped in increasingly desperate situation...are of doubtful value."

It may have been important to assuage a worried public, but the Top Secret *Graybook* listed some forty ships lost to *Kamikazes* by that month.

Meanwhile, Una had been issuing her own "Walker Family" communiqués throughout the war, which she transmitted to family and friends, including Nimitz. Lamar wrote that Walker *Communiqué* No. 36 was "thoroughly enjoyed by me and the Fleet Admiral. Your letters are so cheery and gay that I look forward to receiving each one with much enthusiasm. Of course, the Boss loves to read them too."

With the frenzy of war off Okinawa dominating *Graybook*, in a letter of May 2nd, Lamar mentioned that Nimitz needed some time off at Muliwai to escape the demands of command. "Your remarks about 'Muliwai' brought back so many pleasant memories. The Boss needs a trip to that lovely spot now and I am waiting for an opportune time to bring the matter up. After all, you can be harassed by people who come to 'see' you just so long." They expected to see Hanko in the near future "when the admiral threatens to walk his legs off."

The next day, Nimitz thanked "Our good angels from Honolulu" who "generously provided me and my mess with four large bottles of Vermouth for Martini cocktails."

Lamar echoed Nimitz, asking Una to "Tell Sandy that I have used the new Vermouth and it produces a swell martini."

For breakfast, Nimitz's steward brought him "with great pride a yellow fig about an inch in diameter, which is the first fig to come off the fig plant you sent us." The "orchid plants you sent" were "doing well." He was about to take "two or three news correspondents for a walk to Mount Tenjo" and wished "you two could come along." He closed, wistfully, "The descriptions of your week-ends at Muliwai make us all filled with nostalgia." Enclosed was a signed photograph of Nimitz dated May 3, 1945, that now hangs in the author's office:

Nimitz inscription, May 3, 1945: "To Una and Sandy Walker—With great affection."

May 8th brought two reasons for celebration. It was Victory in Europe Day (VE Day), when the Allies formally accepted the unconditional surrender of Germany, thus recognizing the end of World War II in Europe. And it was the 61st birthday of the new President of the United States, Harry Truman. With the end of the war in Europe, the United States turned most of its attention and resources to ending the war in the Pacific, although reading the *Graybook*, it appeared as business as usual for Nimitz and his fleet. However, except for a grand finale, Japan was already doomed, with the Allies setting its "Rising Sun."

In Late April, Nimitz wrote, "Your 'young hopeful'—Hanko [will] soon have a new boss whom I am quite sure you know well." He was referring to Capt. Stuart S. "Sunshine" Murray, with whom he recently had dinner, who would take command of *Missouri* in May. Nimitz wrote that he would soon "have the pleasure of having Hanko at my table," after they took "a long walk with my usual walking group."

That pleasure took place on May 18th, when the *Missouri* pulled into Guam. To the extreme displeasure of the ship's jealous Executive Officer, a message from Nimitz's headquarters invited only the ship's Commanding Officer, Captain Callaghan, and Ens. Henry A. Walker, Jr., to dinner.

The next day, Nimitz wrote, "You will be pleased to hear that a very handsome and slender young ensign, nicely tanned, sans mustache, named Hanko, had dinner with me last night in my quarters. He was in the best of health and bubbling over with good spirits," and "enjoys, according to his account, the distinction of being the senior ensign in the ship, ranking a number of new Naval Academy ensigns who are already aboard…. In that capacity he is entitled to be called 'The Bull Ensign'—a distinction which goes to the senior officer of each rank."

The Walkers had a roast beef in reserve for his next visit, but Nimitz suggested they not keep it "in the ice box too long, because the tempo of war at present is going to keep us pretty close to our posts[,] and there is no telling when any of us will have a chance to enjoy a visit with you. However, when such a chance comes, I hope we can celebrate it at Muliwai."

Hanko explained that during his short visit, Nimitz asked him to make one of his special old-fashioned drinks:

> *We went ashore, [Missouri Captain William M.] Callaghan, [Admiral] Spruance and a small group of senior officers. It was a very pleasant evening for the opportunity of enjoying a cocktail ashore was always a very pleasant occasion. A bar was set up in the Admiral's quarters to refresh his distinguished guests. Nimitz turned to me and casually said, "Henry, please make me an 'old fashioned.' You know how I like them." I promptly did, carefully remembering the tablespoon of dark run he liked floating on the top.*
>
> *Nimitz, as always, was gracious. On such occasions, as indeed on earlier occasions in Honolulu, the Commander in Chief, Pacific, spoke of the broad strategy he was employing in maneuvering his forces. He never minded questions from his subordinates and in fact encouraged them. I always listened very quietly, fascinated. These were the senior military commanders of the Pacific discussing the intimate secrets of Pacific war strategy.*[357]

Nimitz also cryptically wrote that he had "returned on the 17th from a two-day visit to an Old Friend." He related taking a present of "Midway peanut candy" for the "Old Friend's son," advising his mother "to ration him one bar each day." Instead, the son proceeded to eat the entire box, becoming "ill enough to 'toss his cookies'."

Who was the Old Friend? Chet Lay figured it out. *Graybook* reveals that Nimitz was in Manila for a conference with CINCAFPAC. Hence, the Old Friend was none other than MacArthur. The child vomiting his candy was his seven-year-old son, Arthur MacArthur IV. It seems likely that Nimitz's reference to an Old Friend was a bit of tongue-in-cheek.*

Because MacArthur commanded half the western Pacific forces, Nimitz had to deal with him. But were they truly friends? I posed that question to Chet Lay.

> In response, Chet said people often asked Nimitz's four children that question. They replied that Nimitz never discussed him or any other officer, other than to praise him. (Edwin Layton claims that when Nimitz was asked why he kept a photo of MacArthur on his desk, he replied, "to remind me not to be a horse's ass." [358] Chet doubted he used such words.)
>
> In his December 5, 1944, letter to Catherine, Nimitz lamented an article by columnist, Drew Pearson, in the Honolulu Star-Bulletin† "trys [sic] to stir up trouble between MacArthur & me where <u>none</u> exists…What a trouble maker he is! Apparently[,] many people like to read such rubbish."

---

* On June 15th, Nimitz sent King a personal message, after Gen. Henry "Hap" Arnold, Chief of the Army Air Forces, mentioned a proposal that MacArthur's headquarters move to Guam for the invasion of Japan. Nimitz "had no objections," but "had repeatedly invited MacArthur to visit my headquarters" which "he never accepted," so "doubted MacArthur's willingness to come to Guam." If he did, because of space limitations, Nimitz "would care for MacArthur only on the same basis of 'double up and share' as is now used for Spruance." *Graybook*, 3270. (MacArthur would never have accepted less than the most elegant private quarters.)

† The article reads under "Navy-MacArthur Feud, Once Patched Up, Resumes": *"Navy-MacArthur feuding has broken out all over again. It was bad during the early stages of the war two years ago, but was patched up by Admiral Nimitz and MacArthur personally. … Now MacArthur blames the navy for letting Japanese troops sneak ashore on Leyte, while the navy blames 'Doug-out Doug' for jumping the gun with far too optimistic communiques."*

> However, about a dozen years ago, Chet's mother Kate was having a drink with a neighbor, noted Civil War historian and Ulysses S. Grant biographer, William McFeeley. McFeeley mentioned research he was doing on Christopher Columbus.
> "Oh," Kate replied, "I have a biography of Columbus that dad had at the Academy—you're welcome to it." Kate retrieved Nimitz's old book and handed it to McFeeley.
> A couple of days later, McFeeley returned with a broad grin across his face. "Have you ever read this book?" he asked.
> "No," Kate replied. "Why?"
> McFeeley opened it to a page with an engraving of Columbus, who had just disembarked from a small boat and was wading ashore. It was captioned, "Columbus arrives in the New World." In the margin, Nimitz had written in pencil "An early MacArthur?"
> "So," Chet concluded, "Now we know!" *

Nimitz had been planting maidenhair ferns, ginger, bird of paradise,

---

* From Chester Nimitz "Chet" Lay's speech, February 24, 2014, Nimitz's hundred twenty-ninth birthday, at the U.S. Naval War College for the unveiling of the digitized on-line version of Nimitz's *Graybook*. This author recently read a book about Pearl Harbor with many errors. Nimitz arrived in Pearl Harbor on December 25th, a momentous event not mentioned. On December 31st, it has Nimitz six thousand miles away in DC (it's five thousand miles) in white uniform (if he was in the east, he'd be in blues). While Nimitz assumed command of the Pacific Fleet on December 31st on the submarine *Grayling* in Pearl Harbor, the book still has him in the East Coast taking command the next day, January 1st. Chet related that his mother has a biography falsely claiming that when Nimitz flew over Pearl Harbor the first time he sang under his breath, "O come all ye faithful." In her father's style, Kate wrote in the margin in pencil, "Christ!"

Vanda and *dendrobium* orchids, "'Spathoglottis'* (sounds like something in the body near the throat)," and other flowers and various trees on Guam flown in from Hawai'i as seeds or seedlings from the Walkers. "Not long ago, Hal, [Doc] Andy, and myself," Nimitz wrote, "took a walk with our pockets filled with monkeypod seed, [Algarroba] seed, and a few flowering tree seeds which we carefully planted at intervals along the roadside as we walked up to Mount Tenjo. Johnnie Appleseeds we were, but happy to think that we might improve the locality for some future residents."

By the end of May, Nimitz asked that they not "send any more plants now as every space we have is full." He later apparently belayed that injunction because the Walkers continued to send plants and seeds.

Hal Lamar, Nimitz & Schnauzer. "Mak," CinCPacFlt Guam Headquarters

---

* A *spathoglottis* (with two "t's") is a type of orchid that grew profusely in the Walkers' gardens.

Michael A. Lilly

At Pearl Harbor, Nimitz kept a pet Schnauzer named "Mak" (short for Makalapa) which he took with him to Guam. Mak had an angry disposition, except with Nimitz and Lamar, and was frequently mentioned in letters as a companion on their many hikes, bounding up hills and into the water when walking along the beach. Enclosing a photograph of Mak, Nimitz and himself outside their Guam quarters, Lamar dispatched the letter on the next plane to Pearl Harbor.

The next day, Nimitz wrote, "In a few minutes, [Commodore] Austin, Sherman, Andy, and I, accompanied by Mak and an armed orderly, will take a walk out into the country, in which I wish you could join. Lamar cannot go, because he is down at our signal station where one of our young signalmen was killed by a piece of stone from blasting operations nearby. Austin will probably take this letter back with him," on the flag plane to Pearl Harbor.

In the first week of May, Mak had a beauty treatment—"everything but a wax job and now looks quite handsome." Shortly after the beauty treatment, Nimitz and Lamar took Mak to the beach. "He liked the water and was doing fine" until some guns were shot "and Mak took off for the mountains at sixty knots and hasn't come home yet."

Nearly every letter expressed sorrow on Mak's departure. On May 21st, Nimitz wrote, "Mak is still A.W.O.L. but I am sure he is alive and well, because there is plenty of water on the island and he has been sighted at various camps where he goes for food. He is too wild to let anyone come near him, but" Nimitz added in handwriting, "...he has found a dog companion."

It was not until July 27th that Lamar reported "The most exciting news of the week...the return of 'Mak'. A marine found him while on patrol in one of the native villages...He is covered with battle scars and sores," and is being sent for treatment at the marine dog hospital. Doc has assured us that Mak will receive 'Admiral's treatment'."

Mak was not the only one who went AWOL. "After losing Mak," wrote Lamar, "the next excitement was 'losing' the Boss's son-in-law [Cdr. James T. Lay, Jr.]." Soc was on Okinawa and expected to fly back to Guam with Jim and his boss Admiral [Theodore S.] Wilkinson in time for dinner.

Unfortunately, Jim "was outranked by some Captains and Colonels and got left behind. We were all waiting to get our necks chopped off, when he suddenly arrived in time for dessert tonight." In a letter later that month to the Walkers, Nimitz hoped they'd have a chance to meet "Junior Lay" who was "somewhere in your area," noting he was "a particularly good cribbage player."

No doubt they did meet him.

Michael A. Lilly

Chapter 23

The Woo Pen

EVERY DAY THROUGH May, Nimitz initialed grim reports of the ferocious Japanese defense on Okinawa and the mounting numbers of troops dying on both sides. *Kamikazes* continued raining down and sinking Allied ships.

By June 1st, the *Graybook* reported over sixty-two thousand enemy killed in action. That number would rise to over a hundred thousand, a staggering ninety-two percent death rate. "There were numerous surrenders, individual and group suicides, and shooting[s]" of Japanese "trying to surrender by their own comrades." (The Japanese naval commander, Admiral Minoru Ota, "committed suicide in his cave" with a pistol.)[359]

On June 18th, Lieutenant General Buckner's last act was to wire Nimitz that "Enemy resistance in Okinawa broken today."[360]

Buckner was watching the last marines wade ashore from a forward observation post, when he was struck and killed by shrapnel. The good friend of Nimitz and the Walkers was only fifty-eight years old and the most senior U.S. military officer killed during World War II.

The *Graybook* recorded on June 19th that the "Collapse of Jap defenses across the entire line was increasingly evident," and on June 20th that the enemy was "confined to three pockets on the southern end of the island." Two days later, it was over. "The U.S. colors were formally raised on the island of Okinawa at 1000." [361]

The costly Battle of Okinawa was over, but its bitter lessons weighed heavily on leaders such as Nimitz. The Japanese defense was so fierce and their deaths so heavy, that some strategic planners predicted another half million to a million Allied casualties to invade the homeland in *Operation Downfall*.

Nimitz cautioned, however, that the "Previous successes against ill fed and poorly supplied units" should not be "used as the sole basis for estimating the type of resistance we will meet" in Japan, "where the enemy lines of communication will be short and enemy supplies more adequate." [362]

Nimitz was on the verge of a huge conquest, but at a projected enormous expense that fueled his insomnia. Fortunately for him, the B-29 firebombing of Japanese cities was directed by the Army's Major General Curtis LeMay, who was thirty-eight, and not Nimitz. Nimitz commanded all the forces in the Northern and Central Pacific with the exception of LeMay's 21st Bomber Command, which reported directly to Gen. Henry "Hap" Arnold, Chief of the Army's Air Forces.

The killing of hundreds of thousands of citizens, and the millions more rendered homeless in the last months of the war, might not have sat well with the gentlemanly Fleet Admiral. What would have been a war crime, had the tactic been employed by the Japanese, was, however, lauded, until later times when the carpet-bombings of Germany and Japan were severely criticized. (Historians continue to disagree on the subject.) At the time, Secretary of War Henry Stimson, who failed to stop it, nevertheless said the "practice" could give America "the reputation of outdoing Hitler in atrocities." [363] Fortunately, Nimitz had no direct involvement in that strategy.

Soc McMorris traveled to Oahu and spent the weekend at Muliwai, returning to Guam laden down with gifts of *spathoglottis* orchids, ginger, Bird of Paradise, maidenhair ferns and tales of Muliwai, which Nimitz envied. "Although the future is very uncertain," Nimitz wrote, "we can always hope for repeats on those fine visits we had there."

Hanko, who Nimitz sometimes referred to by his childhood nickname, "Walking Bird," was "no doubt having an exciting time at this very instant. I believe that when you next hear from him he...will undoubtedly have much of interest to write you." In a postscript, the Commander in Chief of the Pacific Fleet and Pacific Ocean Area gave Hanko a "new title—'Hanko, the Walking Bird and the Scourge of Japan's Coast!'"

In late June, Nimitz flew to California for what would become his last war meeting with King. Nimitz's close friend and next-door neighbor in Berkeley was Y. C. Woo, a prominent businessman and Executive Director of the Bank of Canton in San Francisco. Woo presented Nimitz with a gold-capped Parker 51 Pen, costing a whopping $50 in 1945, asking, "When you have defeated Japan you can sign the peace treaty with it." [364]

Woo was born in 1898 in Shanghai, China. His father was a prominent banker who expected his sons to follow him into the family business, but Y. C. had other aspirations. His first love was the sea, wanting to become a sailor instead. Given his youth, the opportunity for a strong education, and older brothers ahead of him at the bank, Woo spent his teen years learning seamanship. He attended two of the five naval colleges in China, beginning with the Mercantile Marine College in Woosung, and finishing at the highly regarded naval college at Chefoo. But after graduation, he acceded to his father's requests and returned to the family banking business.

"I do think," his grandson Paul said, "his calling to the sea was trumped by his fidelity to father and family."

Before Shanghai fell to the Japanese, the Woo family relocated to Hong Kong and finally the United States in early 1940. They settled in Berkeley, becoming neighbors of the Nimitz family, when Catherine moved in next door. Catherine and Woo's wife Eching developed a close friendship during the war. With his quarterly meetings in San Francisco, Nimitz also became close to Y. C. Woo. The two loved playing cards, swimming and fishing together. Their natural and mutual affinity for the sea added to the relationship. Pocketing the gold-tipped pen that would soon make history, Nimitz departed San Francisco.

During Nimitz's trip, he stopped in Honolulu in both directions. The state of his health shocked the Walkers. Nimitz had lost weight, gaunt from stress and suffering from chronic diarrhea. Nimitz's malaria from Guadalcanal caused him to suffer periodic flu-like symptoms and may have exacerbated his condition.[365] Una expressed her concern in a confidential letter to Doc in Guam:

> *Your Chief had dinner with us last night, and Sandy and I were shocked at his physical condition. He told us on his way through the other way, that he had this ailment, had had it for two weeks, and we had expected he would get medical treatment on the Coast and be cured by his return. In place of that, it had apparently grown worse....*
>
> *Here in Honolulu, that is considered a very serious ailment, and according to Dr. Arnold, who is a specialist in stomach diseases, every hour that it lasts makes it harder to cure. I had a similar touch in February and his treatment was very severe, no eggs, milk, meat, vegetables or fruit of course, absolutely quiet in bed etc. I lived on bread, potatoes and rice for five days, and it is monotonous as it can be, but it cured with a few medicines.*

Sandy, who would not have commented unless he was extremely worried, recommended hospitalization. "Knowing the Chief's usual vigor and dislike for fussing, we know that will be hard to do. However, to have him invalided out of the [N]avy at this stage of the game would be more than a tragedy for the country, for him and for you." (Una asked Doc to keep her letter confidential, which he did.)

Walker Family Communiqué No. 44 of July 7 wrote of Muliwai:

> *The inspiration for this week's communiqué springs from the tranquil skies, lofty mountain-tops, peaceful atmosphere and broad seas of Muliwai, with all its happy associations of cheery friends and loving family...It arose from the feeling of nearness of you all, from the memory of all the lovely days spent there together and from the hope of those that will come in the future.*

Continuing, Una spoke of family and friends, including Nimitz, enjoying the beauty of Muliwai:

> *Hanko, Walking Bird, you are always there in your faded blue, favorite shorts in and out of the water with your fish-nets and boat, forever trying to start your motor, with cheery, smiling face...Ginger dear, sunning and tanning, putting the gremlins to bed or waking them up, sleepy-eyed babies with sunburned faces...Flags immaculate and shining with gay, happy laughter and dancing feet...The dear Doctor hovering over broiling steaks with Sandy, or with cocked cigar, wondering the advisability of entering the pot in poker...And then of course the Chief [Nimitz], bravest and strongest, the reason and center for everything.*

Nimitz had sent the Walkers a lovely piece of tapa, which they hung over the Victrola as it is so much prettier and lighter than the one that was there. Her Red Cross work broke all previous records and shipped over a million dressings. Concluding, Una asked that the "Flags, take notice...Your tonic is still at Muliwai. *Haina ia mai ana* *kapuana la*[*]...you are all constantly in our thoughts and we pray for your health and happiness."

Two days later, Lamar responded that he and Nimitz read the Communiqué and "enjoyed hearing from you so much. I must confess that the news about the fun at Muliwai made us even more sorry that we couldn't have enjoyed our planned visit there." Lamar noted that Nimitz's stomach ailment had subsided, and he was "feeling much better." They had brought a station wagon from Pearl Harbor to use instead of the jeep, Grey Ghost. "The first day we used it was almost our last. A great water truck ran into us and smashed our side in. Fortunately we were not hurt, but the station wagon had to have a complete beauty treatment."

---

[*] Meaning "and so the story is told," a phrase often starting the last verse in Hawaiian songs.

Chapter 24

War's End: The Atomic Bomb

IN LATE JULY, a Top Secret letter from King was hand-delivered to Nimitz, informing him of a secret new super weapon that would forever change the world. He and Layton watched the devastating power of the Atomic Bomb in films of its explosion and mushroom cloud at Alamogordo, New Mexico. Nimitz shared the news with Lamar. But he was never an advocate of the Atomic Bomb, thinking it "somehow indecent, certainly not a legitimate form of warfare."³⁶⁶

After the war, Nimitz said, "I would consider the atom bomb as an inefficient weapon because it cannot be pinpointed on a military objective and destroy that alone." ³⁶⁷

Lamar's next letter to the Walkers revealed nothing about the war or that a revolutionary bomb would soon alter the course of history. Lamar shared that under their daily regimen, they "leave the office at 1200 and drive down to our special beach. From 1230 to 1300 we have a sun bath and then swim for half hour." They were "up to a quarter of a mile and some morning I expect the Admiral to strike out for Japan. We are back at headquarters at 1400 feeling fit and ready for the afternoon's business." (Envious,

Una started to practice long distances [at Muliwai] to keep up with the marathon swimmers in the far west.)

A swim on August 1st, however, "was almost too strenuous," wrote Lamar. Swimming out too far in a strong current with Nimitz and a Commodore Carter, it suddenly dawned on them they would have trouble getting back. Nimitz had wisely turned around before Lamar and Carter and made it back safely. Lamar swam across the channel to the reef to get some extra breath before getting help, when he saw some Marines struggling with a boat to bring the Commodore in. "After watching the Marines try to row a boat in a strong current, I now propose some lessons in seamanship for these 'sea soldiers' in case we have to call on them again."

On another day, Lamar wrote, "the Boss and I were out with just a marine and got lost in a deep valley. When we finally emerged the Boss whistled gaily at an Army truck and we came riding home like three bags of meal, or should I say 'Kona' coffee." (In those days, Sandy's American Factors produced coffee from its Kona coffee plantations.)

On July 23rd, Walker Family Communiqué No. 45 mentioned Muliwai with a few friends. In response, Lamar wrote, "One of the nicest things we have in Guam are your communiqués. They always are highlights of the day for both the owner [Nimitz] and me when they arrive. We read them word for word forward and sometimes even let the doctor in on the special news…The owner [Nimitz] asked particularly that I tell you how nice it was to hear from you and also his thanks for his own private note."

He requested, "Send me some of your 'Philodendron' [orchids] which I shall plant in the bamboo vases with great pride and pleasure." Concluding, Lamar wrote the "Bugler just sounded 'call to quarters' which gives me 15 minutes before taps so I had best get on my horse and get home before the curfew. We still have that out in the forward area."

A week later, Nimitz sent the Walkers a package with a note: "The papers say there 'ain't' no Bourbon in Honolulu. Here is a flask of my personal brew."

Una responded, "How very nice of you to send Sandy and me the perfectly wonderful bottle of your own brew of Bourbon." (The label said, "For the personal use of the Commander in Chief.") "We shall keep this beautiful bottle unopened and admired, until your next visit, when we shall open it for a celebration, and we hope that it will be soon and at Muliwai."

Lamar assured Una that he had given Nimitz's new deputy in Pearl Harbor, Adm. John H. Hoover, the word as to who is who in Honolulu and that "you are always to get the seat on the right. He has had little experience in social affairs and I told him he could get the 'word' from you if he got in a tight spot."

On August 4th, Hanko, aboard *Missouri,* received a coded message directing all ships to "Keep away from the Japanese coast near the city of Hiroshima and to avoid any clouds emanating from that sector." [368]

At first, the message puzzled Hanko.

The *Graybook* recorded a prohibition of "friendly aircraft" within a radius of fifty miles of Hiroshima and its two alternate targets. Two days later, what had been a closely-guarded secret among only a handful of Nimitz's staff for two weeks, suddenly became known worldwide.

The *Graybook* chronicled that "President Truman has announced that Hiroshima was bombed…with an atomic bomb with explosive power equal to 20,000 tons of TNT." [369] (The bomb was released from the belly of the B-29 Superfortress Enola Gay, killing tens of thousands.)

The next day, Hanko received another message warning about Nagasaki. Two days later, a second bomb exploded over the port city of Nagasaki. (The *Graybook* records that Kyoto, the historic capital of Japan, was an original target for the bomb, but the Secretary of War replaced Kyoto with Nagasaki, because the former was "an important cultural center that he did not wish destroyed.") [370]

Nimitz Awarded the Order of Knight Grand Cross of the Bath[371]

The previous January, Nimitz learned that the British King George would be honoring him with the Order of Knight Grand Cross of the Bath (military) for the liberation of the British islands in the Pacific. The Order was the highest and only honor of that rank given to any American during the war. After receiving congratulations from Churchill, Nimitz facetiously wrote Catherine, "Lamar will address you hereafter as 'Lady Catherine'— and you may expect to receive mail under that title from time to time."[372]

Because MacArthur was awarded a lesser rank, Nimitz, in rare bluster, wrote Catherine, "Are we puffed up!!" [373]

The award ceremony was held on August 10, 1945, aboard the Royal Navy Battleship HMS *Duke of York* off Guam. At 11:00 a.m., Admiral Fraser bestowed Nimitz with the scarlet ribbon representing his knighthood. Lamar described it as "full of good English cheer," although it was blistering hot.

Upon Nimitz's return to Guam, he received a message from King that "Tokyo has indicated in ultra channels that Japan wishes to bring about peace immediately." [374]

While many in the staff were jumping for joy, Nimitz "merely smiled in his own calm way" and "was as calm, cool and collected as if he'd known all along this was going to happen and as if he'd expected it." [375]

Lamar wrote the Walkers that the headquarters had been all a tizzy "with the excitement of Hirohito deciding to quit and turn in his suit."

However, Nimitz pondered what the Japanese meant by the words, "Cease hostilities." Ever since the enemy "wanted to 'close hostilities,' we have tried to indicate just what that means to the Japs,"

Lamar wrote. "Some have understood, and some have not."

They were "standing by now for a quick run into Tokyo for the surrender ceremony. I hope that the *Kamikaze* boys will behave themselves on that occasion. Once you get people wound up with the 'Do or Die' spirit it is sometimes difficult to call a halt."

Echoing Lamar's sentiments, Nimitz ordered the fleet to end war offensives, but "Beware of treachery of last moment attacks by enemy forces or individuals." [376]

He also sent a message to all Pacific commands, cautioning that Japanese "Counter proposals for the termination of the war must not be permitted to affect vigilance against Japanese attacks." [377]

Isolated attacks continued despite the Emperor's radioed capitulation. On August 18th, for example, the *Graybook* noted that "War is not yet over for some of our subs," in light of enemy air attacks. At the same time, the Japanese asked that Allied forces not approach home waters "...until sufficient time has elapsed for the cease fire order [to] have been fully effectuated." [378]

The next day the Japanese radioed its intention to surrender. Hanko was one of three officers who received that communication aboard the *Missouri*. Shortly thereafter, the following transpired:

> *A marine gunnery sergeant arrived at Hanko's stateroom on the Missouri and said, "Lt. Walker, Admiral Halsey's compliments, will you report to cabin 214 on the 0-2 level [Halsey's stateroom]."*
>
> *Hanko got out of his bunk, put on his marine combat boots and hastened to the flag stateroom. The two other watch officers on duty when the message was received of the war's end were already there. Admiral Halsey's personal orderly gave them a paper bag, saying, "Gentlemen, this is with the Admiral's compliments. A marine will be stationed outside the door until you are finished."*
>
> *The three perplexed officers peered into the paper bag. There they found three cigars, a bottle of Old Grand-Dad bourbon whiskey, three paper cups, a cardboard container of ice and a note, "Gentlemen, please enjoy yourselves. You have done well. WFH."*
>
> *"And we drank the whiskey," said Hanko, "then we lit the cigars and we went down to the wardroom quite obviously bombed, thinking, 'If anyone challenges our condition...check in with Admiral Halsey.'"*
>
> *The next day, Hanko ran into Admiral Halsey and told him, "Thank you, Sir, for the paper bag." Halsey replied, "Walker, I hope that cigar didn't make you sick."*
>
> *It did not.* [379]

Nimitz dispatched a message to all Pacific commands that with the war over, everyone was to be on their best behavior:

Michael A. Lilly

> *It is incumbent on all officers to conduct themselves with dignity and decorum in their treatment of the Japanese," notwithstanding their "treacherous attack on the Pacific Fleet and which has subjected our brothers in arms who became prisoners to torture, starvation and murder...Neither familiarity and open forgiveness nor abuse and vituperation should be permitted.*

The JCS informed Nimitz the disappointing news that MacArthur would sign the surrender document as Supreme Commander of all Allied forces and would continue in that position for the occupation of Japan. The *Graybook* recorded Nimitz's gracious personal message of congratulations to MacArthur on his appointment, but that masked his personal disappointment by the news.[380]

Lamar later said that Nimitz was displeased with the appointment because victory owed so much to the Pacific fleet, and he, therefore, informed Forrestal he would not attend the surrender ceremonies. Realizing he had made a huge public relations error, Truman informed Nimitz he would sign as the U.S. Representative, and that the surrender would take place aboard a Navy ship—the *Missouri*.

John K. Emmerson, a career Foreign Service Officer assigned to MacArthur in Japan, lamented that Nimitz was not selected to command the occupation forces. "Navy men, who thought *they* had won the Pacific war, were disappointed that their chief [Nimitz] was not awarded command of the Occupation of Japan. One wonders what the difference would have been had this genial, warm-hearted seafarer ruled the island empire instead of the imperious MacArthur."[381]

Una wrote Nimitz's wife, Catherine, of their displeasure that Nimitz would not be Supreme Commander, but sent also their "sincerest felicitations" in "this hour of victory":

> *Sandy and the men of Hawai'i who have watched the progress of the war, and have seen the Navy, under the*

> brilliant leadership of your Fleet Admiral, winning the Battle of the Pacific, feel very disappointed that he was not chosen to be the Supreme Commander. However, there is probably more important work for him to do, now that the war is won, and with his usual modesty and fine view of everything, he is already endeavoring to promote the common good for all.
>
> Our hearty congratulations to you and to your Fleet Admiral for the magnificent accomplishments of the Pacific War.

She hoped that if Catherine and Nimitz came to Hawai`i, the Walkers would host "A party of welcome for you in our garden" in part return for "the lovely party in your darling garden in the autumn of 1943."

In response, Mrs. Nimitz intimated how her husband had spent his career preparing himself for the central role he played in winning the Pacific war:

> Indeed we are proud of the splendid part Chester has played in this war. His strength and stability have played a major part in the winning of the war. As I look back thru the years and remember how much study he put into the subject of battles on land and sea, and strategy in all its forms, and how he has always made himself familiar with the terrain and seas in the area where he was stationed, I realize how splendidly he was preparing himself to take his place as a leader when his country needed him.

Mrs. Nimitz ended with "Best good wishes to all the Walkers" on "this great day for the world and one that the Nimitz family in particular will never forget."

In late August, Lamar complained about having "No let up in the number of distinguished guests being fed" and cared for. One evening, they entertained Catholic Archbishop (later, Cardinal) Francis J. Spellman of New York, who also served as the "military's curate," Andrew Higgins, Vice Adm. Adolphus Andrews, Rear Adm. John J. Ballentine, and a *Chicago Daily News* correspondent.

As Lamar described it, the evening started out fine, with so many interesting and successful guests. Admiral Andrews was Chairman of the Navy's Manpower Survey Board in Washington D.C. who, Lamar wrote, held "the surgical dressing division of the Red Cross in Honolulu," which Una chaired, "in very high regard," a "sentiment which I share wholeheartedly, particularly in view of your outstanding record with 'broncho-scopy' sponges." Ballentine was Commander, Fleet Air in Seattle, who received the Silver Star for heroism while commanding an aircraft carrier in the western Pacific.

Higgins, a one-time logger and truck driver, was a self-made millionaire who founded a successful boat-building enterprise, Higgins Industries. His company designed and built a variety of PT and landing boats (including the famous LCVP or "Higgins Boat") critical to the war effort in the Atlantic and Pacific. (After the war, Gen. Dwight Eisenhower said Higgins "is the man who won the war for us.") [382]

When the moon-faced and portly fifty-six year old Archbishop Spellman arrived on Guam that day, the tropical climate was so hot and humid that his purple mozzetta sartorial cape bled through, badly staining his white shirt underneath.

"Your Eminence," said Lamar, "You can't wear this sort of uniform on Guam. Let us get you some khakis."* So, Spellman's elaborate vestments of a Catholic Archbishop were exchanged for ordinary war khakis.

After cocktails, the party settled down for dinner, which began well, Lamar wrote, but soon began to deteriorate. "Higgins

---

* Interview with Hal Lamar, 81. Later, when Lamar, an Episcopalian, wanted to marry his Catholic fiancée, then-Cardinal Spellman granted him dispensation to marry into the Catholic Church.

was an outspoken, rough-cut, hot-tempered Irishman," who, perhaps like Halsey, "hated red tape, loved bourbon, and was the sort who knocked down anything that got in the way." [383]

With Archbishop Spellman incognito in khakis at the table, Higgins was in full form, boisterously telling "one story after another, and each story getting a little more ribald" and the Archbishop beginning to frown and squirm in his seat. [384]

Higgins, Lamar continued in his letter to the Walkers, finally told "one of those stories which are not suited for the ears of a Catholic Archbishop. The story caused quite a few tense moments for genteel Nimitz and his aide, whose red faces reflected their mutual embarrassment.

Spellman finally brought the evening to an end, saying, "Admiral, I should like to go and say my prayers, both for myself and," slowly fixing blue eyes magnified by rimless glasses on Higgins, "for you gentlemen." [385]

The following should dispel any notion that Spellman was unduly pious, without any humor. On another occasion, after Spellman left Guam, Nimitz related numerous entertaining stories around the dinner table. An old friend expressed amazement at Nimitz's remarkably large collection of stories. "These aren't mine," replied Nimitz. "I told mine last night to Archbishop Spellman, and these are the ones he told me." [386]

Lamar was still infatuated with the Walkers' daughter Ann. In early May—two months after entertaining Ann at the Hawaiian Room in New York—Lamar grieved over not having heard from her. "Last Saturday was the 8th month anniversary of our first day together at Muliwai. It was really an important night for me."

In another letter, he sulked, "Now that there is no curfew in Honolulu and Ann is staying out late, I don't seem to get any word from there. Am I in the dog house?"

On May 13th, he lamented not flying to Pearl Harbor "tomorrow your time to help celebrate Ann's birthday. Since I can't be there please bail me out with Ann. I would have loved to come but the war seems to be interfering somewhat."

Later, he waxed amorously that he "really should be writing to Ann tonight. We have one of the biggest tropical moons shining all over the place that I ever saw. It just radiates romance with all the trimmings. Ann owes me a letter, however, and as much as I should like to write her too I am waiting hopefully for a reply to my last letter." (Poor moonstruck Lamar. Beautiful Ann had plenty of beaus in Honolulu keeping her company.)

Tony & Ginger Lilly, Hal Lamar, Ann Walker, and unknown Lieutenant, Pearl Harbor Officers Club, 1944

Brawny Ben Kanahele, the thrice-shot hero of Una's favorite war song commemorating his killing a Japanese pilot who crashed on Ni'ihau, recovered from his wounds. On August 15th, he received two Presidential Citations, a Medal of Merit, and the Purple Heart in a ceremony at Fort Shafter in Honolulu. Although he was a civilian and not entitled to the Purple Heart, Washington provided special dispensation for his justly-earned award. Hawai'i's Military Governor and the Walker's and Nimitz's friend, General Richardson, presented the awards while the Army bank played,

"They Can't Take Ni'ihau No-How!"

Una's Communiqué No. 48 of August 25th reported, "From the latest news about the signing of the surrender, it would appear that at least three of our poker players would be present."[*] She continued that if Doc Anderson could be spared from his important work and be there, it would increase the count to four, making a mighty good percentage of our game. Also, Sandy missed Doc at this poker table as well as Muliwai. Oh, how happy we were to read that the flag of the Commander in Chief would fly from the 'U.S.S. MISSOURI' B.B. 63."

Lamar summarized their arduous trip from Guam to Tokyo Bay and the surrender ceremonies:

> *The trip to Tokyo was out of this world. And I shall try to give you some of the highlights other than those which appeared and were heard in papers, movies and radios. We were all set to leave on the 27th but the weather and General MacArthur couldn't get together. Finally on the 29th the CinC, plus Admiral Sherman, Flags, and other selected staff members took off before dawn from Guam in one of the plush jobs. At Saipan we shifted to two seaplanes and shortly after lunch were over Sagami Wan.*[†]

Nimitz entered the cockpit and had the plane circle the massive fleet of two hundred fifty-seven Allied ships anchored in Tokyo Bay. Nimitz told the pilot he had waited forty-eight years to see the Japanese World War I-era Battleship *Nagato,* moored at Yokosuka Naval Base below them. The last surviving Japanese battleship, *Nagato* still showed battle damage from an attack by Halsey's carrier planes in July.

"Landing in Tokyo Bay," continued Lamar, "we were picked

---

[*] The three were: Nimitz; Lamar; and Sherman.

[†] Sagami Wan is about forty-five miles south of Tokyo.

up by a motor launch and taken aboard the [Battleship USS] *South Dakota* [BB 57], which broke the boss's flag in prescribed style. Soon, visitors, led off by Admiral Halsey, and messages started arriving in large number which kept us busy until late in the night. The next morning we had more guests, this time headed by Admiral Fraser, Royal Navy, who was anchored close by in the [Royal Navy Battleship HMS] Duke of York [17]."

Lamar states that "In the afternoon we went ashore and inspected the Yokosuka Naval Station." Unfortunately, the "trip was marred somewhat by the fact that someone had run off with the nice sedan I had sent up for the Chief."

They had great difficulty with the car of a Japanese Admiral, which had been redesigned under war strictures to run on alcohol.

"The next morning we went to call on the General [MacArthur], whose radio call by the way is 'SCAP'" for Supreme Commander of the Allied Powers. "MacArthur went steaming into Yokohama at a fast clip in a destroyer and had a great visit. Afterwards we visited the prisoners of war in the hospital ship [USS] Benevolence [AH 13]. Some of them were in pretty bad shape."

Nimitz wrote to his daughter that four hundred fifty former POWs on board *Benevolence* "were recovering from their bad treatment, and they were badly treated, too, beatings, starvation rations, solitary confinement, and so forth." [387] They also visited Admiral Fraser again, as Nimitz wrote his daughter Kate, "partly on official business, partly because I like him, and mostly to get a Scotch and soda before dinner because our ships are dry." [388]

Lamar concluded that the "Rest of the day was spent quietly getting ready for the ceremonies the next morning, September 2, 1945, aboard the *Missouri*.

Chapter 25

Victory: September 2, 1945

ON JANUARY 29, 1944, the senior Senator from Missouri, Harry Truman, spoke as his daughter Margaret christened the battleship before it slid down the spillway into the Brooklyn Navy Yard Basin. "The time is surely coming when the people of Missouri can thrill with pride as the *Missouri* and her sister ships sail into Tokyo Bay."

Eighteen months later, the Senator was President, and the battleship named for his home state, the fourth to bear the title since 1842, indeed sailed into Tokyo Bay, destined to play a role as momentous as the devastation her guns had wrought against the Japanese Empire.

"As the Admiral has already written you," Lamar wrote the Walkers, the surrender ceremonies "went off in great shape and Hanko was right there in the middle. He looked great and what a pleasure to see him again. He and his good ship will soon be taking part in more ceremonies but this time the Admiral will be the central figure."

The "Mighty Mo" was the flagship of the U.S. Navy's Third Fleet Commander, Adm. William F. "Bull" Halsey. Ironically,

Michael A. Lilly

Japanese officials guided the battleship to its anchorage in Tokyo Bay through wartime minefields. On that fateful day of September 2, 1945,[*] Hanko was standing watch on the bridge of the *Missouri* then anchored in Tokyo Bay on the very spot where Commo. Mathew Perry anchored in 1854, when he forced Japan to open itself to the world. At Halsey's request, the U.S. Naval Academy hand-delivered Perry's flag to the *Missouri* and prominently displayed on the 0-1 deck overlooking the surrender ceremonies.[†]

Among scores of military and political dignitaries aboard that day, were the two giants—General of the Army Douglas MacArthur and Fleet Admiral Chester Nimitz. Hanko later told me, "The uniform for the surrender had been a subject of great debate. Should the allies wear neckties or leave their shirt collars open? Back and forth opinions went. Finally, Admiral Nimitz and General of the Army MacArthur settled it. We had fought the war without ties. We would sign the surrender without ties."

> *Suddenly, the 1MC (the ship's loudspeaker) blared, "LT. WALKER, YOUR PRESENCE IS REQUESTED IN THE WARDROOM!"*
>
> *Nimitz had just boarded the battleship and, because of his friendship with the Walkers, Hanko reckoned "It was very likely he would send for me." Hanko hastened from the bridge to the wardroom three decks below.*
>
> *As Hanko stood alone in the wardroom, Nimitz and Halsey entered from the starboard (right) side, and MacArthur came from the port side.*
>
> *In 1998, Hanko and I toured the Missouri not long after its arrival at its final resting place in Pearl Harbor. Pointing to a spot in the center of the*

---

[*] The surrender date had been set for August 31st, but was delayed for two days because of a series of typhoons between Okinawa and Japan.

[†] A replica now hangs on the 0-1 deck of the *Missouri*.

wardroom, Hanko said, "MacArthur, Halsey and Nimitz were right here. "I stood hat in hand 15 or 20 feet away unnoticed as they turned toward each other. Nimitz hadn't seen me. None of them had.

"MacArthur, with his rich voice, went up to Chester, clasped his hand and said, 'Chester'. He took his other hand and put it on Halsey's and said, 'Bill. Chester. This is the day toward which we have strived for so long.' They stood there for a frozen moment. It was history, boy. And there I was alone watching it." (I felt as though I was standing there with Hanko during that historic meeting.)

Shortly afterward, "Halsey took MacArthur and began to go up toward his flag officer's quarters. Nimitz looked around and saw me and said, 'Oh, Henry, I saw your parents two weeks ago and they're fine. I just wanted to tell you that your ship the Missouri will be coming to Guam next week and you'll have dinner with me at my house on Guam.' Then he looked at me and said, 'Henry, where the hell are your collar bars?'

"I said, 'Oh, Sir, I left them in my room.'"

Remonstrating, Nimitz told Hanko to "Go get your collar bars. We may sign the surrender without neckties, but we sure as hell will wear the insignia of our rank." (Nimitz's collars sported rings of five stars.)

Then, as Hanko tells it, Nimitz shook his hand, "smiled his wintry smile and followed Halsey and MacArthur." [389]

From that encounter, 23-year-old Ens. Henry A. Walker, Jr., learned firsthand, as Lamar later reported, that Nimitz "had those steely blue eyes...." Lamar continued, "He could look at you with a twinkle and tell you what you were doing wrong and make you realize it without getting mad at you—or without you getting mad." [390]

At 9:00 a.m., the formalities began on the 0-1 surrender deck (one deck up from the main deck). Hanko says that he stood watch on the "Navigation bridge on the starboard side looking right down on the surrender ceremony 20 feet below me, and I truly believe I had the only unobstructed view of what took place."

Nimitz wrote to the Walkers, "What a story young Henry will have to tell you all—over and over again—when he returns" about "how he helped put Hirohito out of business and how he personally witnessed the surrender scenes."

The *Missouri* was crowded with observers. Uniformed service members packed the sixteen-inch gun turrets and hung from every window and over every rail. Despite the crowds, Lamar recalled that a "dead silence" prevailed.[391] Hanko also recalled a "captain's skimmer" bringing the Japanese emissaries to the starboard side. "They were, of course, all in cutaway coats with striped trousers and top hats as befitted the solemnity of the occasion. The allied uniform...was standard khakis and obviously less formal."[392]

The scene was reminiscent of the surrender of the Confederacy at Appomattox in 1864 with General Grant in his war blues and General Lee in his finest dress gray uniform.

With the ceremony proceeding, Hanko told me, the front row of Russian soldiers on top of the packed Number 2 turret stood up to intentionally block anyone behind them from taking pictures. "There were screams and outcries [from the photographers behind the Russian soldiers] and [they were] finally put down but very few photographs, therefore, were taken of General MacArthur signing for that reason."[393]

Other cameras and photographers, fortunately, had unobstructed views of the ceremony on a platform cantilevered out from the 0-1 deck over the Bay.

Each signatory sat before an ordinary mess deck table covered with green felt and signed two unconditional Instruments of Surrender—a leather-bound version for the Allied forces and a canvas-backed version for the Japanese.

Below Hanko, a somber and diminutive Japanese Foreign

Minister Mamoru Shigemitsu, who boarded the ship wearing a silk top hat and formal morning dress, found himself flanked by the tallest marines they could find. He had difficulty walking on an artificial leg from an assassin's bomb. Because of that disability, Hanko recalled, the Japanese asked that the surrender take place on the main deck. MacArthur refused.

From the main deck, Shigemitsu hobbled up a broad ladder and stepped onto the 0-1 level, next to the powerful Number Two sixteen-inch gun turret. A hushed stillness overcame the Battleship and its hundreds of expectant witnesses.

Shigemitsu, with cane in hand, clip-clopped toward the surrender table. Suddenly, his cane dropped. Stooping, he picked it up with difficulty. At the table, he pulled two watches from his pockets and removed his top hat. He leaned forward and penned his name in *kanji* on behalf of the Japanese government at precisely 9:04 a.m. Shigemitsu was followed by the uniformed General Yoshijiro Umezu, Chief of the Imperial General Staff.

Once the Japanese representatives signed, MacArthur announced through a microphone that he, the "Supreme Commander for the Allied powers will now sign in behalf of the Allied nations at war with Japan."

MacArthur used five pens, the first of which he handed to a still gaunt General Jonathan Wainwright, the highest-ranking American POW who endured over three years of extremely harsh conditions in Japanese prison camps in the Philippines.[*]

Nimitz followed, signing on behalf of the United States, with MacArthur, Halsey and Sherman looking over his shoulder. Nimitz approached the table, pulling two fountain pens from his left khaki pants pocket. He sat down and placed the pens to the right of the surrender documents.

One was an ordinary green Parker Duofold pen he had carried

---

[*] Although Wainwright was a close friend, MacArthur overruled a recommendation that he be awarded the Medal of Honor, apparently for having surrendered Corregidor.

with him throughout the war. The other was the gold-capped Parker 51 Pen given to him by Y. C. Woo three months before in San Francisco.

Even without glasses, Nimitz could clearly read the two halves of the large Instrument of Surrender, each twenty-two and a quarter by fifteen and a half inches. The left side proclaimed Japan's "Unconditional surrender to the Allied Powers." Half-way down on the right side, below MacArthur's signature, was a line under which appeared the simple words, "United States Representative."

Nimitz removed the gold cap of the Woo Pen and held it firmly between his thumb and first two fingers, leaned his stocky body forward, his back ramrod straight. His right hand reached out and penned his name to the Allied copy of the Instrument of Surrender, adding two dots like tiny eyes above "Nimitz." [394]

He recapped the Woo Pen and, while holding it in his left hand, picked up his old fifty-cent green Parker Pen, with which he signed the Japanese copy of the surrender document.

Nimitz later wrote to Catherine that he signed the Allied surrender document "with the Woo gift pen and the second copy with my old green Parker pen." [395]

Nimitz appeared to everyone the invariably calm and cool Fleet Admiral, but admitted later to his wife and Hanko his hidden trepidation.

Perhaps the most famous photograph of the surrender captured the historic scene.

Nimitz inscribed photo: "To Una and Sandy Walker – With best wishes, warm regards and great appreciation of your contribution to the war effort which made possible the above scene." Signed, "C.W. Nimitz, Fleet Admiral, USN."

Representatives of eight other Allied nations—China next—followed Nimitz.

"Let us pray," said MacArthur in a moving statement in his baritone voice after the surrender documents had been signed, "that peace be now restored to the world and that God will preserve it always. These proceedings are closed."

Hanko wrote his mother that from his vantage point above the ceremony on the Navigation Bridge, the "surrender was very exciting. I almost burst as I watched all the signing." Mentioning Nimitz, he continued, "The boss looked very happy. It must have been a load off his chest."

After the ceremony and everyone departed the 0-1 deck. Only one Soviet General, Lieutenant General K. Derevyanko, and a cameraman remained. Hanko, who was still on the bridge, watched Derevyanko sit at the surrender table while being photographed pounding "the table and shaking his finger at an imaginary Japanese on the other side." Hanko at first thought, "This guy is nuts," but soon realized he was making a documentary "for propaganda purposes, dictating the surrender terms."

Hanko imagined that the film would show only the Russian general present during the surrender. In fact, the Russian version of the surrender "showed Derevyanko accepting the Japanese surrender aboard an unidentified warship—a great Russian victory!" [396] When the Soviet Union later claimed it played a major role in the defeat of Japan, Nimitz replied its contribution was "practicably negligible," since they did not declare war on Japan until after the Atomic Bomb had decimated Nagasaki. [397]

"Japan made many strategical mistakes," summed up Imperial Japanese Rear Admiral M. Kanazawa who concluded with perhaps the greatest understatement of all, "but the biggest mistake of all was starting the war." [398]

The day of the surrender, Una, Sandy and Ann drove to 37 Makalapa to plant a lichee tree in honor of Nimitz and to hear the surrender broadcast live at Nimitz's quarters, as reported in Walker Family Communiqué No. 49. "At 3:45 HWT, a little lichee tree was planted carefully with Sandy officiating and Ann wielding the spade with proper style and form...After the planting, we went in to the well-known room and radio to listen to the broadcast from the 'MIGHTY MOE' which began at 4 HWT. It came through so clearly, we could feel the impressive scene and all waited to hear the voice of the Chief. Finally it came with his fine, measured tones, clear and true, giving the credit of winning the war to all the services in the Pacific, with never a thought of praise to himself."

The Missouri Plan of the Day for September 10, 1945, pointed out that, "Many precedents were broken with the signing of the historic document aboard the USS *Missouri*. Never in all the history of the United *States* had such an event taken place aboard a ship of war."

In 1998, exactly fifty-three years later, the ceremony was reenacted aboard the *Missouri* at her final resting place in Pearl Harbor. The most moving words during the ceremony were those of a successor to Nimitz—Adm. Archie Clemins, Commander in Chief, U.S. Pacific Fleet. He quoted from a poignant letter, written by a third class petty officer to his son on the day of the surrender. The petty officer commented first-hand about finally arriving, after four long years of war, in Tokyo Bay. "Over our heads this morning was one of the greatest air-powers ever flown. There were so many planes, that they looked like birds. This bay was full of ships of all descriptions. Now the day I am waiting for is when I can come home to you and your mother for good. May this be kept until you grow old enough to take it and save."

The letter was signed, Archie C. Clemins, EM3—Admiral Clemins' father. Many in the audience were so moved by the words that tears welled up in their eyes. For it was extraordinary to hear Nimitz's successor use his own father's letter in a ceremony honoring that day.

As Archie said of this father, "He would have been surprised that fifty-three years later I would become a part of a commemorative ceremony on the USS *Missouri*. Although he was just a young sailor, he knew he was viewing history on that day. He knew he had been through a difficult journey and he hoped his letter would someday help his son to remember the lessons of the past."

Nimitz and his staff "had a pleasant trip back from Tokyo Bay. We took off at 7:00 a.m. Tokyo time and after circling twice over Tokyo City low enough to see plainly the terrific damage done by our bombers," reminiscent of the devastation facing Nimitz when he landed in Pearl Harbor after the attack. Revenge is a bittersweet reward. Continuing, Lamar wrote, "We headed for Saipan where we landed in our seaplane about 4:30 p.m. Thence to Guam by land plane – and back at my quarters by 6:45 p.m." [399]

At first, Lamar and Nimitz expressed disappointment at not

receiving the Walkers' Communiqué No. 49 which was due. However, Lamar wrote, "You can imagine how happy both the Admiral and I were when we returned [to Guam] late on the third to find the good Doctor in charge of the precious document, which was really tops. The owner [Nimitz] and I did enjoy getting the news so much. ... Both the owner and I can hardly wait for a steak with luau at Muliwai."*

Doc Anderson thanked the Walkers for the communiqué. "The Admiral looks fine," he wrote, "although a little thin..., but as strong and active as ever. The Admiral's little digestive difficulty is much better and you were entirely right ...that he should have gone to a hospital. I tried to persuade him but you know the Chief."

Nimitz sent the Walkers one of the famous photographs of his signing the Instrument of Surrender on the *Missouri*. At the bottom, he wrote, "To Una and Sandy Walker—With best wishes, warm regards and great appreciation of your contribution to the war effort which made possible the above scene." Signed, "C.W. Nimitz, Fleet Admiral, USN."

He also sent photos of himself, Sherman and Lamar aboard the Nineteenth Century Japanese battleship *Mikasa*. The vessel had been the flagship of the famous Japanese Admiral Togo when he defeated the Russian fleet in 1905.

Nimitz realized the *Mikasa* needed protection and ordered a marine guard to prevent looting and damage. (Years later, Nimitz learned that the *Mikasa* had fallen into disrepair. Accordingly, he wrote an article for a Japanese publication, reminding every Japanese citizen of Togo's legacy embodied in the *Mikasa*. Nimitz donated his fee for the article to a *Mikasa* restoration fund, inspiring the Japanese to restore the vessel, which was achieved on May 27, 1961, the fifty-sixth anniversary of the Russian defeat.)

---

* "Luau" refers both to a traditional Hawaiian meal or, as Lamar intended it in his letter, a mixture of taro tops and coconut milk cooked into a consistency similar to spinach.

(L to R): Marine sentry, Nimitz, Adm. Richard Turner, Lt. Gen. Roy Geiger, Adm. Forrest Sherman and Hal Lamar Aboard the 19th Century Japanese Battleship Mikasa[400]

Nimitz sent each Gremlin a One Yen military currency signed by him on the front, and stamped on the back, September 2, 1945 "USS South Dakota," "Tokyo Bay – V-J Day":

Michael A. Lilly

One Yen Currency Stamped USS *South Dakota*, Nimitz's Flagship, and inscribed to Maile (Major Gremlin) and Sheila (Minor Gremlin), Tokyo Bay, September 2, 1945

To Ginger he sent a poem written by a Capt. Gordon Beecher, Jr., entitled "By Nimitz—and Halsey—and Me."

The poem recounted the war with Japan and ended with the surrender in Tokyo Bay:

Nimitz at Ease

Me—and Halsey and Nimitz
Are anchored in Tokyo Bay.
The place is just drippin' American shippin',
They stretch for a helluva way.
We hear that the fighting is finished,
And that is the way it should be.
Remember Pearl Harbor – they started it then.
We're warnin' 'em never to start it again.
For we have a country with millions of men
Like Nimitz—and Halsey—and me.

Nimitz inscibed the poem, "To our Ginger – with best wishes and great aloha from CinCPac – Cincpoa – C.W. Nimitz – Fleet Admiral."

Back on Guam, Lamar was hastily tying up boxes for their return to Pearl Harbor. "Since Admiral Sherman left there has been only the owner [Nimitz] and me for the daily swim."

Although beset by a small tropical storm and rain and high water, they swam nonetheless. "As I write I can hardly see the trees outside my window for the heavy sheet of rain coming down."

A week later, *Missouri* steamed into Apra Harbor, Guam. That evening, Hanko dined with Nimitz at his quarters located on a bluff overlooking a peaceful tropical beach not unlike Muliwai.

Discussing the surrender ceremonies and perhaps evoking a Parker 51 pen advertisement of the day describing it as so "Feather-light" that it "warms your heart as it glides with effortless smoothness," Hanko told Nimitz, "You looked very calm and very cool."

Nimitz's signature may have looked effortlessly smooth, but he felt neither calm nor cool. "Oh, Henry," Nimitz replied with a warm smile, "I was anything but. I shook so with excitement I could hardly sign my name." [401]

To his wife, Nimitz confided, "When it came time to sign, I confess to nervous excitement, but I did sign in the correct places." [402] Not everyone did. One signatory, Canadian Representative

Colonel Lawrence M. Cosgrove, nearly created an international incident, which to this day is a conspicuous embarrassment whenever one looks at the Japanese copy of the Instrument of Surrender. After the ceremony, a Japanese foreign office aide angrily told Lamar their copy of the surrender document was invalid. Instead of signing on the line designated for Canada, Cosgrove had erroneously signed the next line below—the one designated for France. The French representative had to sign on the line for the Netherlands and so forth. Four signatures wound up on the wrong lines. Nimitz and MacArthur told Lamar and Lt. Gen. Richard K. Sutherland, MacArthur's aide, to "Change the thing." They quickly scribbled changes to the document. Under Cosgrove's signature, they struck the words, "Provisional Government of the French Republic Representative" and added in pen the words "Dominion of Canada Representative" and so forth for the next three signatures. Next to each, Sutherland wrote his initials, satisfying the Japanese representative.[403]

When the *Missouri* stopped in Honolulu on its triumphant return, Hanko wrote that waiting on the pier were a host of senior officers along with Nimitz and Hanko's "mother and father and my sister Ann, then a tall, lovely eighteen year old with hair down to her shoulders."[404]

The Captain gave Hanko special permission to stay with his parents while the ship was in port and, thus, he was the first person down the gangway.

The Walkers invited the battleship's entire complement of a hundred twenty-five officers to a lawn party at their Nu'uanu home. About a hundred attended. They played tennis, swam in the pool, and played softball on a diamond laid out in the yard with lime by Sandy. Una rounded up all the young ladies in Honolulu she could find, including Ann, and Sandy corralled vast amounts of fresh milk and, of course, beer, hot dogs, hamburgers, tons of potato and fresh vegetable salads, all items not in plentiful supply on a ship long at sea."[405] The party was a great success, with the officers returning to the battleship sunburned, exhausted, and somewhat inebriated.

In the last Walker Communiqué, No. 50, dated September 23, 1946, Una wrote from the "Same Poker Table ... Same Upstairs Sitting Room" to "Dearly beloved family and friends, poker players, and others...."

> *Haina ia mai ana kapuana la ... Our Aloha ... Sandy and Ann join in sending love. God bless you all deal poker-players and others, and may we gather again round this table with happy hearts and cheery faces....*

Michael A. Lilly

Chapter 26

Post War

FLEET ADMIRAL CHESTER Nimitz returned to Hawai'i long enough to enjoy one Muliwai weekend.

While the *Missouri* was in port, Nimitz hosted a reception aboard the Battleship on September 28, 1945, which the Walkers and all of Nimitz's Honolulu poker friends attended. On the cover of a bi-fold invitation was the photograph of Nimitz signing the Instrument of Surrender.

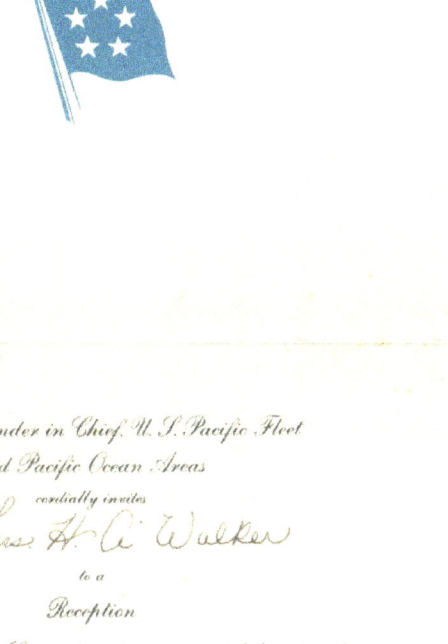

Invitation to September 28, 1945 Reception

Nimitz flew to the mainland on October 2nd. Landing in Oakland at 11:00 a.m., Lamar reported that they were "met by a large group including the [California] Governor [Earl Warren]" * and, after a few speeches, adjourned to the "Bohemian Club for a few drinks and lunch."

Nimitz spent the night with his wife Catherine in Berkley. "Many people asked what I would do with the [Woo] pen", Nimitz had previously written to his wife. "I told them I would give it to a Chinese friend." [406]

That afternoon or evening, Nimitz met with his next-door neighbor and good friend, Y. C. Woo, presenting him with a folder containing the same inscribed surrender photo he had given the Walkers along with the Woo Pen on the gold cap of which he had engraved the words, "Victory Pen." An accompanying note read:

> *I take pleasure in sending you herewith the "Victory Pen" I used as Representative of the United States in signing the first copy of the formal Surrender terms today. This is the pen you presented to me in Berkeley this summer "with best wishes and speedy victory." Your wishes for a speedy victory have been fulfilled. With best wishes—sincerely yours, C.W. Nimitz.* †

At 8:00 p.m. on October 3rd, Nimitz's plane landed at Patuxent, Maryland before flying into Washington. "The Capital's welcome and parade was the biggest and best in history, according to all reports and left nothing to be desired." Nearly a million people lined the streets to greet Nimitz's Caesar-like triumphal return. A "Thousand Navy planes droned overhead…the most planes ever seen—and heard—over an American City."

One squadron spelled out the name:
N I M I T Z[407]

---

* Warren later became Chief Justice of the U.S. Supreme Court.

† The note, together with an autographed photograph of Nimitz signing the Instrument of Surrender with the Woo Pen, are in the possession of Woo's grandson, Paul Woo.

Nimitz gave an address before an appreciative joint session of Congress. President Truman awarded him a Gold Star in lieu of a third Distinguished Service Medal for "Exceptionally Meritorious Service…from June 1944 to August 1945."

On October 9th—dubbed by New York as "Nimitz Day"—Nimitz was honored at a tickertape parade on Fifth Avenue. He was back in Pearl Harbor nine days later. Between then and November 24th when Nimitz turned over his command to Admiral Spruance, he spent a lot of time traveling and speaking on the mainland.

Nimitz asked the Walkers for a personal favor. Navy Day, October 27, 1945, was to be a big day for him. The Daughters and Sons of Hawaiian Warriors were to invest him as a "High Chief of Hawai'i," in a ceremony on the steps of 'Iolani Palace. President Franklin Roosevelt had been the last prominent person so honored in 1934. Nimitz wanted to give a short speech in Hawaiian. To do so, he could not have wished for more knowledgeable friends than the Walkers. From their close personal relationship, he knew that Sandy grew up speaking fluent Hawaiian, and Una had a conversational understanding of the Polynesian language. What he wanted to say in Hawaiian was, "To my good friends of dear Hawai'i, I give my overflowing thanks and my very fullest aloha. Aloha, aloha for all of us."

The Walkers were delighted to accommodate their dear friend and proceeded to translate it into Hawaiian, dutifully typing the words on a five by seven-inch card on which Una added its rough translation in pencil.

Surrounded by a motorcycle escort, Nimitz in choker white uniform, travelled from Pearl Harbor in an open convertible limousine with Hawai'i Governor Ingram Stainback and Honolulu Mayor Lester Petrie along a road built during the war that has been since known as "Nimitz Highway." Arriving at the Palace grounds fronting King Street, Nimitz saluted smartly to a standing-room-only crowd of ten thousand grateful citizens, who gave him a welcoming cheer. Here was the man who had rescued Hawai'i in its darkest hour. The man who had raised the Pacific Fleet from *Davy*

Jones' Locker. Who had saved the islands from invasion and occupation. Who, like David against Goliath, had destroyed the Japanese Imperial Navy and forced its Empire to capitulate. The jubilant audience, which included the Walkers, adored their *kama'aina* Fleet Admiral.

Climbing sixteen steps to the broad Palace lanai, Nimitz was seated between the Mayor and Governor and flanked by Hawaiians attired in traditional feather cloaks and *mahiole* (helmets), *holoku* (missionary-like dresses) and leis, and carrying *kahili* (long poles decorated at the top with a barrel of feathers). At the written invitation of Governor Stainback, as honored guests, Una and Sandy Walker were seated in the VIP section.

Nimitz could not help but recall Sandy's poignant account of the momentous events that took place, where he was sitting nearly fifty-three years before. Sandy's father, J. S. Walker, Sr., had been a member of King Kalakaua's cabinet for many years and a close confidante of his successor Queen Liliuokalani. The senior Walker had approached his Queen in the Palace on January 17, 1893, with a painful duty, reluctantly informing her that a "Committee of Safety" had demanded her abdication, which she at first refused. However, when U.S. marines had lined up on King Street, not two hundred feet from Nimitz's chair, to support the revolutionaries, the Queen relented.

Sandy's father and four older brothers, who supported the Monarch, were briefly detained in the medieval, castle-like Iolani Barracks (to Nimitz's right). Despite repeated publications that the overthrow had been "bloodless," Queen Liliuokalani accurately recorded that Sandy's father had perished "by the treatment he received from the hands of the revolutionists. He was one of many who from persecution had succumbed to death." [408]

Sadly, those revolutionaries included some of the senior Walker's closest friends and associates. Sandy said the overthrow was an injustice and proudly proclaimed the Walkers a family of "Royalists and not missionaries."

Thinking about 'Iolani Palace behind him, Nimitz may have

smiled at a shared prank. He and Sandy enjoyed a poker game with friends sitting at King Kalakaua's koa poker table in a sitting room next to the King's second floor bedroom.

Opening a small drawer, Nimitz and Sandy noticed that others had inscribed their names. Looking at one another, they exchanged knowing smiles instantly realizing what they were about to do next. Nimitz used a pen with blue ink to write his name "CWNimitz". Sandy added his initials "HAW" to the left in pencil. A little joke a friend of Sandy's grandson did not discover until seventy-four years later.

Nimitz's and Sandy's Initials on a Drawer of King Kalakaua's Koa Poker Table, 'Iolani Palace[409]

Looking across the spacious Palace lawns and mature trees and beyond King Street, Nimitz caught sight of the massive eighteen-foot tall bronze statue of King Kamehameha, which had been erected in front of the Hawai'i Supreme Court building in 1883. The statue's gaze and outstretched right hand beckoned beguilingly to Nimitz, as the ceremony began with the haunting sound of a conch shell blown by David Kahea, followed by the Kamehameha chant by Malea Kau. Governor Stainback rose to issue a proclamation declaring that day "Navy and Nimitz Day." A formation of two hundred Navy fighter planes flew overhead in perfect unison. "All the pomp and color of old Hawai'i was revived for a few moments, and even the heavens obliged with a hint of a shower that brought a vivid double rainbow which the Hawaiians have always considered a good omen." [410]

The Governor's wife placed violet leis around Nimitz's neck. A Hawaiian *wahine* (lady), wearing colorful leis on her head and around her neck draped what the newspapers described as a brilliant yellow, feather cape (an *'ahu 'ula*) over his broad shoulders.[*]

Two spears held by Hawaiian men were crossed over his head. Nimitz's name was entered in the roll of Hawaiian *Ali'i* (hereditary chiefs) forever linking him to the *aina* (land) and Hawai'i's people.

It was Nimitz's turn to speak. Standing before the expectant crowd, he pulled Una's card from his pocket and read his appreciation in Hawaiian:

> E na hoaloha Maikai o Hawai`i, Nei, Ke Haawi Aku Nei Au, I Kuu Hoomaikai Piha, Ame Kuu Aloha Nui Loa, Ia Oukou Apau, Aloha, Aloha Kakou

> (To my good friends of dear Hawai`i, I give my

---

[*] DeSoto Brown, the Bishop Museum archivist, told the author, "Feather garments were no longer being made in the 20th century. There were lots of reasons: rarity or extinction of the birds that provided the feathers, and the incredibly painstaking and time-consuming work to make the foundation netting, as well as tying innumerable tiny bundles of feathers to it. This latter process was daunting, even if you used modern dyed feathers from chickens or ducks." After reviewing a newspaper photo of Nimitz with the feather cape, he believed it was "a crepe paper cape and not a feather one" similar to a cape shown in the book *Hawai'i: Royal Isles*, which was published by the museum in 1980.

overflowing thanks and my very fullest aloha. Aloha, aloha for all of us.)

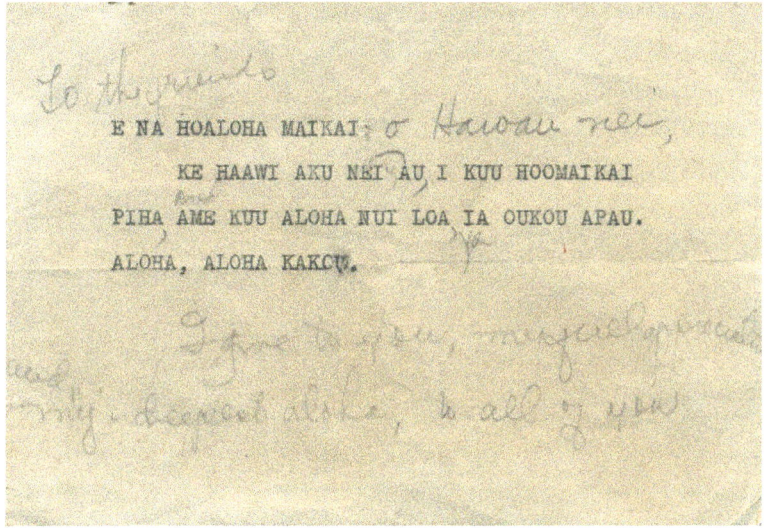

Nimitz's Speech Translated in Hawaiian by Una & Sandy Walker, October 27, 1945

That short speech, given in the native language of Hawaiʻi, brought a rousing ovation from the crowd and tears to the Walkers' eyes. After the ceremony, spear-bearers escorted Nimitz to his limousine, in which he travelled to the pink Royal Hawaiian Hotel in Waikiki for a luncheon, hosted by the Honolulu Chamber of Commerce in his honor.

He was presented with an oil painting by the late artist, Lionel Walden, of sea waves crashing against a rocky shore with the Waianae range in the background. The painting was a gift of civic associations and several thousand citizens of Hawaiʻi who contributed $1 each.

Nimitz had, at one time, unwittingly placed the bug in the Walkers' ear that he admired Walden's paintings. His wish became their command that Navy Day 1945.*

At 12:45 p.m., Nimitz stood before a clutch of microphones at the Royal Hawaiian and gave an address, which was broadcast nationwide before a live audience that included Sandy and Una. From his experiences in the war, he had changed his mind about unifying the armed services.

"The people of Hawai'i," he said, "have seen our fleet rise from the mud of Pearl Harbor.... [Hawai'i] will remain the cornerstone of sea power in the Pacific."

Relating a classic lesson from the victory over Japan, he said America was a maritime nation. "Without sea power we would not be the victors today. Without adequate sea power, we cannot ensure our children the fruits of that victory tomorrow. Sea power is our birthright. Let us appreciate it and keep it." [411]

He continued that, while we won the war, if Japan had followed up its attack with an invasion, "Our capacity for recovery here might have been destroyed and the war might have been indefinitely prolonged or even lost."

He warned that America "must maintain occupying forces in troubled areas of the world to insure that we will not lose much or all that we have gained at great cost." Those words ring as true today as they did seven decades ago.

Before the day was out, Nimitz inscribed another photograph of himself "To Una and Sandy Walker":

---

* The painting now resides over a table at the Boston home of Nimitz's granddaughter Sarah Smith.

To Una and Sandy Walker—
With best wishes and great appreciation of all you have done for me and our officers and men throughout the war with the Japanese.
Affectionately, C.W. Nimitz, Fleet Admiral.

Although there is no record of it, in the remaining month, no doubt Nimitz and the Walkers got together and enjoyed a weekend or two at Muliwai. We will never know for sure.

On November 24th at 11:30 a.m., under sunny skies, Nimitz relinquished command to his dear friend and war colleague, Spruance. Nearly four years before, he had assumed command, during the darkest days of the war aboard the submarine USS *Grayling* (SS 209). Now, he turned over command on board one of the Navy's newest submarines, USS *Menhaden* (SS 377). "It is appropriate," he said, "that I am relinquishing command aboard a submarine in Pearl Harbor, and it is appropriate that Admiral Spruance is relieving me."

He continued that it "was from Pearl Harbor that this fleet fought its way across the Pacific to victory. And it was under the able leadership of Spruance that the Japanese navy was severely crippled." Nimitz's flag was struck, and Spruance's broken out. For the first time since December 31, 1941, Fleet Admiral Nimitz no longer commanded the Pacific Fleet.

৵ ৵ ৵

Whether Nimitz would become the next CNO remained uncertain, until he met with another friend of the Walkers, Edwin W. Pauley, a power in the Democrat Party, who helped install Truman in the Whitehouse. During a private conference at the Damon Kailua property, Nimitz convinced Pauley that he should be CNO. To Nimitz's astonishment, Pauley picked up the Damon's phone, called Truman long distance, and told him so. * 412

On December 15th, Nimitz replaced Fleet Admiral King as Chief of Naval Operations. He and Catherine moved into their new official residence, the historic U.S. Naval Observatory on Observatory Hill in Washington, D.C. A few days before, he wrote

---

* The following year, Truman nominated Pauley as Secretary of the Navy. Harold Ickes resigned as Secretary of the Interior in protest, claiming Pauley had tried to bribe him. The scandal doomed Pauley's nomination.

to the Walkers, "Within a few days after you receive this letter, I expect to be in my new job as Chief of Naval Operations without having had a moment's time off."

He said that he "pictured you all at Muliwai enjoying charcoal steaks, walks on the beach, swims, etc. How I miss all of that!"

Hanko received a letter from Joe Lyle, the Supply Officer who had attended many Walker gatherings, including Una's fifty-seventh birthday party. Lyle had seen Nimitz in D.C., since becoming CNO, and described him as "busier than a one-armed paper hanger."

Although Nimitz "has his hands full," Hanko wrote his parents that he was surprised to receive a very long and slender package in the mail from the Fleet Admiral. At the time, Hanko was aboard the *Missouri,* anchored in the middle of the harbor of New York City. Inside the package was a special gift—the samurai sword of Rear Admiral Keiji Shibazaki, the Imperial Japanese commander of the Gilbert Island of Betio who had perished under Spruance's bombardment on November 20, 1943. Attached to the sword was a small tag, "To LIEUT (jg) HENRY A. WALKER, Jr., with great aloha, C.W. Nimitz, Fleet Admiral, USN."

Hanko assured his mother that he had thanked the Fleet Admiral profusely for the thoughtful gift.[*] In his thank-you letter to Nimitz, Hanko expressed, "How very much I owe you my deep gratitude for all you have done for me." (Even though Hanko never sharpened it, when I pulled the sword from its scabbard sixty-eight years later, its blade was still razor sharp and extremely dangerous.)

Sandy and Una traveled to the East Coast for two months in the spring of 1946 for business and pleasure. Hanko had become engaged to the former Nancy Johnston, with their wedding set for March 10th in New York. Three days before, he had taken leave

---

[*] Years later, Hanko tracked down the Admiral's family in Japan, offering to return the sword. The offer was refused because the sword "had been lost honorably in battle with its owner giving up his life for his country." *Memoirs,* 34.

from the *Missouri* and rushed to Washington D.C. to see his parents. When Nimitz got wind of the nuptials, he "insisted on holding my bachelor's party at his home [the U.S. Naval Observatory]" the next evening.

"Not bad for a lieutenant junior grade!" concluded National Geographic Associate Editor and author, Frederick Simpich Jr. [413]

Lamar and Sandy were present at the bachelor's party, along with other young friends. "Although it was not a boisterous or licentious affair, there was plenty of conviviality, and Nimitz provided numerous old-fashioneds with his distinctive spoonful of dark rum floating on top." [414]

No sooner did Hanko and Nancy marry, but Hanko departed on the *Missouri* on March 22nd for a tour of the Mediterranean. Una reminded him to thank Nimitz for the bachelor's party and all the many advantages the Fleet Admiral had provided. "Yes, Dear Mar," Hanko responded. "I already had written Adm CW a five page report on our Mediterranean doings." He had "thanked him effusively for making it all possible" and "made it quite apparent he was my guardian angel." Because Nimitz had yet to meet Nancy, "I told him I wanted to come down this summer and show him Nancy."

Meanwhile, Sandy and Una remained in D.C., until the end of April, meeting with their friend Nimitz from time to time. On Monday April 1st, Nimitz and his wife Catherine hosted cocktails for the Walkers and their Honolulu friends, the Phillip Spaldings. On April 29th, Nimitz wrote, "I hope Sandy's mission in Washington has been successful and that your return to those lovely Islands in the Pacific will be comfortable and safe and that it may not be too long before we are privileged to meet again."

In May, Hanko applied to the Columbia School of Business and pondered whether to ask Nimitz for a recommendation because "he'd already done so much for me already, and made my naval career a proud and happy experience." Deciding to do so, he wrote "Boss," saying, "If he didn't or felt he'd rather not write the letter, I would be terribly grateful anyway. He wrote me immediately back one of the cheeriest letters he ever has written saying how happy he was to do it, enclosing a copy of the letter he'd sent to Columbia and it was something. He didn't spare the superlatives."

Nimitz's letter to the Dean of Columbia said that the "Walkers have been very good friends of mine…and I feel sure that Henry…will make a student you will be proud to have in your school." With such an endorsement, Hanko was promptly admitted.

In late May 1946, Una and Sandy wrote to Nimitz, enclosing a photograph of their first grandson born to Ginger, a nine-pound, seven and one-half ounce boy. Responding, Nimitz congratulated the Walkers and Lillys on my birth:[*]

> *Congratulations to the Parents and Grandparents on the safe arrival of another heir. My! What a husky and healthy young fellow he is.*

Nimitz also waxed longingly of the times he spent on Hawai'i beaches during the war: "Just the thought of the beach at Kailua and at Muliwai fills me with nostalgia."

As well it should, being so far away from the tropical shores of La'ie that provided so much solace from the toils of war. As CNO, Nimitz was spending more time at work than when he was in command of the Pacific Fleet. Spruance visited him in July 1946, and from his post in Newport, Rhode Island, as President of the U.S. Naval War College, wrote to Una, lamenting Nimitz's lack of exercise:

---

[*] Adm. John Towers' wife, Pierrette, sent Ginger a note on my birth, "Congratulations, indeed to you all…but it's not a baby, it's an elephant!"

Hanko, still aboard the *Missouri* at sea, gave my arrival "Five hundred blasts," writing his mother "It sure is cheery to have a bouncing young nephew."

> *I saw various of our friends in Washington including, of course, Nimitz. He was looking well, but he told me that he did not get away from his office until six p.m., and was not getting much exercise these days. He ought to have at least one month's leave with nothing on his mind, but I am afraid he will never get that as long as he is C.N.O. Washington was at its usual summer temperature, and I was glad to leave it and get back to cool Newport.*

Nimitz did, however, begin a routine of walking the six-and-a-half-mile roundtrip between work and Observatory Hill, sometimes arranging to meet Catherine on the way home.[415]

He also continued tossing horseshoes, arranging frequent games with his newfound friend and equally matched opponent, President Harry Truman. One day, a visitor boasted about being particularly good at the game. Nimitz "promptly phoned the President. 'Mr. President,' he said, 'I've got a live one here. Can we make a date?'" They did, to the likely chagrin of the visitor, when he realized who his opponent was.[416]

In early 1946, Sandy and Una constructed a separate, large cottage with fireplace at Muliwai, filling it with elegant Monarchy-era Koa furniture. A Hawaiian *Kahu*—priest or minister—blessed the structure.

Christened the "Nimitz Cottage," Nimitz and Catherine were invited to visit and stay, but it was never to be. Nimitz never returned to Hawai'i or saw Muliwai again.

From his letters, however, we know that for the rest of his life, he recalled those enchanting Muliwai weekends with a sense of wistful nostalgia.

The Author, Climbing the Steps of the New "Nimitz Cottage," Muliwai, 1946

That September, Una recorded that Hollywood mogul, Samuel Goldwyn, stood on the lanai of the new Nimitz Cottage, looking out over the mountains. Echoing Nimitz's sentiments, Goldwyn said in his philosophical way that he could feel a happiness and soul in Muliwai.

Una, thinking of those many weekends during the war entertaining Nimitz, told Goldwyn the aura he felt arose "from the associations of loving friends and family, from the memory of all the lovely days spent there together, and from the hope of those to come." Her words resonated with the artistic heart of the famous movie producer.

In response to Hanko's Christmas card that December, Nimitz invited him to D.C. Hanko thought better of it, writing his mother, "He has his hands so full and he is so busy I thought I might inconvenience him. So I have contented myself by writing at length how very much I owe him and my deep gratitude for all he has done, and my happiness in my assignment. He sent me a large colored photograph of the *Missouri*, and I shall write him a thank you this morning."

Michael A. Lilly

In February 1947, Nimitz travelled to the Columbia School of Business to receive yet another in a long line of honorary degrees. He wrote that he "had hoped for and fully expected to have an opportunity to chat with Hanko and his bride, but to my great disappointment I did not see Hanko." (Unfortunately, Hanko was not aware he had been there, until he received a letter from Nimitz.)

Sometime during his service as CNO, Nimitz was treated to a final accolade from his connection to Hawai'i. Neither he nor Eisenhower, with whom he had served on the Joint Chiefs of Staff, had any political ambitions. However, they did discuss the possibility of one or both of them being drafted for political service. A Hawai'i veterans' group "introduced a resolution that they favored Ike for the next president. Hawai'i was Nimitz country, however, and a spirited debate on the resolution took place to the end that it was Nimitz the group endorsed for the presidency."

Nimitz gave a press release of the endorsement to his colleagues on the Joint Chiefs "and then with mock seriousness observed to Eisenhower that he had clearly defeated him in the first test of presidential strength." [417]

Nimitz continued as Chief of Naval Operations until December 15, 1947. When Tony Lilly had duty in Washington D.C., the family occasionally met with the Fleet Admiral. In one meeting with Tony, Nimitz asked about Ginger and the girls. Nimitz knew they tried to see him while in San Francisco, but he had already left for the East Coast and was sorry to have missed them. In late 1948, Tony heard Nimitz was in the Pentagon and went to see him. At first, the Fleet Admiral looked like a lonely soul, just sitting by himself in an office seemingly without very much to do. But he beamed when he saw Tony and said, "Tell me all about Ginger and the children and please say hello and give them my good wishes."

In March of 1949, Nimitz accepted the position of Plebiscite Administrator in Kashmir for the United Nations. Ginger wrote her mother that Nimitz had been "going between Wash. and N. York preparing for his departure to Kashmir at the end of the month. Mrs. N. is going too, and they'll be there 15 months."

Tony had again met with the Fleet Admiral at the Pentagon. Nimitz was delighted to see him and asked after the family. During the conversation, Nimitz mentioned Kashmir. Eyeing Tony's braided gold aiguillettes of an admiral's aide, he said wistfully that he had been searching for an aide, strongly hinting the job was Tony's if he wanted it. When Tony arrived home, he discussed the "offer" with Ginger and later with a Navy detailer, weighing its pros and cons for several days.

On the last day of March, Tony attended a stag party of naval officers including Nimitz, who asked him again to "send my best wishes" to Ginger and the children. Nimitz told Tony, "I'm up to my neck in this Kashmir business," and mentioned anew he was "still looking for an aide." For a moment, "Tony almost offered" to accept the position, Ginger wrote, "but thought better of it." While being Nimitz's aide in Kashmir would have been a great honor with extra pay, it would have removed him from the normal career path for a naval officer, which was command at sea. Tony's Navy detailer said, with the post-war draw down, some of his classmates would not be promoted, so he should get a year of command as soon as possible.

"Tony is very anxious to get sea duty for his record," but "What an interesting time" it would have been to work for Nimitz, Ginger mused. It was fortunate Tony did not take the job. While Nimitz was appointed Plebiscite Administrator, he never actually took up the post, because the conditions of appointment, including an agreement between India and Pakistan, were never fulfilled. And in less than a year, Tony, a young Lieutenant Commander, took command of the second of his five ship commands, the patrol frigate USS *Newport* (PF 27) in Yokosuka.

Sometime that year, Nimitz received a manuscript from William A. Simonds of a book he was writing on the Centennial of American Factors entitled *Kamaaina—A Century in Hawaii*. He had asked, because Sandy figured prominently in the book, if Nimitz would be willing to write its Introduction. Nimitz was delighted to do so, and in three paragraphs summarized the history of the company from the days of the gold rush to the end of World War II and closing with a tribute to his dear friend Sandy Walker:

> *I have known Hawaii for a good many years, both in peace and war, and am proud of the many friends I have there. One of them is H. Alexander Walker, [P]resident of American Factors, Ltd. During World War II the company, led by President Walker, made its land available for military installations, loaned its equipment to help in their construction, diverted sugar land to the production of food, made available to the military government the services of its organization from its President on down, and, in short, cooperated wholeheartedly and patriotically to the fullest degree with the armed services in the conduct of the war in the Pacific.*
> C.W Nimitz
> *FLEET ADMIRAL, U.S.N.*[418]

Nimitz and the Walkers continued corresponding for the next nineteen years. On March 21, 1951, he wrote Hanko in long hand, "Give my love to Sandy & Una and tell them both—I never forget their wonderful hospitality and friendship during the war years."

In February 1955, Una was visiting friends and family in the Bay area. One evening, she attended the opera in San Francisco and ran into Nimitz and Catherine—the last recorded meeting between the families. They had a cordial, if brief, reunion. Later that month, Nimitz thanked the Walkers for their "birthday greetings and good wishes, which arrived on my seventieth birthday. Although the official records say I am seventy—I do not feel quite that number of years and I credit that feeling to lesser responsibility—and more gardening and horseshoe pitching. It was good to see Una at the opera house...and to hear about your very large family of grandchildren. We still have only six."

In his last communication, a handwritten letter dated March 16, 1965, Nimitz thanked the Walkers "a million for your telegram of Birthday congratulations & good wishes on my 80th BD." He had been so "swamped by cards, telegrams & letters" that he had "now sworn off birthdays, interviews and anything that attracts mail."

He still suffered from a bad fall in 1963, which "severed a tendon in my right leg" and destroyed a kneecap, but was "lucky to have reached four score years." For the vigorous, exercise-loving Fleet Admiral, his physical infirmity was dismaying.

best of health and spirits, We have kept well inspite of added years - but I still suffer from the effects of a bad fall I had in Oct 1963, an accident that resulted in a severed tendon in my right leg - at the knee. However - I am very lucky to have reached four score years. I am sure you two nice people revel in the proximity of so many handsome children + grandchildren - Our six grandchildren live in the East - 3 in New Canaan, Conn. + 3 in Newport R.I. Out here we have our two younger children Nancy - unmarried in Santa Monica + Mary - Sister M. Aquinas, OP. A Dominican nun who teaches Science at the Dominican College, San Rafael - Warm + affectionate regards + good wishes to you both — Amanda — Chester W. Nimitz

Last Letter from Nimitz

As a Fleet Admiral, Nimitz remained on active duty for the rest of his life until he passed away in his quarters at Treasure Island Naval Station eleven months later on February 20, 1966, just four days shy of his eight-first birthday and the day after Sandy Walker's eighty-first birthday. Carrying out his directions, he was buried at Golden Gate National Cemetery, San Bruno, California, alongside his lifetime naval companions, Admirals Spruance, Richmond K. Turner and Lockwood. Nimitz's simple headstone bears five stars, "Chester W. Nimitz, FADM," and his dates of birth and death.

The great Civil War Gen. William T. Sherman could have been writing of Nimitz when he expressed to Grant on March 10, 1864, that "You are as brave, patriotic, and just, as the great prototype Washington; as unselfish, kind-hearted, and honest, as a man should be; but the chief characteristic in your nature is the simple faith in success you have always manifested, which I can liken to nothing else than the faith a Christian has in his Saviour." [419]

Looking back on Nimitz's life and the scope of his achievements on behalf of all mankind, calls to mind the French war hero and novelist André Malraux's quote, "Man is the sum of his actions, of what he has done, of what he can do, nothing else." [420]

In Nimitz's case, that sum is a very large number.

After his death, Catherine Nimitz felt like her husband had "just gone to sea and, as I have done so many times in the past, some day I will follow him." [421]

She followed him in 1979 and was buried next to him.

Michael A. Lilly

Afterword

SOMETIME AFTER THE war, Y. C. Woo gave Nimitz a huge, stuffed, largemouth bass as a present. In return, Nimitz gave Woo, who was shorter than the tall Fleet Admiral, a small, stuffed, red snapper, saying "A small man gave a big fish to a big man; a big man gives a small fish to a small man."

Woo's grandson Paul proudly displays the small, red snapper in his Chicago home. Y. C. Woo passed away in 1983. The eulogy described him as a naval officer.

On September 2, 2013, the USS Missouri Memorial Association celebrated the 68th anniversary of the signing of the Instrument of Surrender aboard the USS *Missouri*, as it does every year. During the ceremony, the Navy Order of the United States unveiled a magnificent eight-foot bronze statue of Fleet Admiral Chester W. Nimitz on the pier next to the *Missouri*. The Navy Order selected *Missouri* over 22 other competing locations. Nimitz's twin grandsons, Chester Nimitz ("Chet") and Richard "Dick" Lay were present. I was honored to speak for the Association about Nimitz, his close relationship with the Walkers during World War II, and a few of the anecdotes chronicled here, before welcoming Chet to the podium.

"This is the anniversary of the signing of the surrender of

Japan, September 2, 1945, here on the battleship *Missouri*," said Chet. "I think we're honoring not just our grandfather but all the veterans who fought and died in World War II." (Chet, Dick and I have since become good friends).

Nimitz had donated the green Parker 51 pen with which he signed the Japanese Instrument of Surrender to the Naval Academy Museum. But what happened to the Woo Pen, with which he signed the Allied surrender document? For seven decades it was lost to history, until with determination and a great deal of luck, historian Jeff Harding and Paul Woo tracked down the Woo Pen. Woo had given it to a member of Chang Kai Shek's Nationalist Chinese Government, but it was left behind when his government fled China from Mao Zedong's onslaught to Taiwan. The pen eventually wound up in the Nanjing Museum, where it rests to this day.[422]

I wanted Nanjing Museum to loan the Woo Pen to the USS Missouri Memorial Association for the seventieth Anniversary of the Surrender aboard the battleship on September 2, 2015. My friend and former Deputy Assistant Secretary of the Navy, Bill Cassidy, suggested I write to the Chinese Ambassador, Cui Tiankui, in Washington D.C., which I did. I explained that the loan would represent a great opportunity to "highlight…the alliance between our two nations in bringing World War II to a victorious conclusion."

The Ambassador agreed and opened doors leading to an agreement between the USS Missouri Memorial Association and Nanking Museum for a loan of the Woo Pen. The U.S. Naval Academy also loaned Nimitz's green Parker® Pen. For the first time in seventy years, the two pens Nimitz used to sign the Instruments of Surrender were reunited.

The photo shows me together with Paul Woo holding the Woo Pen and Chet Lay with the green Parker Pen.

Michael A. Lilly

Paul Woo with Nimitz's Woo Pen, Chet Lay with his grandfather's Green Parker Pen, and Michael A. Lilly, aboard the Battleship Missouri on the seventieth Anniversary of the Surrender, September 2, 2015

In a poignant postscript, in 2012 Woo's grandson, Paul, and granddaughter, Yvonne, visited Nimitz's grave to pay respects to him and Catherine. Paul recounted: "We stood for several minutes in silence before the marble tablet on a beautiful California morning. Drawing back, we gazed on the acres of such tablets—the final home of so many service men and women. Walking among those silent graves and reading their inscriptions brought to mind many things, chief among them, what the Fleet Admiral likely knew, that his command decisions were extraordinarily important and difficult, and countless resulting sacrifices would be necessary to bring victory and return peace. What made Nimitz such a great man was that, like the small red snapper he gave my grandfather, he knew his mission was much greater than any one man. His humility is part of that which made the Fleet Admiral such a superb leader and person."

Chester W. Nimitz, Jr., retired in 1957 as a Captain, but was awarded the honorary "tombstone" rank of Rear Admiral for his brilliant war record. Because of failing health in 2002, he and his wife of sixty-three years sadly chose to end their lives in a suicide pact.

Fleet Admiral Ernest King was awarded a third Distinguished Service Medal by President Harry Truman, a Congressional Joint Resolution of Appreciation, and an Honorary Degree from Harvard University. He left active service after relieved by Nimitz as CNO and died at the age of seventy-eight on June 25, 1956.

Adm. Raymond A. Spruance, as most military history buffs know, commanded the U.S. forces in our victory at the Battle of Midway in June 1942. I have never seen it published anywhere, but my grandfather told me that Spruance told him that, once he set the battle in motion, he retired to his stateroom to read a mystery novel. He figured if he meddled, he would likely screw things up. Spruance relieved Halsey as head of the fleet, then renamed the Fifth Fleet, and later succeeded Nimitz as Commander in Chief, Pacific Fleet. The Walkers continued entertaining him, with weekends at Muliwai, until Admiral Towers relieved him. Spruance's last position was as President of the U.S. Naval War College in Newport, Rhode Island, where he served with distinction until his retirement in 1948. Although recommended by Nimitz, he never received the five-star rank his outstanding service to our nation deserved. He passed away at age eighty-three on December 13, 1969.

Fleet Admiral William Halsey wrote his memoirs in 1948, *Admiral Halsey's Story*, a self-aggrandizing revisionist account of his poor judgment during the Battle of Leyte Gulf. Astonishingly, he blamed Rear Adm. Thomas Kinkaid for letting Kurita's fleet catch Task Force 77 by surprise. His finest hours were Doolittle's raid on Japan and Guadalcanal. Like many dynamic wartime military leaders, however, Halsey found ennui and too much alcohol in peace. He passed away in 1959 at the age of seventy-six.

Vice Adm. Charles H. McMorris (Soc) went on to command the 14th Naval District in Pearl Harbor where he continued a close relationship with the Walkers, and occasional weekends at Muliwai, until he retired in 1952. Sherman wrote to the Walkers in 1946 that Soc was in the running for Surgeon General of the United States, but it was not to be. Just a short ten years after the many days, evenings and weekends of activities with the Walkers chronicled here, he passed away on a trip to Chile in 1954 at the young age of sixty-three.

Hal Lamar, Nimitz's consummate Aide, retired from the Navy as a Commander. He was still pining over Ann when he wrote her—"Dearest Ann"—on July 25, 1946, aboard the amphibious flagship USS *Appalachian* (AGC 1), observing the Bikini Atoll atomic bomb test "Baker." "The second bomb went off on schedule this morning and made quite a splash. We were much closer this time and had an excellent view. We are now anchored on the edge of the lagoon waiting for the scientists to say the water is safe from radio activity. It's hot as hell and no breeze. I miss you!"

Unfortunately for Hal, Ann had met and fallen in love with C.E.S "Frank" Burns, Jr., a Hawai'i sugar plantation manager; they were married seven months later.

In 1984, the Admiral Nimitz Foundation published a forty-four-page booklet by Hal Lamar, *I Saw Stars: Some Memories of Commander Hal Lamar, Fleet Admiral Nimitz' Flag Lieutenant, 1941-1945*. Considering he was an eyewitness to the most significant events of America's war in the Pacific and the incredible movers and shakers with whom he rubbed shoulders during that time, the book is sadly deficient of historical content. But he never forgot the times he spent with the Walkers.

Lamar's last letter to the Walkers in September 1948, was addressed to Una, in advance of her fifty-ninth birthday:

This afternoon while reading a story about the month of

> *September, I found the following under the date of the 19th [Una's birthday]: "Ambitious, energetic and a hard conscientious worker, you help those dear to you even at the cost of your physical well being. You are colorful, accurate, discreet and somewhat fastidious. You love music, dancing and literature and make an interesting conversationalist. You are loving and kind and will be contented." Sounds a little like the dearest and sweetest lady in all Hawai`i. Since I can't deliver my aloha in person this year, I take this means of wishing you a happy birthday and many more to come.*
>
> * * *
>
> *I look back over our days in Hawai'i together with most nostalgic memories. They will always be the happiest days of my life and I shall never be able to thank you for your many, many kindnesses. The Walkers will always be my favorite family.*

Una responded that Lamar's letter "was a masterpiece and touched my heart. There never was lady born with all the attributes you credited to me, although I was greatly complimented by your words. Your loyalty to your 'favorite family' is unsurpassed, and all join to thank you for your letter."

Wherever he was and whatever he did, "We hope that you are happy and well...." Lamar passed away in 2002 in Marietta, Georgia, at the ripe old age of ninety-one.

Thomas C. "Doc" Anderson, who graduated from the U.S. Naval Academy in 1914, was promoted to the permanent rank of Rear Admiral on January 8, 1946. After serving as Fleet Surgeon, he became Medical Officer in Command of the National Naval Medical Center, Bethesda, Maryland. In 1969, he described Nimitz as "The calmest man in the face of great problems that I have ever known." [423]

Adm. Royal Eason Ingersoll remained as Commander, Western Sea Frontier until his retirement in 1946, and the command disestablished. He passed away in 1976 at the age of ninety-two.

Adm. Forrest Sherman, Nimitz's Deputy Chief of Staff, regularly corresponded with the Walkers. While commanding the Mediterranean fleet in 1948, he wrote, "I miss you and my other friends there. There is nothing like them over here, and few like you anywhere. Some day I must bring my bride out there."

In October 1949, Sherman became the youngest Chief of Naval Operations until Elmo Zumwalt in 1970. He wrote the Walkers that if he landed in Honolulu, he hoped to "hang my hat in your house" as it was "a fine secluded spot and might not have quite such complex personality problems as may exist elsewhere."

In fact, in early February 1950, the Walkers entertained Sherman and the Joint Chiefs of Staff at Muliwai.* The JCS Chairman, General of the Army Omar Bradley, thanked the Walkers for their "delightful luau dinner at your home. It was a special treat ... to hear fine Hawaiian music again." After dinner, Una had entertained the JSC with her ukulele.

Sherman's last letter dated July 5, 1951 was mailed after a stopover in Honolulu, noting, "How much I enjoyed seeing you and Sandy and our relaxing forenoon at Mulewei [sic]." Just seventeen days later, while on a diplomatic mission to Europe, Admiral Sherman died after a series of heart attacks at the young age of fifty-four. Yet he had already cheated death by six years. Lamar wrote the Walkers from Guam on March 27, 1945, that while Sherman was taking off from Iwo Jima, "a Jap sniper put a bullet through the exhaust of one engine" of his plane, the "Pink Lady." Soldiers believe there is only one bullet with your name on it; that one was missing the name, "Sherman." Lamar facetiously concluded that

---

*The four members of the Joint Chiefs at the time were General of the Army Omar Bradley, Sherman, Gen. L. Lawton Collins, and Gen. Hoyt S. Vandenberg. They were in Honolulu for three days on a return trip from the western Pacific and a strategy meeting with General MacArthur.

their flag plane, the Pink Lady, had been "recommended for the purple heart."

Adm. Thomas C. Hart, after completion of his one-man inquiry on June 15, 1944, returned to retired status, but not anonymity. In 1945, he was appointed U.S. Senator from Connecticut to fill a vacancy, but declined to run for reelection. He passed away on July 4, 1971, at the age of ninety-four.

Adm. John Towers relieved Spruance as Command in Chief of the Pacific Fleet in 1946. In 1947, he was appointed the first Commander in Chief of the Pacific Command, served only two months, and retired at the end of that year. He passed away in 1955 at the age of seventy.[*] He and his wife Pierette Anne are buried at Arlington National Cemetery.

Secretary of the Navy Frank Knox, who attended parties at the Walkers' Nu'uanu home and Muliwai with Nimitz and his staff, died of a heart attack on April 28, 1944, at the age of seventy. Knox went to the grave without acknowledging his personal culpability in not timely informing Kimmel that he expected a surprise attack by the Japanese on Pearl Harbor within three hours.

James Forrestal, the reclusive if brilliant politician who succeeded Knox as Secretary of the Navy, became the first peacetime Secretary of Defense in 1947. To the graduating U.S. Naval Academy class of 1946—which included the future President Jimmy Carter and Vice-presidential candidate Vice Adm. James Stockdale—he spoke of the humble origins of the Navy heroes of World War II. King's father was a "railroad employee."

> *Nimitz came from a small town in Texas where his grandfather ran a small hotel...Halsey was "the son of a naval family.*
>
> *Mitscher's father was one of the first settlers of*

---

[*] As mentioned, Charlie Bryant, the PBY pilot who, the night before Pearl Harbor, poo-pooed Ginger's concerns about the fleet being in peril, became Towers' flag lieutenant.

Michael A. Lilly

Oklahoma...Turner's father was a '49er in California."

Forrestal thanked "God that the Naval Academy produced men of [such] patriotism, talent and discipline."

When in Hawaiʻi, he visited the Walkers, staying at Muliwai or for dinner in Nuʻuanu as guest of honor. On March 28, 1949, Truman fired Forrestal as Secretary of Defense.* Rumors circulated that Forrestal was "unbalanced," but Tony told Ginger "Everyone at the Pentagon says it's not true."

Perhaps it was. Two months later Forrestal jumped to his death from a window—suicide brought on by extreme depression at a time when "His nation... probably needed him more than ever before." [424] He was only fifty-seven. In 1954, the Navy launched the first "Supercarrier," USS *Forrestal* (CV 59).

Adm. Husband E. Kimmel, though exonerated by the 1944 Naval Court of Inquiry, was never fully vindicated. He retired as two-star Rear Admiral and died on May 14, 1968, at the age of eighty-six, carrying the unresolved stain of Pearl Harbor with him to his death. His family's repeated attempts to restore his four-star rank were rebuffed by Presidents Nixon, Reagan, and Clinton. In 1999, a non-binding U.S. Senate Resolution requested that the President exonerate Kimmel and General Short and restore their four stars. No action on the Resolution was taken, although four stars are etched prominently on Kimmel's Naval Academy tombstone.

General of the Army Douglas MacArthur, audacious in war but magnanimous in victory, presided over the democratization of Japan. As Commander in Chief of the United Nations Command

---

* Truman sacked Forrestal for several reasons. Forrestal vigorously opposed Truman's reduction of the military forces. Articles exposed Forrestal's disloyal meetings with Truman's Republican opponent, Thomas Dewey, who promised to retain him as Secretary Defense in his administration. Questions about Forrestal's mental stability were also published.

in Korea, he was sacked by President Truman, after bringing the nation to the brink of war with China. He was neither as bad as history has treated him, nor as great as his supporters portray. Despite his faults, MacArthur was largely, though less so than Nimitz, responsible for victory in the Pacific. In a farewell address before Congress, he repeated an old refrain: "Old soldiers never die, they just fade away."

He did in fact fade away, passing away in 1964 at the age of eighty-four. There is no record of MacArthur ever staying at Muliwai, but his nephew, diplomat Douglas MacArthur II, did. In 1956, he wrote Una, "The wonderful atmosphere of relaxation and repose which characterize Muliwai was just exactly what the doctor ordered."

The service of the Waves, such as Cdr. Eleanor G. Rigby and Lt. Winifred R. Quick, received widespread raves from Secretary of the Navy Forrestal ("Your conduct, discharge of military responsibilities, and skillful work are in the highest tradition of the naval service.") and Fleet Admirals King ("For their discipline, their skill, and their contribution to high morale") and Nimitz ("They have demonstrated qualities of competence, energy, and loyalty"). Today, those same women would share equal responsibilities with men, including combat.

Hara, the Walkers' loyal Japanese national cook, who could have poisoned the entire Pacific Fleet high command during hundreds of meals, refused to believe Japan had lost the war.

Hanko wrote that Hara "was convinced Japan had won the war and that a huge lie had been contrived to conceal the truth from the people." [425]

After the surrender, the Walkers paid for Hara's retirement in Japan. "Sadly, though, he returned to Japan to find his country blackened and burned and much around his own home town destroyed. It broke his heart and a short time after his return to Japan, he died." [426]

Suetaro Goto, the Walker's Japanese National gardener, who was prepared to meet the invading Japanese army marching up

Nu'uanu Valley to let them know the Walkers were good people, lived the rest of his life at the Walker Estate, dying on November 2, 1965, at the age of ninety-eight. He left a hundred eight living descendants—five children, thirty-three grandchildren, and sixty-nine great-grandchildren.

H. Alexander "Sandy" Walker, Sr., retired as President of American Factors in 1950. He soon contracted Guillain-Barré syndrome ("French Polio"), a rare affliction that imprisoned him with paralysis for two years. He told me his goal was to walk unaided from the Muliwai *hikie*—large Hawaiian bed—to the ocean. With the aid of his helper, Takeo Higuchi, he painfully inched his way each day—first one step, then two, and so forth. After two years of prodigious effort, he struggled to his feet and plodded by himself the fifty yards or so to the end of the yard, where he gazed past the long-gone barbed wires and command post to his beach, ocean and the Ko'olau Mountains beyond. Nimitz wrote that he was relieved "to hear he is on the mend now," and to "tell Sandy to preserve his health—so that he can enjoy retirement—when it comes."

Sandy survived, but because he had lost most of the feeling in his body, for his remaining days, he rose at 4:00 a.m. to clench and unclench his fists and work his muscles to preserve his ability to function. Recovering, he served as Chairman of American Factors until 1960 and continued to drive, propagate orchids, spend weekends at his beloved Muliwai and enjoy his family.

As a teenager, I spent hours on his back lanai where, two decades before, he, Una and Nimitz played cribbage, and listened to the tales of his life. I learned of his operating a Red Cross relief train across the frigid Siberia steppes at the end of World War I, where he witnessed human privation at its worst, chairing the Leper Hospitals and Settlements, the war years, Nimitz, American Factors, the sugar industry, our family's Royalist support of the Hawaiian Monarchy, and even his friendship with Houdini while at Harvard.

In a hallway leading to the back lanai was a gallery of family photographs; a childhood favorite was Gramps in Vladivostok swathed in heavy sheepskin coat and a fur cap with ear flaps swept up like a Hershey's "Kiss." When that modest giant of a man introduced me to friends and associates as "my grandson Michael," pride would fill my heart. His last words in my presence were to Una, before I left for Officer Candidate School in the summer of 1968. "Aren't I fortunate," he said softly, "to have ten such wonderful grandchildren!"

I was a young Ensign in San Diego on my way to Vietnam on January 14, 1969, when I received a painful call from my grandmother that Gramps had died that day, just three years after Nimitz had passed away, at the age of eighty-three. Neither of us could utter a word over our tears. U.S. Senator Hiram Fong entered a tribute to Sandy into the Congressional Record on January 23, 1969:

> *Mr. President, it is with deep sadness that I deliver this eulogy to the late Henry Alexander Walker a distinguished business and civil leader of Hawai'i who passed away on January 14.*
>
> ൠ ൠ ൠ
>
> *He was among the great builders of the Hawaiian sugar industry. He contributed significantly to the high standing and international reputation which the industry enjoys today.*
>
> *He also gave outstanding service in two world wars, served as a volunteer leader in community health work, and became a world-famous orchid grower.*
>
> ൠ ൠ ൠ
>
> *Hawai'i has lost a most valuable citizen who will be sorely missed by all who had the good fortune to know him over the years.*
>
> *Mrs. Fong and I join the people of Hawai'i in paying tribute to the late Mr. Walker and his life of service and dedication to his nation and island*

community.

Until Sandy's death in 1969, each of Nimitz's successors in command of both the Pacific Fleet and Pacific Command became Walker friends and guests of magical Muliwai, staying in the Nimitz Cottage, renamed the "Admiral's Cottage." They included Adm. Arthur D. "Raddy" Radford. In the early 1950s, Sandy and Raddy designed and constructed a nine-hole pitch and putt golf course on Muliwai, dubbing it "Muliwai Golf Links." Raddy became its first "Chairman," issuing seven rules, including the prohibition of "profane language in the vicinity of the clubhouse." When Radford was Chairman of the Joint Chiefs of Staff in 1956, he wrote Sandy thanking him for the "relaxing week we spent enjoying your hospitality at Muliwai."

Others successors included Adm. Felix Stump who had commanded one of the carrier divisions attacked by Kurita's formidable battle group during Leyte for which he earned the Navy Cross; Adm. Harry "Don" Felt, a diminutive and personable gentleman who commanded an escort carrier during the Battle for Okinawa (He often attended Walker parties and as a Christmas guest.); and Adm. Ulysses S. Grant Sharp, who often played Muliwai Golf, sometimes with me, on weekends.

With the passing of Sandy in 1969, Adm. John S. McCain, Jr., father of Senator John McCain, was the last Nimitz successor to stay at Muliwai. However, one last successor has been to Muliwai. We entertained there my friend, Adm. Richard C. "Dick" Macke, a Navy hero, who succeeded Nimitz as Commander in Chief, Pacific Command in 1994.

Una Walker remained a Grande Dame of Honolulu, opening her gardens yearly to raise funds for her cherished Stratford Hall Plantation, Robert E. Lee's birthplace, on whose board she had been an original director since 1934. She continued, as she had throughout her life, befriending and entertaining celebrities and loving her family. Una never failed to enchant all who came within her sphere. As I was growing up, our Christmas dinners in Nu'uanu (black tie) or garden parties at Muliwai (uniform—swim suit) were attended by diplomats (President & Mrs. Dwight D. Eisenhower, Gen. & Mrs. Chiang Kai-Shek, Secretaries of State John Foster Dulles[*] and Dean Acheson, Secretary of Defense James Forrestal, the King and Queen of Thailand), actors (Loretta Young and Jack Lord) movie mogul, Samuel Goldwyn, famous personalities (Clare Boothe Luce, Henry Luce, and William F. Buckley Jr.), and innumerable flag officers.

In preparation for an oral history recording in 1982 at the age of ninety-five, Una called her old friend, retired Air Force Maj. Gen. Howard C. Davidson in the East Coast, himself 92, to bone up on her volunteer wartime efforts with the Women's Air Raid Defense (WARD) at Fort Shafter. The General commanded a wing at Wheeler Field at the time of Pearl Harbor[427] and later the 7th Air Force in the Pacific, and he had become very close to the Walkers. Davidson had called on the Walkers a few days after Pearl Harbor to assist him with establishing the WARDs program. But he could not recall a thing, telling Una it was all too long ago. Una, ever youthful at heart, said to me, "When I knew him, he was a big strapping handsome man. Full of vigor. You know," my ninety-five-year-young grandmother whispered confidentially, "I think he's gotten old!" (At dinner parties, she refused to sit with older people who bored her and boldly moved name tags around, so she would be next to youngsters.) Davidson passed away two years later.

At about the same time, I suggested that my grandmother write her life story of accomplishments. She looked at me and said very deliberately, "Michael, I am too busy living today and planning for the future to write about yesterday!"

She took me to her front garden by the Wedding Circle and pointed to an area she was developing that would not mature for ten years. That told me a great deal about her personality and

---

[*] "After Dulles became Secretary of State, whenever he was in Hawaii, he would stay at the Walkers' ocean-front retreat, Muliwai, to rest and work in privacy." *Dynasty in the Pacific*, 246.

longevity.

Una was a delightful spirit who departed this world (with all her family, including my wife and me, surrounding her bed) on May 6, 1987, just shy of a hundred years of age. "'Twas a pity," she was heard to whisper when death was near, "I won't reach one hundred!"

Even now, I run into friends who I briefly introduced to my grandmother decades years before, who are still enchanted by the experience. Never in all the years I knew her—not even at her death—did she ever lose her magnetic charm or her *joie de vie*. She left her descendants a note, which spoke of Muliwai as "The most beautiful spot in the world," and of hers and Sandy's love:

> *Our love for you is warm and deep, the most important thing in our lives, and we pray that you will continue to be as happy and adjusted as you are at this time. Never have parents had more appreciative, loving, thoughtful, fine children, daughter-in-law, two sons-in-law, and ten beloved grandchildren than Pasie and I. How fortunate we have been.*

In 1973, Una registered the Walker Estate in Honolulu as an historic site on the National Register of Historic Places. After Una passed away, the family had no alternative but to sell the Estate, which was purchased by Misao Nagaku of Minami Group (USA), Inc. He significantly renovated the interior of the manor house, replacing the four sprawling upstairs bedrooms, lanais and poker room into eight hotel-like en-suite bedrooms.

Without the watchful eyes of Una Walker, Mother Nature slowly absorbed her once-exquisitely-manicured orchid gardens into oblivion. The property has since been sold and is now in the hands of a Taiwan corporation.

If you drive up Pali Highway and just past Jack Lane, you can catch glimpses of the manor house through trees and shrubs that have radically thinned without Una's and Sandy's loving care.

Author as Hawai'i Attorney General with Una, 1985

Paul Woo wondered if the Woos and Walkers ever met. They did. A letter from Una to Catherine thanked her for "the lovely party in your darling garden in the autumn of 1943."

It turns out, the Walkers stayed at the St. Francis Hotel for several weeks in September 1943. Catherine's party would have included their next-door neighbors and close friends, the Y. C. Woos. The Woos, Nimitz's and Walkers were together that autumn day in Berkeley, linking forever the relationships later forged between the grandsons of those three families 68 years later.

Henry A. "Hanko" Walker, Jr., started as a truck driver's helper at American Factors (later Amfac) after the war and, through hard work, drive and a great deal of intelligence, succeeded Sandy as President in 1967. In his years at the helm, Hanko built Amfac from a multi-million sugar company into a multi-billion-dollar diversified conglomerate. He replaced the historic Amfac building with two twenty-story Amfac Towers. Hanko retired as President in 1982, remaining as Chairman until 1988. He and Nancy had two children, Henry A. "Renny" Walker, III, and Susan. In 2000, my dear uncle Hanko passed away. His daughter Susan Walker Kowen described him as having "a really nice touch with people." Any employee, she said, "will say, 'I knew him, he spoke to me, and he asked about my day and he asked about my life.' He wasn't the typical corporate executive."

Muliwai was subdivided into three parcels. The main house went to Ann, who installed a substantial concrete bridge, where Nimitz once crossed Wailele stream on the old arched bridge to play paddle tennis. A middle parcel with the cottage in which Nimitz slept during the war went to Hanko. Ginger received a third parcel, on which the post-war Nimitz Cottage was built before burning down in the 1970s. Hanko and Ginger built new homes on their properties, patterned after Muliwai with cathedral ceilings and walls that slide away into pockets.

Although Muliwai's spacious lawns and gardens are gone, the property still maintains the magical aura Nimitz found so refreshing. In rainy weather, the pond still breaks through the sandbar to the sea. The old 19th century iron pier pilings still march out of the sea like aliens. The same radiant sun bursts from the eastern horizon, turning the night grays to gold and red. The beach is still washed clean during the night for morning walkers. Japanese glass balls are still occasionally found. Nimitz's cottage still commands the bluff over the ocean. The ocean beats a staccato against the shore below, lulling insomniacs to sleep. When the

Nimitz at Ease

Walker grandchildren gather there today, they talk of how gracious Muliwai was, beckoning guests like a long-lost friend. The walls echo the haunting melody of Una's ukulele and the family song, *Muliwai*. Even now, if you spend three days there away from TV, radio and the internet, you become so relaxed as to be "Muliwai-fied." As General Davidson convalesced from injuries, he wrote Una in 1942, "The days spent at Muliwai were so restful and perfect they seem like a dream now."

It remains even today the perfect tonic for anyone with Nimitz's sleeplessness.

Stroll to the foot of Fort Street in downtown Honolulu, and you will come upon a triangular forested garden and memorial to Una and Sandy Walker at the former location of Sandy's American Factors building. The hypotenuse of the "Walker Park" triangle is ironically Nimitz Highway. The Park sports the gate through which Sandy walked to work, a grove of mature shade trees, and a fountain with a unique sculpture—a combination stirrup and poi pounder named "Puna." The stirrup symbolizes Una's love of horses. The poi pounder symbolizes her love of flora. Because her family name, "Puna," also means "fresh spring of water," the sculpture perches in the center of a splashing fountain of "spring water," rolling small waves toward your feet, much like early morning beach walks at Muliwai. Plaques commemorate both Sandy's and Una's contributions to the Hawai'i community they loved and served so well. Una's plaque calls her "A woman of renown" who "campaigned vigorously for Honolulu's cultural development. Her gardens and her hospitality were famous as was her zest for life."

The Park is a serene place, amid the hustle and bustle of downtown Honolulu that faintly echoes the Eden that was Muliwai. Pedestrians pass by Walker Park with no clue of the innumerable contributions the Walkers made to Hawai'i and to the war effort by providing Nimitz his own special R&R (Rest and Relaxation).[*]

---

[*] A web site of interesting waymarks describes Walker Park and Una

Perhaps one reason Nimitz and the Walkers became such close friends was how much alike they were. Humble and unpretentious, they exuded unbridled optimism. They loved good stories and had infectious grins, twinkling eyes (that could turn equally fierce) and a laughter that caused others to laugh as well. They were good conversationalists with a healthy supply of interesting stories to relate.

Equally significant, they were polite listeners to whomever was speaking. All three gave their full attention to a VIP or the lowest sailor, treating everyone impartially, despite their station in life. They associated with people of good will. They were leaders in their own right, Sandy of the largest business in Hawai'i, Una of the Red Cross Surgical Dressing Corps, and Nimitz of the largest naval fleet in history. They intimately understood the responsibilities that came with command. They knew how to delegate, inspire and nurture.

Perhaps unfortunately, today's Navy has an almost zero-tolerance for mistakes. Nimitz's career was not destroyed when he ran one ship aground and another into a vessel at sea. He understood the lessons of mistakes and made allowances for errors of judgment. When a junior officer issued a dispatch without authority, instead of punishing him as recommended by Spruance, Nimitz replied, "It isn't what you or I would have done, but at least he showed initiative and took positive action." [428] Sandy had the same forgiving nature.

As leaders, Nimitz and Sandy were loved and respected by subordinates. Nimitz, as did Sandy, "had the easy touch, the light hand" and found "value in everyone and everything." [429] They were both humane, unpretentious and down-to-earth. Their words were their bond, honestly speaking their minds. One could absolutely rely on their unfailing integrity, a trait perhaps all too often lacking

---

Walker's plaque:
   http://www.waymarking.com/waymarks/WMRHMT_Una_Craig_Walker_Honolulu_Oahu_HI

in leaders then, as well as now. When together, the Walkers and Nimitz relaxed absolutely—free of command or demand. In short, they were alike and simply liked one another.

I pondered a great deal before writing about the incredible relationship between the Walkers and Nimitz, but their connection was an important unpublished footnote to the history of World War II. Nimitz was a great man who is still loved by a grateful nation for winning the war in the Pacific. From the time he stepped from his Coronado Flying Boat in Pearl Harbor, Christmas morning 1941, and assumed the enormous demands of fighting the Pacific war, the Walkers ensured that he always had a private sanctuary with close friends which, perhaps in a small but significant way, helped him and the nation close the final chapter of the most costly war in history.

The Walkers and Muliwai provided Nimitz with the perfect "tonics of companionship, relaxation, active sports and congenial surroundings"—his own private USO.

While Nimitz never returned to Hawai'i, his many letters to the Walkers until eleven months before he passed attest to how greatly he valued their friendship and those magical weekends at Muliwai which, like Camelot, there was "simply not a more congenial spot" for peacefully enjoying time away from the enormous demands of command.

Michael A. Lilly

Acknowledgments

THE AUTHOR IS grateful for the scores of people and institutions who contributed to this work. I first began to learn about the close relationship between my family and Nimitz first hand from my grandparents, H. Alexander "Sandy" Walker Sr. and Una Craig "Puna" Walker, and my mother, Virginia C. "Ginger" Lilly. This book would not have been possible but for my grandmother's diary of 1944 and the hundreds of letters written by Fleet Admiral Nimitz, Hal Lamar, Admirals Sherman and Spruance, the Walkers and Ginger, which my grandmother preserved.

My late uncle, H. A. "Hanko" Walker Jr., added much to this work, both from what he related to me during his lifetime, but also in his priceless *Memoirs*. So did my father, Capt. Percy A. "Tony" Lilly, in the personal stories he told us and from his autobiography, *A Sailor's Life*, completed shortly before he passed away.

A very special appreciation goes to the members of the Nimitz family whom I have come to know and respect during the period this book took shape: Nimitz's late daughter Catherine Nimitz "Kate" Lay contributed previously unpublished anecdotes; his twin grandsons, Chester Nimitz "Chet" Lay and Richard "Dick" Freeman Lay, provided me with enormous quantities of insights and information; as did Nimitz's granddaughter Sarah Smith, daughter of Chester W. Nimitz Jr., who owns the Walden painting. While their grandfather never returned to Muliwai, in 2015 Chet and his wife Marion stayed in our beach house built where the "Nimitz Cottage" stood.

    I am especially indebted to historian Jeff Harding, with whom I have exchanged innumerable emails, and who provided an enormous quantity of helpful information; Y. C. Woo's grandson, Paul Woo, who has been a constant beacon of optimism and information about his grandparents and their relationship with the Nimitz's; MacArthur Foundation archivist, James Zobel; Bishop Museum archivist, DeSoto Brown; USS Missouri Memorial Association curator, Mike Weidenbach; author Brian Sobel; my book agent Donna Eastman; and my copy editor, Tommye Gadol, who corrected my many grammatical and other mistakes. All added immeasurably to details which enriched this account.

    To Ken Coffman and the Stairway Press team, thank you for your dedication and patience in bringing my manuscript to print.

    Friends and relatives who also provided invaluable assistance include my siblings, Maile "Major Gremlin" Arnold, Sheila "Minor Gremlin" Zaretsky, and Anthony "Tony" Lilly; cousins, Susan Walker Kowen, the late Pam Burns and Caleb Burns; author and columnist, Bob Sigall who coined the title of this book; William J. Cassidy Jr., Lindsey Haskin, Paige Merrill Baker, the late Gordon Damon, J.P. Damon, Randy Slaton, Nimitz successor Adm. R.J. "Zap" Zlatoper, USN (Ret.), author Mackinnon Simpson, Allen Adler, and Jean Navarra, who has amassed a large collection of priceless information about Hawai'i during the war.

    I am indebted to the U.S. Naval Institute—my bible throughout this work has been its *Nimitz*, by E. B. Potter. Their interviews with the major players in Nimitz's life are treasures of history, archived and available to the public. The Hawaiian section of the Hawai'i State Public Library was especially helpful with its rows of books and publications on Hawai'i during the war, as was the Hawai'i State Archives, where I found many of my grandfather's letters as Director of Food Control and other original war records.

Michael A. Lilly

While I was writing this book, the U.S. Naval War College digitized the *Graybook*. Chet Lay sent me an advance copy on CD with its thousands of pages of daily war events recorded contemporaneously and initialed each day with his grandfather's "CWN." I am grateful to be one of the first authors to have this invaluable source of information about the Pacific war and Nimitz at my fingertips. With *Nimitz*, Una's diary, and the *Graybook* in hand, I was in the unique position to follow Nimitz's daily life—in war and leisure—for the first time.

Several sources of information were missing. One was the visitor logs kept by Lamar at Nimitz's headquarters. Also, Nimitz's wife, Catherine, burned the many of the letters she received from him, apparently deeming them too personal to share.

Finally, I thank my darling wife, Cindy Walter, whose contributions were immeasurable. A successful author in her own right, having ten books on quilting to her name (one an award-winning, international best-seller), she provided moral support, patience and editing help on her husband's second but most important book. Without her, this work would never have been completed.

About the Author

CAPT. MICHAEL A. LILLY, USN (Ret) is an honor graduate of the University of the Pacific's McGeorge School of Law. He had a distinguished career as Hawai'i's Attorney General and as a successful trial attorney. He obtained the largest jury verdict in state history for wrongful termination and won U.S. and Hawai'i Supreme Court cases. He is a Founding Director of the USS Missouri Memorial Association, which operates the *Missouri* as a memorial and tourist attraction. A Vietnam War combat veteran, his personal decorations include the Legion of Merit, Defense Meritorious Service Medal and two Meritorious Service Medals. He retired as a surface warfare Captain after 30 years of service, active and reserve. He and his wife, Cindy Walter, have four children and reside on O'ahu and Maui.

Michael A. Lilly

Endnotes

[1] *Life* magazine, July 10, 1944 issue, p. 86.
[2] Potter, E. B., *Nimitz*, U.S. Naval Institute Press, 1986, 9. Una acquired my copy of Nimitz in 1986 when she was 99 years old. She passed away the following year.
[3] Frank DeLorenzo, Captain, U.S. Navy (Ret.), March 28, 1999, http://www.johngreavesart.ca/delo.htm
[4] Simpson, MacKinnon, *USS Arizona: Warship Tomb Monument*, Bess Press, 2008, p.88.
[5] Laqueur, Walter, *The Uses and Limits of Intelligence*, Transaction Publishers, 1995, p.354.
[6] *Nimitz*, p.17.
[7] *Honolulu Star Bulletin*, January 1, 1942, p. 1.
[8] Prang, Gordon W., *At Dawn We Slept*, McGraw-Hill Book Company, 1981, p.549.
[9] Simpich, Frederick, Jr., *Dynasty in the Pacific*, McGraw-Hill Book Company, 1974, p.8.
[10] Post-war testimony of A. L. Castle to the Joint Congressional Committee to Investigate the Pearl Harbor Attack, *A Record of Civilian and Industrial Preparedness in the Territory of Hawai`i Prior to December 7, 1941*, Exhibit No. 153, 3412.
[11] *Paradise of the Pacific*, May 1954 issue, p.21.
[12] As told to the author by his mother; and Allen, Gwenfread, *Hawaii's*

War Years: 1941-1945, University of Hawai'i Press, 1950, p.78.
[13] Photograph by *Honolulu Star Bulletin*.
[14] West, Rodney T., M.D., *Honolulu Prepares for Japan's Attack*, MD, self-published, 1992, p.29.
[15] *An Era of Change. Oral Histories of Civilians In World War II, Vol. III*, interview of Warren Nishimoto by Masao Adada, Center for Oral History, Social Science Research Institute, University of Hawai'i at Manoa, April 1, 1994, p.855.
[16] *Dynasty in the Pacific*, 90.
[17] Weintraub, Stanley, *Long Day's Journey Into War: Pearl Harbor and a World at War-December 7, 1941*, Lyons Press, 2001, p.243.
[18] *Memoirs*, p.29.
[19] *Graybook*, p.10.
[20] Chenoweth, Candace A. & Napier, Kam A., *Shuffleboard Pilots: The History of the Women's Air Raid Defense in Hawai'i*, 1941-1945, Tongg Publishing, 1991, p.6.
[21] Simpson, MacKinnon, *Hawai'i Homefront, Life in the Islands During World War II*, Bess Press, 2008, p.17.
[22] *Ibid.*
[23] *Paradise of the Pacific*, May 1954 issue, p.21.
[24] *Hawaii's War Years: 1941-1945*, p.200.
[25] *Ibid.*
[26] Author's collection.
[27] Simonds, William A., *Kamaaina—A Century in Hawaii*, American Factors, Ltd., October 1, 1949, p.95.
[28] *Hawai'i Homefront, Life in the Islands During World War II*, 175.
[29] *Shuffleboard Pilots: The History of the Women's Air Raid Defense in Hawai'i*, p6.
[30] *Ibid.*, p.21.
[31] Ex Parte White, 66 F.Supp. 982, 990 (D. Haw. 1944).
[32] Thomas, Jane, *My Hawai'i: 1938-1968, With Personal Recollections of Pearl Harbor December 7, 1941*, Xlibris Corporation, 2002, p.55.
[33] *The Wartime Cabinet*, p.72.
[34] *Honolulu Advertiser*, December 7, 1942, p.16.
[35] Duncan v. Kahanamoku, 327 U.S. p.304, p.325 (1946) *Indeed, the unconstitutionality of the usurpation of civil power by the military is so great in this instance as to warrant this Court's complete and outright repudiation of the*

action.
[36] Author's collection.
[37] *Dynasty in the Pacific*, p.107.
[38] *Memoirs*, p.30.
[39] *Hawaii's War Years: 1941-1945*, pps.168-69. In a February 1, 1943 letter from H. A. Walker to Brigadier General Frederick Gilbraith, Port of Embarkation, Fort Mead, California, Sandy was finally able to report having adequate refrigeration space for frozen meats.
[40] *Honolulu Advertiser*, July 14, 1942, p.1.
[41] *Honolulu Star Bulletin*, July 16, 1942, editorial.
[42] *Kamaaina—A Century in Hawaii*, p.93.
[43] *Honolulu StarAdvertiser*, February 2, 2011, Business section.
[44] Brown, DeSoto, *Hawai`i Goes to War*, Editions Limited, 1989, p.97.
[45] *Kamaaina—A Century in Hawaii*, p.97 (report by Hawaiian Sugar Planters' Association President H. Alexander Walker in 1945).
[46] *Dynasty in the Pacific*, p.108.
[47] *Kamaaina—A Century in Hawaii*, p.91.
[48] *Memoirs*, p.17.
[49] *My Hawai`i: 1938-1968, With Personal Recollections of Pearl Harbor December 7, 1941*, p.55.
[50] *Hawaii's War Years: 1941-1945*, p.90.
[51] *Honolulu Advertiser*, June 21, 1984, article by Beverly Creamer, Focus section, p.1.
[52] Interview with Hal Lamar, May 3, 1970 by John T. Mason Jr., U.S. Naval Institute, p.20.
[53] Official U.S. Navy Photograph.
[54] Official U.S. Navy Photograph.
[55] Interview with Fleet Admiral Nimitz, January 26, 1965 by John T Mason Jr., p.70.
[56] Keegan, John, *The Second World War*, Penguin Books, 1989, p.279.
[57] *All Hands*, Bureau of Naval Personnel Information Bulletin, December 1944, p.17.
[58] *Graybook*, p.2067.
[59] Hornfischer, James D., *Neptune's Inferno: The U.S. Navy at Guadalcanal*, Bantam Books, 2012, p.10.
[60] Letter to Catherine, January 21, 1945. The letters are held in the archives of the U.S. Naval Academy.

[61] *Ibid.*
[62] Lamar, H. Arthur, *I Saw Stars*, Admiral Nimitz Foundation, 1985, p.16.
[63] Interview with Hal Lamar, p.102.
[64] *Ibid.*, p.40.
[65] *Nimitz*, p.367.
[66] Letter to Catherine, February 13, 1945.
[67] Post-war testimony of A. L. Castle to the Joint Congressional Committee to Investigate the Pearl Harbor Attack, *A Record of Civilian and Industrial Preparedness in the Territory of Hawai`i Prior to December 7, 1941*, Exhibit No. 153, 3415.
[68] MacBride, William M, *Technological Change and the United States Navy*, 1865-1945, The Johns Hopkins University Press, 2000, p.205.
[69] Interview with Hal Lamar, pps.14 & 100.
[70] Morison, Samuel Eliot, *History of United States Naval Operations in World War II: The Battle of the Atlantic, September 1939-May 1943*, University of Illinois Press, 2002, p.115.
[71] Thomas, Evan, *Sea of Thunder: Four Commanders and the Last Great Naval Campaign 1941-1945*, Simon & Schuster, 2007, p.72.
[72] Interview with Rear Adm. William W. Drake, p.22.
[73] *Memoirs*, p.31.
[74] Sobel, Brian M., *Sister M. Aquinas Nimitz, Daughter in the Shadow of Greatness*, unpublished article 1.
[75] *I Saw Stars*, p.43.
[76] *Neptune's Inferno: The U.S. Navy at Guadalcanal*, p.6.
[77] Hansell, Gen. Haywood S., Jr., *The Strategic War Against Germany and Japan: a Personal Memoir*, Diane Publishing Co., 1986, p.174.
[78] Interview with Hal Lamar, p.76.
[79] Churchill, Winston S., *Marlborough: His Life and Times, Book One*, by Winston S. Churchill, Chicago: University of Chicago Press, 2002, p.569.
[80] *Look* magazine, January 9, 1945, p.35.
[81] *Memoirs*, p.32.
[82] *I Saw Stars*, p.4.
[83] Interview with Rear Adm. Edwin T. Layton, March 19, 1970, by E. B. Potter, U.S. Naval Institute, pps.45-6.
[84] Interview with Hal Lamar, 12; *Nimitz*, p.225.
[85] Hastings, Max, *Retribution: The Battle for Japan, 1944-45*, Alfred A.

Knopf, 2008, p.28.
[86] *Nimitz*, p.226.
[87] *Look* magazine, January 9, 1945, p.32.
[88] Interview with Rear Adm. William W. Drake, p.36.
[89] *Nimitz*, p.228.
[90] Hoyt, Edwin, *How They Won the War in the Pacific: Nimitz and His Admirals*, The Lyons Press, 2002, p.122.
[91] *Nimitz*, pps.270-71.
[92] *Ibid.*, p.270.
[93] Interview with Hal Lamar, p.16.
[94] *Ibid.*, p.22.
[95] *Memoirs*, pps.31-2.
[96] Interview with Rear Adm. William W. Drake, pps.11 & 46.
[97] Leverton, Rear Adm. Joseph Wilson, Jr., *Nimitz: A Good-Humored Leader of Men*, USN (Ret.), Published by the Leverton Family, 2002, 1.
[98] *Life* magazine, July 10, 1944, p.82.
[99] Letter to Catherine, January 23, 1944.
[100] Burns, James MacGregor, *Roosevelt: The Lion and the Fox*, Volume One, Harcourt Brace Jovanovich, Inc., 1956, p.149.
[101] Biddle, Francis, *The Wartime Cabinet*, American Heritage Magazine, American Heritage Publishing Co., June 1962, p.67. Biddle served as U.S. Attorney General during World War II.
[102] *Dynasty in the Pacific*, p.91.
[103] *How They Won the War in the Pacific*, p.70.
[104] *Nimitz*, p.227.
[105] *Ibid.*
[106] *Ibid.*
[107] *Life* magazine, July 10, 1944, p.83.
[108] *Look* magazine, January 9, 1945, p.32.
[109] *Graybook*, p.574.
[110] *Ibid.*, p.575.
[111] Walker, Jack, *John Cornwell Walker of Pualani*, self-published, 1990.
[112] *Graybook*, p.576.
[113] *Ibid.*
[114] Peters, Tom and Waterman, Robert H., Jr., *In Search of Excellence: Lessons from America's Best-Run Companies*, Harper & Row, 1982.
[115] *Life* magazine, August 6, 1951, p.30.

[116] Official U.S. Navy Photograph.
[117] Korson, George Gershon, *At His Side: The Story of the American Red Cross Overseas in World War II*, Coward-McCann, 1945, p.11.
[118] *Honolulu Advertiser*, January 15, 1944, p.2.
[119] *Nimitz*, p.227.
[120] *Ibid.*, p.272
[121] Interview with Hal Lamar, pps.16-17.
[122] *Nimitz*, p.273.
[123] *At His Side: The Story of the American Red Cross Overseas in World War II*, p.6.
[124] *Nimitz*, p.197.
[125] Interview with Hal Lamar, p.88.
[126] Fuchs, Lawrence H., *Hawaii Pono: A Social History*, Harcourt, Brace & World, Inc., 1961, p.392.
[127] *Hawaii's War Years: 1941-1945*, p.366. Greer, Richard A., *Dousing Honolulu's Red Lights*, Hawaiian Journal of History, Vol. 34, 2000, p.192 ("On August 28, [1942] the girls turned on the heat with a strike that lasted twenty-two days. They carried signs stating their grievances and picketed the police station and 'Iolani Palace.'").
[128] Bailey, Beth and Farber, David, *The First Strange Place: the Alchemy of Race and Sex in World War II Hawaii*, The Free Press, 1992, p.100.
[129] Anthony, Garner J., *Hawai'i Under Army Rule*, Stanford University Press, 1955, p.40.
[130] *Graybook*, p.1862.
[131] *Memoirs*, pps.31-2.
[132] Interview with Hal Lamar, p.14.
[133] *Memoirs*, pps.31-2.
[134] Photo courtesy of Allen Adler.
[135] *Nimitz*, p.228.
[136] Interview with Hal Lamar, p.15.
[137] *Graybook*, p.1863.
[138] *Nimitz*, p.273.
[139] *Life* magazine, February 7, 1944, p.33.
[140] *Graybook*, p.1867.
[141] Borneman, Walter R., *The Admirals: Nimitz, Halsey, Leahy, and King—the Five-Star Admirals Who Won the War at Sea*, Little, Brown and Company, 2010, p.313.

[142] *Nimitz*, p.226.
[143] *Memoirs*, pps.31-2.
[144] *Graybook*, p.1869.
[145] Chickering, William H., *Letters From the Pacific*, self-published, 1946, p.77.
[146] *Nimitz*, p.275.
[147] *Graybook*, p.1870.
[148] *Honolulu Advertiser* editorial, February 10, 1944.
[149] *All Hands*, editorial, June 1944, p.38.
[150] *Nimitz*, p.421.
[151] Official U.S. Navy photograph.
[152] *Graybook*, pps.1875-76.
[153] Costello, John, *The Pacific War 1941-1945*, HarperCollins Book Publishers, Ltd., 1981, p.448.
[154] *All Hands*, March 1944, p.2.
[155] *How They Won the War in the Pacific*, p.342.
[156] Interview with Hal Lamar, p.12.
[157] *Nimitz: A Good-Humored Leader of Men*, p.16.
[158] As related to Chet Lay by his mother, Kate Nimitz Lay.
[159] *Life* magazine, March 13, 1944, p.24.
[160] *Life* magazine, March 6, 1944, p.41.
[161] O'Reilly, Bill & Dugard, Martin, *Killing the Rising Sun*, John Costello, Henry Holt and Company, 2016, p.233.
[162] *Nimitz*, p.287.
[163] *Life* magazine, July 10, 1944, p.82.
[164] *Nimitz: A Good-Humored Leader of Men*, p.16.
[165] Letter to Catherine, December 21, 1941.
[166] *Nimitz*, p.289.
[167] *I Saw Stars*, p.32. The Walkers frequently gave military leaders and dignitaries long boxes of orchids. This author has many letters from Secretaries of State and the Navy, a Chief Justice of the Supreme Court, admirals, Madame Chiang Kai-Shek, and the like, thanking the Walkers for their thoughtful gift of orchids.
[168] *Nimitz*, p290
[169] *Life* magazine, July 10, 1944, p.84.
[170] *Life* magazine, October 15, 1951, pps.78 & 87.
[171] *Ibid*.

[172] *Nimitz*, p.291 (citing a confidential memorandum from Nimitz to King).
[173] Photograph from the Army Signal Corps Collection, U.S. National Archives.
[174] *Honolulu Star Bulletin*, April 27, 1944, p.1.
[175] *All Hands*, April 1944, p.36.
[176] *Hearings Before the Joint Committee on the Investigation of the Pearl Harbor Attack*, S. Cong. Res. 27, Part 26, Proceedings of the Hart Inquiry, U.S. Government Printing Office, Washington D.C., 1946, p.275.
[177] *Honolulu Advertiser*, April 4, 1944, p.3.
[178] *Graybook*, p.1910.
[179] *How They Won the War in the Pacific*, p.136.
[180] *Ibid.*, p.336.
[181] *Memoirs*, p.32.
[182] Ng, Wendy, *Japanese American Internment during World War II: A History and Reference Guide*, Greenwood Publishing Group, 2001, 24 ("Secretary of the Navy Frank Knox proposed that all Japanese in Hawaii, citizen and alien, be interned on the island of Molokai").
[183] *Honolulu Advertiser*, October 22, 1995, interview with Hal Lamar.
[184] *Nimitz*, p.226.
[185] Official U.S. Navy Photograph inscribed by Nimitz for the Walkers.
[186] *Graybook*, p.1527.
[187] *Hawai`i Homefront, Life in the Islands During World War II*, p.17
[188] *Graybook*, p.1928.
[189] Sigall, Bob, *The Companies we Keep 4*, self-published, 2014, p.123.
[190] *Hawaii Pono: A Social History*, p.133.
[191] *Life* magazine, May 15, 1944, p.30.
[192] *All Hands*, June 1944, p.4.
[193] Summers, Anthony and Swan, Robbyn, *A Matter of Honor*, HarperCollins Publishers, 2016, p.247.
[194] *Graybook*, p.1933.
[195] *Nimitz*, p.293.
[196] *Admiral Nimitz: The Commander of the Pacific Ocean*, pps.102-03.
[197] *Graybook*, p.1939.
[198] *Ibid.*, p.1942.
[199] *Nimitz: A Good-Humored Leader of Men*, p.15. Potter describes the incident in *Nimitz*, p.294.

[200] *I Saw Stars*, p.11.
[201] *How They Won the War in the Pacific*, pps.395-96.
[202] *I Saw Stars*, p.11.
[203] *Graybook*, p.1950.
[204] *The First Strange Place: the Alchemy of Race and Sex in World War II Hawaii*, p.75.
[205] *Nimitz*, pps.294-95.
[206] *Graybook*, p.1957.
[207] *Life* magazine, July 10, 1944 issue, p.84.
[208] *Nimitz*, p.296.
[209] *Graybook*, p.1972.
[210] *Nimitz*, p.219.
[211] *Japan's War*, p.347.
[212] http://www.ibiblio.org/pha/pha/hart/hart-00.html
[213] James, Dorris Clayton, *The Years of MacArthur: 1941-1945*, Houghton Mifflin, 1975, p.523.
[214] *Graybook*, pps.2346-47.
[215] Interview with Hal Lamar, 91. ("Whenever we would sink a carrier he was jubilant. His primary mission was to get rid of carriers. ... He was just simply in seventh heaven when we sunk a Japanese carrier.")
[216] *Nimitz*, p.303.
[217] *Graybook*, pps.2014-15.
[218] Letter to Catherine, January 22, 1945.
[219] Letter to Catherine, January 18, 1945.
[220] *Honolulu Advertiser*, July 13, 1944, p.2.
[221] *Graybook*, p.2027.
[222] *Nimitz*, p.313.
[223] *Ibid.*, p.315.
[224] Official U.S. Navy Photograph.
[225] *Honolulu Advertiser*, July 13, 1944, p.1.
[226] *Memoirs*, p.33.
[227] Pratt, Helen Gray, *Hawai'i: Offshore Territory*, Charles Scribner's Sons, 1994, pps.21-23.
[228] *Memoirs*, pps.33-4.
[229] Letter to Catherine, January 23, 1945.
[230] Harris, Brayton, *The Commander of the Pacific Ocean*, Palgrave MacMillan Trade, 2012, p.139.

[231] Official U.S. Navy Photograph, Pacific Fleet, from the author's collection.
[232] Morison, Samuel Eliot, *History of United States Naval Operations in World War II: The Liberation of the Philippines: Luzon, Mindanao, the Visayas*, 1944–1945, University of Illinois Press, 2002, p.3.
[233] Carroll, James T. and Tucker, Spencer C., *World War II: The Definitive Encyclopedia and Document Collection*, Volume 3, Philippines, U.S. Recapture of (October 20, 1944-August 15, 1945), edited by Spencer C. Tucker, ABC-CLIO, LLC, p.1328
[234] *How They Won the War in the Pacific*, p.413.
[235] Interview with Hal Lamar, p.55.
[236] Lamar's autobiography says he counted 136 stars. *I Saw Stars*, p.25. His interview in 1970 said there were 146. Interview with Hal Lamar, pps.54-5. Both numbers are likely embellished.
[237] *Graybook*, p.2045.
[238] *Ibid*, p.2053.
[239] *Nimitz*, p.126.
[240] *Ibid.*, p.320.
[241] *Graybook*, p.2055.
[242] *Memoirs*, p.34.
[243] *Ibid.*, p.35.
[244] Official U.S. Navy photograph.
[245] Shay, Frank, *The Best Men Are Cooks*, Coward-McCann, Inc., 1941, pps.195-96.
[246] *Graybook*, p.2072.
[247] *Hawai'i Homefront, Life in the Islands During World War II*, p.142.
[248] *Nimitz: A Good-Humored Leader of Men*, pps.6 & 11.
[249] *Hawai`i Goes to War*, p.135.
[250] Journal of Social Hygiene, American Social Hygiene Association, Volume 32, 1946, p.74.
[251] *Hawaii's War Years: 1941-1945*, p.366.
[252] September 20, 1944 letter from Governor Ingram Stainback to Nimitz.
[253] September 23, 1944 letter from Nimitz to Governor Stainback.
[254] *Honolulu Advertiser*, September 22, 1944 editorial page.
[255] Alexander, Joseph H., *Storm Landings: Epic Amphibious Battles in the Central Pacific*, U.S. Naval Institute Press, 1997, p.104.
[256] *Ibid.*, p.105.

[257] *The Rubáiyát of Omar Khayyám*, translated by Edward Fitzgerald, George Routledge and Sons, Limited, 1904, p.158.
[258] Official U.S. Navy Photograph.
[259] *Graybook*, p.2090.
[260] *Honolulu Advertiser*, September 16, 1944 editorial page.
[261] *Graybook*, p.2091.
[262] *History of United States Naval Operations in World War II: The Liberation of the Philippines: Luzon, Mindanao, the Visayas*, p.5.
[263] *Graybook*, p.2083.
[264] *Ibid.*, p.2117.
[265] *Honolulu Star Bulletin*, October 11, 1944, p.1.
[266] *Ibid.*, p.4.
[267] *Graybook*, p.2127.
[268] *Ibid.*, p.2412.
[269] *Life* magazine, July 10, 1944, p.84.
[270] *The Second World War*, p.559.
[271] *Graybook*, p.2414.
[272] *Rhetoric and Community: Studies in Unity and Fragmentation*, edited by J. Michael Hogan, article *On Rhetoric in Martial Decision Making* by Ronald H. Carpenter, The University of South Carolina Press, 1998, p.123.
[273] Warner, Denis and Peggy, *The Sacred Warriors: Japan's Suicide Legions*, Avon Books, 1984, p.119.
[274] *All Hands*, May 1944, p.36.
[275] *Graybook*, p.2142.
[276] *Ibid.*, p.2303.
[277] Wilhelm, Donald, *Your Son and Six Fighting Admirals*, American Brake Shoe Company, 1944.
[278] *Memoirs*, p.16.
[279] *Honolulu Advertiser*, December 7, 1942, p.3.
[280] *A Matter of Honor*, p.58.
[281] *Life* magazine, *Report from Tokyo: An Ambassador Warns of Japan's Strength*", by Joseph C. Grew, July 12, 1942.
[282] *All Hands*, December 1944, p.19.
[283] *Graybook*, p.2164.
[284] *Nimitz*, p.346. A year later, he would sign the Instrument of Surrender as the United Kingdom representative.
[285] Wukovits, John, *Admiral "Bull" Halsey: The Live and Wars of the Navy's*

Most Controversial Commander, Palgrave MacMillan, 2010, p.212.
[286] Letter to Catherine, November 30, 1944.
[287] Letter to Catherine, December 3, 1944.
[288] Official U.S. Navy Photograph.
[289] Letter to Catherine, December 3, 1944.
[290] *Nimitz*, p.296.
[291] Letter to Catherine, December 3, 1944.
[292] Letter to Catherine, December 9, 1944.
[293] Letter to Catherine, December 7, 1944.
[294] *All Hands*, December 1944, p.75.
[295] Letter to Catherine, November 30, 1944.
[296] Letter to Catherine, December 11, 1944.
[297] *Nimitz*, p.287.
[298] Letter to Catherine, December 14, 1944.
[299] Letter to Catherine, December 19, 1944.
[300] *Nimitz*, p.351.
[301] Letter to Catherine, December 31, 1944.
[302] *Ibid.*
[303] *Ibid.*
[304] *All Hands*, November 1944, p.6.
[305] *Ibid.*, p.7.
[306] Letter to Catherine, December 31, 1944.
[307] Interview with Hal Lamar, p.43; Interview with Rear Adm. Edwin T. Layton, p.115.
[308] Letter to Catherine, January 7, 1945.
[309] Letter to Catherine, January 13, 1945.
[310] *Graybook*, p.2521.
[311] *Ibid.*, p.2519.
[312] *All Hands*, February 1945, p.45. Modern audiences can still watch the *Fighting Lady* on YouTube.
[313] *All Hands*, March 1945, p.14.
[314] Letter to Catherine, January 11, 1945.
[315] *Ibid.*, January 13 & 14, 1945.
[316] Letter to Catherine, January 19, 1945.
[317] *Memoirs*, p.36.
[318] *Henry Alexander Walker Jr.*, Watumull Foundation Oral History Project, p11.

[319] *Memoirs*, pps.37-8.
[320] Letter to Catherine, January 21, 1945.
[321] *Ibid.*
[322] Letter to Catherine, January 20, 1945.
[323] Letter to Catherine, January 23, 1945.
[324] Letter to Catherine, January 27, 1945.
[325] *Graybook*, p.2548.
[326] *I Saw Stars*, p.26.
[327] Letter to Catherine, January 28, 1945.
[328] *I Saw Stars*, p.27.
[329] *And I Was There: Pearl Harbor and Midway—Breaking the Secrets*, p.493.
[330] *Ibid.*, p.492.
[331] *Memoirs*, pps.45-7 and as related to the author many times over the years.
[332] Official U.S. Navy Photograph
[333] *Graybook*, p.2565.
[334] *All Hands*, March 1945, p.2.
[335] *Hawaii's War Years: 1941-1945*, p.200.
[336] *Graybook*, p.2594.
[337] Though it began "in the middle of the Great Depression, the Hawaiian Room" had more than a half million patrons "in its first two years," grossing more than $1 million. When it closed in 1966, "an era came to an end." *The Companies we Keep 4*, pps.74 & 85.
[338] *Honolulu Star Bulletin*, March 13, 1945, p.2.
[339] *Ibid.*
[340] Letter to Catherine, January 3, 1945; and Interview with Hal Lamar, pps.56-57. Nimitz took the yacht "Catherine" with him to Washington D.C. when he was appointed CNO.
[341] Alonso, Harriet Hyman, *Robert E. Sherwood: The Playwright in Peace and War*, University of Massachusetts Press, 2007, p.248.
[342] Official U.S. Navy Photograph
[343] Official U.S. Navy Photograph
[344] *Nimitz*, p.367. Some references quote Nimitz as having said, "Among the men who fought on Iwo Jima, uncommon valor was a common virtue." See National WWII Museum factsheet, http://www.nationalww2museum.org/focus-on/iwo-jima-factsheet.pdf.

[345] *Graybook*, pps.2597-98.
[346] Letter to Catherine, February 8, 1945.
[347] Letter to Catherine, January 14, 1945.
[348] *Graybook.*, p.2624.
[349] *Retribution: The Battle for Japan, 1944-45*, p.399.
[350] *Life* magazine, April 9, 1945, p. 94.
[351] *I Saw Stars*, p.26.
[352] Letter to Catherine, January 27, 1945.
[353] Letter to Catherine, February 14, 1945.
[354] As related to the author by Henry A. Walker Jr.
[355] *Ibid.*
[356] *Graybook*, p.2868.
[357] *Memoirs*, p.50.
[358] Layton, Edwin T., *And I Was There": Pearl Harbor and Midway—Breaking the Secrets*, U.S. Naval Institute Press, 1985, p.484; and Interview with Rear Adm. Edwin T. Layton, p.78.
[359] *Graybook*, pps.2720 & 2723.
[360] *Ibid*, p.2724.
[361] *Ibid.*, pps.2725 & 2729.
[362] Spector, Ronald H., *Eagle Against the Sun: the American War Against Japan*, MacMillan, Inc. New York. 1985, p.544.
[363] Borgwardt, Elizabeth, *A New Deal for the World: America's Vision for Human Rights*, 2005, Belknap Press, p.252.
[364] *Spokane Daily Chronicle*, October 4, 1945, AP story.
[365] Interview with Hal Lamar, p.34.
[366] *And I Was There: Pearl Harbor and Midway—Breaking the Secrets*, p.492; *Nimitz*, p.181.
[367] *Evening Independent*, September 4, 1962.
[368] *Memoirs*, p.54.
[369] *Graybook*, p.3316.
[370] *Ibid.*, p.3529.
[371] Photo courtesy of Chet Lay.
[372] Letter to Catherine, January 22, 1945.
[373] Letter to Catherine, September 3, 1945.
[374] *Graybook*, p.3536
[375] Interview with Rear Adm. Edwin T. Layton, p.111.
[376] *Nimitz*, p.389.

[377] *Graybook*, p.3465.
[378] *Ibid.*, p.3331.
[379] As related to the author by Henry A. Walker Jr.
[380] *Graybook*, p.3375.
[381] Emmerson, John K., *The Japanese Thread: A Life in the U.S. Foreign Service*, Holt, Rinehart and Winston, 1978, p.249 (emphasis in original).
[382] Ambrose, Stephen E., *D-Day, The Climactic Battle of World War II*, Simon & Schuster, Touchstone Edition, 1995, p.45.
[383] Strahan, Jerry E., *Andrew Higgins and the Boats that Won World War II*, LSU Press, 1998, p.1.
[384] *I Saw Stars*, p.28.
[385] *Ibid.* "After the war, Higgins was beset by problems, some of his own making. He was not a good businessman. ... He Went bust, Higgins Industries went under." *D-Day*, p.47.
[386] *Nimitz*, p.357.
[387] *Ibid*, pps.392-93.
[388] *Ibid*, p.393.
[389] As related to the author by Henry A. Walker Jr.
[390] Interview with Hal Lamar, 59-60. Lamar similarly wrote that Nimitz "had a calm and cool manner of dressing down an ensign or even Admiral Halsey when and if he needed it." *I Saw Stars*, p.43.
[391] *I Saw Stars*, p.38.
[392] Henry A. Walker Jr., January 16, 1967 letter to Harmon L. Graff.
[393] *Ibid.*
[394] *Long-Lost WWII "Victory" Pen Located*, J. J. Harding, undated draft article.
[395] *The Admirals: Nimitz, Halsey, Leahy, and King—the Five-Star Admirals Who Won the War at Sea*, p.457.
[396] Kalisch, Col. Bertram, *Photographing the Surrender Aboard the USS Missouri*, U.S. Army, U.S. Naval Institute, Proceedings Magazine, August 1955.
[397] *Time-News*, Hendersonville, N.C., September 3, 1951, p.2.
[398] *Kokomo Tribune*, September 7, 1945, p.4.
[399] September 3, 1945 letter from Nimitz to Catherine held in the U.S. Naval Academy archives.
[400] Official U.S. Navy Photograph
[401] As related to the author by Henry A. Walker Jr.
[402] *Nimitz*, p.397.

[403] Interview with Hal Lamar, pps.66-67.
[404] *Memoirs*, p.62.
[405] *Ibid* and as related to the author by Henry A. Walker Jr.
[406] Letter to Catherine, September 3, 1945.
[407] *Los Angeles Times*, October 6, 1945.
[408] *Queen's Book*, Chapter 47, http://digital.library.upenn.edu/women/liliuokalani/hawaii/hawaii.html.
[409] Photo by Ric Noyle from *'Iolani Palace—A Metaphor for Two Centuries of Hawaii History*
[410] *Honolulu Advertiser*, October 28, 1945, p.1.
[411] *Honolulu Star Bulletin*, October 29, 1945, p.2
[412] *Nimitz*, p.407.
[413] *Dynasty in the Pacific*, p.247.
[414] *Memoirs*, p.70.
[415] *Nimitz*, p.425.
[416] *Nimitz: A Good-Humored Leader of Men*, p.15.
[417] *Ibid.*, pps.15-6.
[418] *Kamaaina—A Century in Hawaii*, Introduction.
[419] Volume II of the *Memoirs* of General William T. Sherman.
[420] *Man's Fate*, by André Malraux, Random House, Inc., 1961, p.242.
[421] *The Admirals: Nimitz, Halsey, Leahy, and King—the Five-Star Admirals Who Won the War at Sea*, p.466.
[422] *Long-Lost WWII "Victory" Pen Located*, p.5.
[423] *Guiding Lights: Monuments and Memorials at the U.S. Naval Academy*, by Nancy Arbuthnot, U.S. Naval Institute, 2012.
[424] *Life* magazine October 15, 1951, p.77.
[425] *Memoirs*, p.32.
[426] *Ibid*.
[427] In the 1970 movie about Pearl Harbor, *Tora! Tora! Tora!*, Davidson was portrayed by actor Edward Sheehan.
[428] *How They Won the War in the Pacific: Nimitz and His Admirals*, p.238.
[429] *Nimitz: A Good-Humored Leader of Men*, p.18.

www.ingramcontent.com/pod-product-compliance
Lightning Source LLC
Chambersburg PA
CBHW050929240426
43671CB00020B/2966